Whitehall and Westminster

Government informs Parliament:
The changing scene

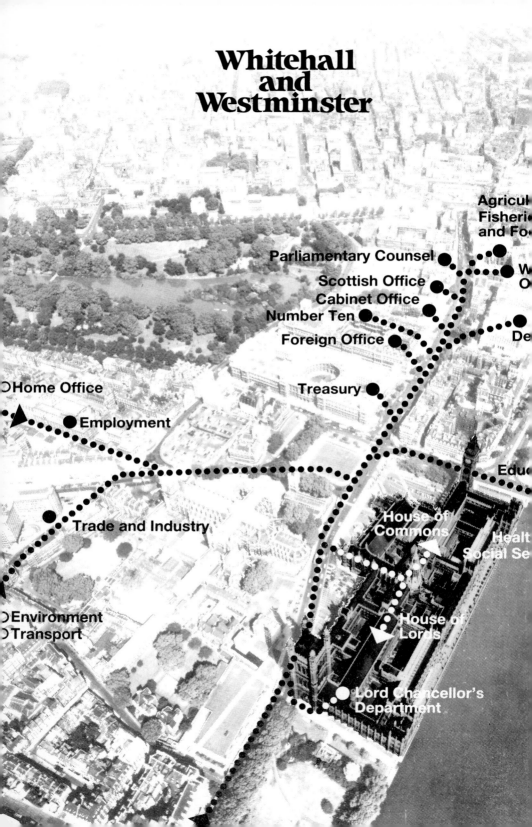

Whitehall and Westminster

Agricul
Fisheri
and Fo

Parliamentary Counsel

Scottish Office

Cabinet Office

Number Ten

Foreign Office

W
O

De

Treasury

Home Office

Employment

Edu

House of
Commons

Healt
Social Se

Trade and Industry

Environment
Transport

House of
Lords

Lord Chancellor's
Department

Whitehall and Westminster

Government informs Parliament: The changing scene

Dermot Englefield

Longman

WHITEHALL AND WESTMINSTER
GOVERNMENT INFORMS PARLIAMENT: THE CHANGING SCENE

Published by **Longman Group Limited**, Longman House,
Burnt Mill, Harlow, Essex CM20 2JE, United Kingdon

First published 1985

British Library Cataloguing in Publication Data

Englefield, Dermot J.T.
Whitehall and Westminster: Government informs
Parliament: the changing scene.
1. Great Britain—Government publications
I. Title
070.5'95'0941 Z2009

ISBN 0–582–90272–X

Typeset by The Word Factory, Lancashire BB4 6HN
Printed and bound by Bath Press, Bath BA2 3BL
Cover design by Archetype, London SE20 8AJ

CONTENTS

TABLES

PLANS

ABOUT THE AUTHOR

Dermot Englefield joined the House of Commons Library in 1954 and has been Deputy Librarian since 1976. He has acted as consultant to the Council of Europe (1970), the European Parliament (1973), the abortive Scottish Assembly (1978) and the Northern Ireland Assembly (1982). He edited a microfilm edition of *The Printed Records of the Parliament of Ireland 1613–1800* (1978) and is author of *Parliament and Information: The Westminster Scene* (1981). He is also editor or co-editor of *Commons Select Committees: Catalysts for Progress?* (Longman, 1984), *Information Sources in Politics and Political Science: A Survey Worldwide* (1984) and *Today's Civil Service: A Guide to its Work with Parliament and Industry* (Longman, 1985).

To my parents
Henry Wotton Englefield
Blanche Englefield

PREFACE

Whitehall is shorthand for many hundreds of thousands of individual people we call civil servants. They travel to work, most of them to execute the already decided policies of Government, while a few, to whom the shorthand most usually applies, are there to advise the Government of the day concerning their policies for the future. Their working methods are formal even hierarchic, their accountability via their minister to Parliament and the context of their work is private. They need eventually to promulgate some of the information they assemble.

Westminster is shorthand for the thousand or so active members of both Houses of Parliament. Their procedures are formal but their relationships are unhierarchical and the context of their work is public. Their accountability is to their party and constituency in particular and to the country in general. They feel committed, therefore, to use and often to promulgate all the information they secure.

Government is shorthand for the hundred or so people at Westminster who lead the majority party and who individually are ministers running departments and collectively are governing the country. Their working context is private in their department and public in Parliament. They bridge the two worlds.

The nuances of these three different groups of jobs are subtle yet far-reaching, though all those concerned come together in seeking to achieve the Queen's business, namely serving the country.

Standing on the touchline are members of the media and the press, observers who are important yet frustrated. They are important because they report Whitehall and Westminster to over 50,000,000 UK citizens and also abroad. They are important too because they report Whitehall and Westminster to each other. They are frustrated because though Parliament is almost entirely open (not politics, but that is another matter), Government necessarily is not. This frustration leads to reporting which is a mixture of exciting, often personalised distortion and surprising insight, written of course to be read during other pressures of the day. In consequence, it is not always easy to get a clear and steady picture of the way in which Whitehall and Westminster link with each other.

This book describes just one aspect of this working relationship, namely the ways in which Government and Whitehall present, willingly and occasionally unwillingly, information to Parliament. It is concerned then with the daily practice of accountability, not with the excitements of "leaks" or Section 2 of the Official Secrets Act. And it is written at a time when Westminster has seen important changes in its circumstances and in its methods of work. We need reminding that only a few years ago ministers never appeared before select committees, the latter took evidence only in private, the proceedings of Parliament were not broadcast, MPs were nearly all part-time with no allowance for personal staff, there was no Parliamentary Commissioner to probe Whitehall

ix

at the request of Members and we were not of course members of the European Communities. Westminster, which unlike Whitehall is an ancient institution and recently commemorated the 700th anniversay of Simon de Montfort's Parliament, has belied charges of being arthritic by introducing these and other changes during the last few years. Whitehall, as the quoted evidence of a number of senior civil servants in the book shows, is increasingly conscious of these changes.

Working in an institution as varied yet as small as the House of Commons is a continuing education and there are many Members and colleagues of both Houses who have unconsciously contributed to this book. The same might be said of a small number of people, some friends, some acquaintances, in Whitehall. I am in their debt. More particularly I would like to thank Sir David House, formerly Black Rod, for his agreement to my publishing The Ceremonial to be observed at the Opening of Parliament; Donald Limon of the Clerk's Department for help on the chapter on financial matters; Terence Skemp, Speaker's Counsel, for help on delegated legislation; and, from the Library Department, Ruth Wheatman for assistance on the subject of POLIS and Sylvia Warren and Marion Chantry for prodding me to meet deadlines. Finally, Alan Day of Longman has been as usual most helpful throughout.

DE

Crystal Palace
June 1985

ACKNOWLEDGEMENT

We are indebted to Granada Television for permission to reproduce an extract from an episode entitled 'A Law in the Making : Four Months inside a Ministry' in the series *The State of a Nation: Parliament*, distributed by Granada International, 36 Golden Square, London W1.

PART ONE: BACKGROUND

1. Introduction

The contest for political power is one of the main themes of a society's history. Parliament in this country has been at the centre of this struggle for many centuries. The centre of power moved from Crown to Parliament in the 17th century and has moved from Parliament to the Executive in our own. The rise of the Fourth Estate (a 19th century term for the press) and the growth of the modern broadcasting media, together with the recent extension of the vote to all over 18 years of age, are changes which have seen yet a further redistribution of political power.

If you read through the pamphlets published either by the Crown or by Parliament during the first months of the Long Parliament in 1641, you find yourself caught up in a debate which illuminates the first significant shift of political power since the Tudor monarchy led the country out of the divisions of late mediaeval civil war. By 1640 the dominant stance of a Henry VIII or the icon-like authority of Elizabeth I were neither tolerable nor relevant. James I and his son had huffed and puffed so much about "divine right" and "personal rule" that Londoners and others might well claim that monarchs "did protest too much". They turned to support Parliament as it abolished the prerogative courts together with other trappings of the Crown and finally prepared the way for the eclipse of the King himself.

This shift in power from Crown to Parliament was completed with a second angry outburst of parliamentary debate and publishing during the 1680s. From the end of that decade through the next two centuries power rested firmly with Parliament. The situation was held stable by having no truck with democratic ideas such as extending significantly the franchise (despite rumblings prior to the 1832 Reform Act), by avoiding the build-up of a large civil service or Executive and by absorbing unsatisfied initiative through founding first an American and later an Eastern empire. The country's energies were further caught up in the challenge of creating the world's first industrial revolution.

Towards the end of the 19th century, however, it became clear that the coming decades would see a further distribution of political power. There were new problems to be solved in a society where aspirations were rising. The Reform Act of 1867, which almost doubled the electorate, was followed by the 1870 Education Act, and before long a mass press was started to match the consequent mass literacy. As society's expectations increased, a career civil service was established both to administer agreed changes and to prepare new ones. The tentacles of the Executive began to spread. Even so, A.J.P. Taylor was able to write at the beginning of his book on the first half of the 20th century: "Until August 1914 a sensible law-abiding Englishman could pass through life and hardly notice the existence of the state."[1]

In many ways it was the First World War which ensured a change in the balance of power between Parliament and the Executive, as gradually the whole country became involved with the centralised organisation which this first total war required. It took time — conscription, for instance, was only introduced in 1916; but by the end of the war, it is clear in retrospect, the scales had moved in favour of the Executive and against Parliament. One small illustration in the field of published information reflected this change. For generations up to the First World War Parliament's papers had formed by far the bulk of what might be loosely called official publishing; during that war, however, there was a severe reduction in this parliamentary publishing, and official publishing subsequently became much more a matter for Government than for Parliament. This growth in the Government's power to initiate and distribute information is illustrated by the following figures of volumes of printed parliamentary papers.

Session	Volumes	Session	Volumes
1912/13	123	1919	54
1913	80	1920	52
1914	102	1921	43
1914/16	85	1922	24
1916	35	1923	27
1917/18	39	1924	28
1918	27		

This decline in parliamentary publishing was reaffirmed after the War when the Treasury stepped in and issued Circular No.38/21 on 6 September 1921. It laid down:

> Papers issued by order of either House or in response to an address to the Crown will continue to be printed under the present arrangements. With this exception . . . , that the present practice of issuing departmental publications as Parliamentary papers should be drastically modified, not only in the urgent interests of economy but to meet the expressed wishes of the authorities of the House of Commons.
> The presentation by departments to the Houses of Parliament of papers "by command" should be discontinued except in the cases of documents relating to matters likely to be the subject of early legislation, or which may be regarded as otherwise essential to Members of Parliament as a whole to enable them to discharge their responsibilities. Other documents hitherto issued as command papers should in future be issued as Stationery Office publications or, wherever possible, be discontinued.[2]

It might well be argued that the change of balance between Parliament and Government, hastened by the First World War, was extended still further by the Second. This latter involved the entire country coming under executive regulation from the very beginning; moreover, after the war the introduction of a Welfare State needing sustained regulation and development by Government was approved by the electorate voting in a Labour administration in 1945. Since then it has been accepted that quite large tracts of a citizen's life and of our society's priorities are subject to various forms of government intervention and often regulation. It therefore seems unlikely that the balance of power between Government and Parliament can be more than marginally adjusted in the latter's favour.

There is indeed an argument that Parliament suffered a serious crisis of self-confidence between about 1950 (before which it was active in legislating for a new post-war society) and the mid-1960s. During this period there were hardly any significant reports on parliamentary procedure. Moreover, the House of Commons had no real machinery to control its own services, such as accommodation, and in some respects it lacked staff and even elementary facilities. Worried Members, academics and others wrote books with titles such as *Can Parliament Survive?* (Christopher Hollis) and *The Passing of Parliament* (G.W. Keeton). It is likely that historians will judge that by the mid-1960s Parliament had reached a nadir in its power relationship with Government and the Executive. But things were to change.

Outside Parliament 1964 saw the founding of the Study of Parliament Group, a small body of parliamentary officials and academics interested in and anxious about the institution's future. Some of its members drew up evidence for the House of Commons Select Committee on Procedure, aiming to suggest ways of strengthening Parliament's role. Books such as Bernard Crick's *The Reform of Parliament* — the author himself was a founder member of the Group — were setting a new tone.

Within Parliament the House of Lords had, since 1958, been brought more up-to-date through the introduction of life peers to supplement the hereditary element. In 1965 the House of Commons took over control of its own working environment through the setting up of the House of Commons (Services) Committee, with sub-committees covering accommodation and administration, catering, the Library and, later, computers. From the end of the 1960s Members of the House of Commons started to receive increasing allowances for their personal staff, namely secretaries and later research assistants, while Members themselves were tending to regard their job as full-time. In 1967 legislation established the Parliamentary Commissioner or "Ombudsman", who works at the behest of Members checking abuses in the Executive's administration. This helped further to strengthen the position of Members, notably in that the Parliamentary Commissioner works with and reports regularly to a select committee of the House. In this period improvements in the select committee system generally were introduced, initially under Richard Crossman. Two types of ad hoc committees were created, covering departments and subjects, and at the beginning of the 1970s the Estimates Committee was replaced by the more broadly remitted Expenditure Committee. It became more usual for ministers to come and give evidence to the committees. Finally, following further procedural investigation, by 1979 the House was ready to set up a proper scheme of departmental select committees required to conduct a continuing examination of the work of each of the major departments of state. In the early 1980s Procedure Committees examined the supply and the finance procedure of the Commons, which was felt to require modernising and bringing more into line with other reforms. At the beginning of 1984 there was established a National Audit Office headed by the Comptroller and Auditor General and working for the Public Accounts Committee.

Partly as a result of these moves, the permanent staff of the House of Commons was doubled between 1964 and 1979, with the Library and research services being especially strengthened. The Committee Office in the Clerk's Department was generally enlarged and the departmental select committees took on temporary specialist advisers to help them, together with a number of research staff. When the plans to build extensive new accommodation collapsed, the House of Commons took over the Norman Shaw Buildings to provide Members and their personal and permanent staffs with adequate space. At the end of 1983 the Government announced phase 1 of the New Parliamentary Building on the corner of Bridge Street and Parliament Street. This is designed to release more accommodation for Members in the Palace of Westminster, by moving out members of the present staff to the new building, due for completion by 1990.

Although no one would suggest that by the 1980s, following these and other changes, there has been or is likely to be any really significant shift of power from Government back to Parliament, there is little doubt that the last 15 years have seen some very real readjustments. One small but important instance is that since 1979, when the House of Commons Administration Act (1978) came into force, Parliament's own estimates for its services are no longer under the control of the Treasury. Parliament is an institution not subject to cash limits and is quite independent of Government. The House of Commons Commission, consisting of the Speaker as chairman, the Leader of the House and four other Members, is not only responsible for preparing the Estimates but also acts as employer of the permanent staff of the House and issues annual reports which are published as House of Commons papers. In recent years, then, the House of Commons, which has increased its membership from 635 to 650 partly to cater for a growing popultion, has also increased its small staff considerably, as follows:

1969/70	1978/79	1984/85
351	521	889

It must be noted that the 1984–85 figure includes for the first time the staff of the refreshment department, numbering 235. This means that of the 1984–85 total, about 400 staff are engaged in club-like activities of catering for some thousands of people (including "strangers" in the Palace of Westminster), keeping facilities charged and in order, and carrying many hundreds of messages daily. Other marks of growth at Westminster include expenditure on Members' personal staff:

1969/70	1978/79	1984/85
£94,000	£2,300,000	£8,000,000

Finally there is the overall cost of both Houses of Parliament (excluding certain services rendered by government departments such as the Property Services Agency and HMSO):

1969/70	1978/79	1984/85
£3,800,000	£20,400,000	£56,000,000

While this increase has been going on and especially during the period of writing this book, the Executive or civil service, as a matter of government policy, has been reduced in size as set out below:

1979 (April)	1984 (April)	1988 (proposed)
732,300	630,000	593,000

It is against this altering background that this book has been written. It is concerned not so much with the two individual institutions themselves, but with an account of one aspect of their relationship, namely how the first informs the second.

INTRODUCTION

Following this Introduction there is a chapter outlining the way in which government departments are organised to inform Parliament and subsequently a chapter outlining the way in which the parliamentary session is shaped to meet the needs of both Parliament and Government. Then, in Part Two, which starts with an examination of the Queen's Speeches, there are chapters dealing with various forms of parliamentary work including general debates, questions, statements, legislation and select committee work, all looked at from the viewpoint of how Parliament secures information from Government. A number of chapters on specialist aspects follow, including financial affairs (which have their own special calender cutting across the normal session), foreign and European Community affairs and the the Ombudsmen. Finally, the distinctive contribution of the House of Lords is noted.

Part Three is concerned with the papers which carry much of this information. After a chapter describing this "published record" in detail, a further chapter deals with the indexes, both traditionally printed ones and the House of Commons Library's computer-based indexing system (POLIS) which, day by day, gathers together so many thousands of references to Parliament's work.

After a Conclusion seeking to draw together some of the main themes of the book, there follows a series of appendices containing reference material germane to the foregoing text. In Appendix 1 there is a portrait of a normal-length parliamentary session running from November to October (1980/81 in this case) and covering work in the two Chambers, the standing committees of the House of Commons and the select committees of both Houses. It tabulates just how much work goes on in the Palace of Westminster day after day and suggests just how little of it is recognised by the media and thence the public at large. Five further appendices reprint instructions to civil servants regarding government information, of particular note being Appendix 4 on the latest (February 1985) encapsulation of prevailing conditions.

Every three years on average some 42,000,000 of us are invited to vote and return a Member of Parliament to represent us at Westminster. This is the moment when each of us may contribute our mite to the electorate's decision. Within a few hours of the poll closing, we know not only who is to be our Member at Westminster but also the nation's judgement of the political priorities the country needs. Assuming a change in the majority party in the House of Commons and the consequent resignation of the Prime Minister, the Queen will immediately invite the leader of the newly victorious party to form a Government. This is to be the Queen's Government, as she makes clear when reading the Speech from her throne in the House of Lords when opening the new Parliament. It is also our Government, at least until it returns to the polls for our verdict on its achievements.

Before the Queen opens the newly-elected Parliament, the press and the television cameras outside 10 Downing Street will record the comings and goings of the actual formation of Government. This takes several days, as the new Prime Minister appoints the secretaries of state for the major departments, the ministers of state and the parliamentary under-secretaries. When the job is done, about 100 members of the Prime Minister's party will have been given posts, and about 22 of these, holders of major posts, will make up the Cabinet. As ministers of the Crown they will all receive ministerial salaries in additon to part-salaries as Members of Parliament.

Once entrusted with the seals of ministerial office by the Crown, the members of the new Government will scatter down the corridors of the departments of state until they reach their offices. There they will meet members of the Executive, their civil servants, who are there to advise them and to carry out their policies, and who are employees of the Crown. The civil servants, who hold their posts permanently and who have just concluded working for the previous Government, are required to switch their allegiance to the Government just formed. (They are also required to lock up the confidential papers of the previous Government.) The new Government, on the other hand, keeps its power and place only while it retains a majority in the House of Commons.

I have spelt out the distinction between Parliament (the Crown and Members of both Houses), the Government (ministers of the Crown in Parliament) and the Executive (civil servants) because we are considering a quite complicated relationship, namely the way in which the Government, and on its behalf the Executive, informs Parliament (on which Government is based and to which it is responsible) on a great range of public affairs. But the starting point of this Parliament, you will remember, was our vote in the polling booth. Government, by informing Parliament, will with the help of its publications and of the press and the media also inform us, the electorate. This responsibility for informing Parliament rests with the Cabinet collectively and with ministers individually.

An interesting small instance of this responsibility is a special category of documents in the House of Commons Library known as "deposited papers". These papers, covering a wide miscellaneous range of subjects, have been deposited in the Library by a minister "for the information of Members" and the collection, which dates back to 1836, is kept permanently among Parliament's records in the Victoria Tower. It is normal for the minister concerned to indicate that he has made the paper available to Members "in the Library of the House". The fact is often mentioned in *Hansard*, and the civil servant who sends the paper indicates that it is sent on behalf of his minister. For this reason, if there is an enquiry other than from a Member for one of these papers, and it is unpublished, the enquirer is referred to the department. Other than ministers, only Mr Speaker may add to this collection of deposited papers.

Because of this ministerial responsibility to Parliament, the House of Commons remains very sensitive about being informed first over quite a range of matters. Accordingly, lobby correspondents and other privileged journalists are very careful about honouring the embargoed times on government papers which they receive for review in advance of Members themselves. Mistakes of course occasionally occur and then, if it is the department's fault, the minister concerned may be accused of "discourtesy to the House". This sounds a mild enough rebuke but "the House" is an institution made up of 650 equal Members, of whom the minister is one, and they work and indeed spend much of their time in close proximity to each other, all using the same corridors, dining rooms, libraries, etc. Partly for this reason, no minister wishing to be successful in Parliament — and that is vital both for the Government of which he is part and in personal terms — will survive many serious charges of "discourtesy to the House".

The 100 or so Members who form the Government are therefore a bridge from the two parliamentary Chambers and their committee rooms at Westminster, right into the heart of Whitehall. The Executive, depending on the size and role of the department, is organised to respond to their ministers' needs, including their accountability to Parliament. Parliament is the body to whom the minister ultimately reports, just as at its dissolution it is we who pass final judgement on that Government's achievement by voting in the next.

NOTES

1. A.J.P. Taylor, *English History, 1914–1945* (Oxford University Press, 1965), p.1
2. Quoted in J. Pemberton, *British Official Publications* (Pergamon Press, 2nd ed., 1974), p.18

2. The Organisation of Government to inform Parliament

Government comes together in one room, either in 10 Downing Street or occasionally in the Prime Minister's office in the House of Commons, when 22 chairs are drawn back from the long coffin-shaped table and the office-holders listed in Table 1 sit down.

Table 1

Her Majesty's Government: Members of the Cabinet

Prime Minister, First Lord of the Treasury and Minister for the Civil Service
Lord President of the Council and Leader of the House of Lords
Lord Chancellor
Secretary of State for Foreign and Commonwealth Affairs
Secretary of State for the Home Department
Chancellor of the Exchequer
Secretary of State for Education and Science
Secretary of State for Northern Ireland
Secretary of State for Energy
Secretary of State for Defence
Secretary of State for Scotland
Secretary of State for Wales
Secretary of State for the Environment
Lord Privy Seal and Leader of the House of Commons
Secretary of State for Social Services
Secretary of State for Trade and Industry and President of the Board of Trade
Chancellor of the Duchy of Lancaster
Secretary of State for Employment
Minister of Agriculture, Fisheries and Food
Chief Secretary to the Treasury
Secretary of State for Transport
Minister without Portfolio

The Cabinet is in session and they will be assisted by the Secretary of the Cabinet taking brief minutes and by two or three other senior civil servants.

The Cabinet itself, as one would expect, works through a series of cabinet committees which have the power to co-opt more junior ministers. Some are ad hoc committees to deal with emergencies or other temporary problems, while others are standing committees. Traditionally great secrecy has surrounded these committees, not just their work and relationship with the main Cabinet but also their title and membership. However, early in Mrs Thatcher's Government the following question and answer was published:

Mr Mike Thomas asked the Prime Minister if she will now answer questions on the membership and terms of reference of cabinet committees.

The Prime Minister: I have established four standing committees of the Cabinet: a defence and overseas policy committee and an economic strategy committee, both under my chairmanship; a home and social affairs committee under the chairmanship of my right hon. friend the Home Secretary; and a legislation committee under the chairmanship of the Lord Chancellor. Attendance at these committees will vary according to the subject under discussion. Where appropriate, sub-committees of the standing committees will be established. Membership and terms of reference of the standing committees or their sub-committees will remain confidential.[1]

There have been no further revelations other than the fact that the chairman of the Legislation Committee is now the Lord Privy Seal. The classic position with regard to the responsibility of the cabinet committees is set out below:

Mr Austin Mitchell asked the Prime Minister, pursuant to her answer on Oct. 26, in what way it would infringe the principle of collective responsibility to give further details of cabinet committees and sub-committees.

The Prime Minister: Under the principle of collective responsibility, all members of the Government are jointly responsible for all the Government's policies and decisions. The publication of details of cabinet committees and sub-committees would tend to imply that ministers shared responsibility only for decisions in committees of which they were members.[2]

Journalists have spent many hours trying to penetrate this secrecy. The most recent list, concerning which there has been no government comment, appeared in April 1984.[3]

It is from decisions made at meetings of the Cabinet that information flows out as urgent memos to permanent secretaries, through press conferences and notices, through libraries of leaflets to the citizen and, not least, through the machinery of Government and the procedures of Parliament to our elected representatives. A key figure in this last relationship, which is the subject of this book, is the minister.

Ministers are normally one of three grades: secretaries of state, in which case they are in the Cabinet and have ultimate responsibility for their department of state; ministers of state in the second rank; and parliamentary under-secretaries in the third rank. Terminology may vary a little between departments for historical reasons, but Table 2 (see next page) sets down their distribution between the main departments at the end of 1984.

The textbooks on Government tell us quite accurately that the distinctive element in the Westminster parliamentary system is that ministers are members of and responsible to either the House of Commons or, in a few cases, the House of Lords. What is important is their dual role of Member and minister, sometimes spending the morning in their department, the evening at the House and the afternoon at either one or the other depending on the demands of parliamentary business and of their department. One of the strengths and weaknesses of the system is that Ministers seldom hold the same post for more than three or four years. In some ways this strengthens the position of the civil servant, with his wealth of information and his matured departmental viewpoint. On the other hand, such changes of ministers can be unsettling for a bureaucratic system which otherwise might tend to complacency. For the

Table 2

Departments of State and Ministers

Agriculture, Fisheries and Food	Minister
	Ministers of State (2)
	Parliamentary Secretary
Defence	Secretary of State
	Ministers of State (2)
	Under-Secretaries of State (2)
Education and Science	Secretary of State
	Under-Secretaries of State (2)
Employment	Secretary of State
	Ministers of State (2)
	Under-Secretary of State
Energy	Secretary of State
	Minister of State
	Under-Secretaries of State (2)
Environment	Secretary of State
	Ministers of State (2)
	Under-Secretaries of State (4)
Foreign and Commonwealth Affairs ..	Secretary of State
	Ministers of State (4)
	Under-Secretary of State
Health and Social Security	Secretary of State for Social Services
	Ministers of State (2)
	Under-Secretaries of State (3)
Home Office	Secretary of State for the Home Department
	Ministers of State (3)
	Under-Secretary of State
Law Officers' Department	Attorney-General
	Solicitor-General
Lord Advocate's Department	Lord Advocate
	Solicitor-General
Lord Chancellor	Lord Chancellor
Management and Personnel Office ..	Prime Minister and Minister for the Civil Service
	Chancellor of the Duchy of Lancaster
Northern Ireland Office	Secretary of State for Northern Ireland
	Minister of State
	Under-Secretaries of State (3)
Privy Council Office	Lord President of the Council and Leader of the House of Lords
	Lord Privy Seal and Leader of the House of Commons

12

Scottish Office	Secretary of State Minister of State Under-Secretaries of State (3)
Trade and Industry	Secretary of State Ministers of State (3) Under-Secretaries of State (4)
Transport	Secretary of State Minister of State Under-Secretaries of State (2)
Treasury	Prime Minister, First Lord of the Treasury and Minister for the Civil Service Chancellor of the Exchequer Chief Secretary Financial Secretary to the Treasury Minister of State Economic Secretary Parliamentary Secretary to the Treasury
Welsh Office	Secretary of State Minister of State Under-Secretary of State

minister such change ensures that they do not grow stale in their job and that lessons learnt in one position may be used in other.

There are then two tempos: the quick tempo of the sometimes accident-prone political change, running against the slow rhythm of administrative needs. Naturally this variety can cause problems. It can also lead to ironic situations, such as a minister authorising the closure of an institution which a decade ago, when policial priorities were very different, he had opened as a more junior minister — having held two or three other portfolios in the meantime.

The minister is not just in charge of a department; he is also a politician and leads a life quite different from his civil servants. As a Member of Parliament he has a direct responsibility to his constituents and to his political party and indeed may on occasion use both as a source of information. This dual role of ministers is clearly shown in the holdings of the House of Commons Library, where a collection called "Ministers' Speeches outside Parliament" (to distinguish them from their speeches reported in *Hansard*) consists of a mixed file of press releases, some from their department if they speak as a minister and others from their party headquarters if they speak as a politician. Unlike the civil servant, the minister therefore spans two worlds. His double needs have been recognised to a modest degree in recent years when some ministers have appointed political advisers to work for them within their department and to try and reaffirm a political dimension to their information. Again, as the minister has his constituency responsibilities (because he is a Member), he employs a personal secretary and possibly a research assistant to help him deal with this aspect of his job; these personal staff really have nothing to do with his civil servants and his work as a minister.

Finally, the minister is a member of that strange institution, the House of Commons — a mixture of legislature, examining tribunal, national forum, school for Government and genial club. While most of these elements play a role in his ministerial life and in that of his civil servants, the last ("a genial club") gives him an existence very separate from his department. Most parts of the Houses of Parliament which he inhabits as a Member, such as the Members' Dining Room, the Tea Room or the Library, are out of bounds to all except Members and senior parliamentary staff; other areas, such as the Smoking Room, the Chess Room and the lobbies behind the Chamber, are forbidden to all but Members. This means that a word between Member and minister during a division, a hand on the shoulder in a corridor or a relaxed talk about a problem at dinner or over a drink, are very much part of a minister's life within the House of Commons and are quite distinct from the day-to-day worries of his civil servants.[4]

Back in his department, the minister deals mostly with a very small number of senior civil servants. The numbers of the three senior administrative grades in the civil service at the beginning of 1985 were as follows:

Grade	Type of Job
39 permanent secretaries	head of department
141 deputy secretaries	head of major area
490 under-secretaries	head of large division

While the whole department is geared up to support its minister and feels a genuine loyalty to his position and often to him personally, information for the minister, and especially any information for Parliament, will rise up through this impressive hierarchy.

Departments themselves are sometimes thought of as falling within two groups: (i) the large ones, which are executive as well as national policy orientated, of which Defence, Health and Social Security, and Trade and Industry might serve as examples, and (ii) the small departments sharply focused on national policy (where executive action, if it is required, is not through central Government), such as the Treasury, Cabinet Office and in many respects Education and Science. There is therefore no standard organisation, because the history and role of departments varies greatly; but major policy divisions in a department will often be run by an under-secretary with the aid of a small number of assistant secretaries.

Before turning to the more detailed Whitehall organisation which responds to Parliament, mention must be made of the minister's parliamentary private secretary. These are Members of Parliament personally appointed by the minister as unsalaried assistants. They are an important link between the civil servants and their minister, especially within the Houses of Parliament, because as Members they have access to all parts of the building. Of considerable importance, for instance, is their role in the Chamber as message-carriers between the minister and his civil servants, because the latter have no access to the floor of the House of Commons. A parliamentary private secretary may also be an important sounding-board for the minister before he takes a political decision or for a civil servant before approaching the minister.

Although all the energies of a department can be quickly concentrated on supporting the Minister (especially in the case of the senior civil service), the two organisations which specifically concentrate on this role are (i) the private office, which offers direct support to the minister, and (ii) the parliamentary branch, which even today is occasionally part of the private office and in any case generally comes under the minister's principal private secretary. Both organisations are vitally concerned with supporting their minister's performance, especially vis-à-vis Parliament. In recent years, as a result of a regrouping of responsibilities, the number of departments has been slightly reduced; in most of them there is a ministerial structure of secretary of state, minister of state and under-secretary of state, although departments differ in their needs and terminology for ministers.[5] The private office is normally run by the secretary of state's principal private secretary with more junior ministers rating a private secretary each. The principal private secretary is appointed by the minister on the advice of the permanent secretary, and should there be incompatability it is the private secretary who would have to be moved.

In a smaller department such as the Department of Education, the private office would run to about 30 people in a total establishment of some 2,500 posts. The private office is concerned only with the minister in his ministerial capacity; his political relationships are therefore not part of their direct interest, although they are well aware that he is very much a political animal and anticipate problems bearing this in mind. As the grade of civil servant who acts as principal private secretary or private secretary is not a very high one, they tend to be young and of course bright. (The Prime Minister and the Chancellor of the Exchequer are exceptions to this generalisation, as their principal private secretaries are in a higher grade.) It can happen, therefore, that a junior minister, his parliamentary private secretary and to some degree his private secretary are all on a learning curve together.

Ministers are very busy people indeed, playing several roles at the same time. They consider and decide on international and national problems in Cabinet; they deal with problems in the administration of their department; and in the House they act as defender of their department and as a Member deal with the minutiae of their constituents' complaints.

The services offered by the private office to a minister include all those offered to the head of a large organisation from the most mundane to the most sophisticated; but what is distinctive about a minister is his accountability. The results of many of his decisions affect us all and he must seek to convince not only his political colleagues but also Parliament and, often via the media, the public. This is very much his job and explains why information for Parliament is prepared with such care and why Governments worry about "getting the message across". But the arena of their work vis-à-vis Parliament is not always a public one, as Members of Parliament frequently write to the minister personally about detailed matters, sometimes specific constituency points, and these are handled through his private office. A Member will always receive a reply signed by the minister himself and this correspondence is one method whereby the minister learns about the way the department he runs is actually working. If, for instance, legislation leads to too many similar constituents' problems, then it may need looking at with a view to changes. During January 1984 as an example, the Secretary of State for the Environment received 1,124 letters from Members and signed 1,058 letters to Members. The private office drafts such letters as well as speeches; it also checks the parliamentary questions and prepares briefs on visiting delegations, etc., and all this in a manner to match the abilities, needs and style of the individual minister.

The second link in this chain from department to Parliament is the department's parliamentary branch. Headed by a parliamentary clerk of higher executive officer grade (or senior executive officer where the department's remit means more parliamentary work) and equipped with between three and about eight staff, the parliamentary branch is the focal point of each department's parliamentary performance. As such, especially when Parliament is sitting, it is offering not only a very direct service to the minister but also to the department and through the other parliamentary branches to Whitehall as a whole.

Work begins early in a parliamentary branch, as by 8 a.m. the House of Commons Vote Office has normally received and distributed to government departments (among others) the House of Commons Order Paper or "Vote Bundle" for the day.[6] It has been printed overnight in the St Stephen's parliamentary press. These papers need immediate study, to extract parliamentary questions tabled the previous day which may relate to the department, to examine early day motions which also may have been tabled the previous day or which have received further supporting signatures from Members and which impinge on the department's responsibility, to check amendments to government bills or private members' bills which may be of departmental interest. Similarly the House of Lords Minutes of Proceedings need careful study. There is also *Hansard* of both Houses to be examined to check whether problems are arising for departments with contiguous responsibilities as it is the parliamentary branch which needs to provide the department with an early warning system of trouble in the House. Nothing disturbs Government more, especially in its relationship with Parliament, than a problem coming out of the blue.

As the day wears on, the parliamentary branch may have to advise on procedure, respond to enquiries from officials of both Houses, arrange the laying of departmental papers before Parliament or arrange a long list of interdepartmental clearances so that the minister can make a statement in the House. The parliamentary branch may also need to draw up a list of the department's officials who will have to be in the official box in the respective Chambers, supporting the minister or the government spokesman (in the House of Lords) with additional information. It is a hectic life and there are times, if the House of Commons especially is in a demanding mood, when the staff must feel they are skating on rather thin ice. But then the whole of the relationship of Government and Parliament may be seen as challenging and while most civil servants can go about their work with hardly a second thought about Parliament, those who surround the minister are always conscious of the parliamentary dimension of his and indeed their job.

The Government's organisation to inform Parliament, then, is kept slim and supple. Whatever the activity discussed in succeeding chapters, it is the parliamentary branch which is on the end of the telephone hastening replies to parliamentary questions, alerting the private office to unexpected amendments, offering procedural advice to specialist officers inexperienced in Parliament's ways who are drafting information, possibly hundreds of miles from Whitehall, clearing lines with other departments and accompanying groups of staff to select committee hearings, standing committee debates, or to the Chamber itself in order to support their minister. He is, from the viewpoint of the department, not just their champion in Cabinet but their standard-bearer in the House. But looked at from the viewpoint of his fellow Members, he is quite simply accountable to them. It is time we looked at the way in which Parliament organises its timetable to match this accountability.

NOTES

1. HC Deb. vol. 967, c.179w. This situation was confirmed on Nov. 14 1984 (HC Deb. vol. 67, c.243w)
2. HC Deb. vol. 974, c.450w
3. *The Times*, April 30, 1984, p.12
4. For a description of the relationship between civil servants and ministers, see Appendix 4
5. See Table 2
6. For a description of these papers see "Parliament and Information" by Dermot Englefield, Library Association, 1981, pp.11–13

3. The Organisation of the Parliamentary Timetable

The House of Commons sits for about 170 days in each session, the normal session running from early November to the end of October. The sittings of the two Houses coincide in general terms, but the House of Lords normally has more work to do in October than does the House of Commons. Parliamentary recesses are usually three to four weeks at Christmas, a week at Easter and at the Spring Holiday and from the end of July to mid-October.

The daily sittings of the House of Commons are from 2.30 p.m. to 10.30 p.m. Monday to Thursday and from 9.30 a.m. to 3.00 p.m. on Friday. During most weeks of the session the House of Lords sits fewer days and shorter hours. Under these conditions therefore the House of Commons actually sits about 1,700 hours a session, but it regularly continues sitting after 10.30 p.m. on Mondays to Thursdays and in 1980–81, a typical session, this added a further 258 hours or 37 sitting days to its workload. Compared with most other Parliaments, Westminster works for very many days and for very long hours.

The time available for parliamentary work is divided between the Government, the Opposition and private Members. Private Members' time is limited to 20 Fridays a session and this time is usually divided into 10 Fridays for bills and 10 Fridays for motions, i.e. discussion of a subject raised by a private Member. As most of these motions concern government policy, there is normally a minister present who replies to the debate informing Parliament of the Government's view concerning the subject raised. In addition there are four other days that private Members' motions are discussed until 7 p.m. In terms of time in recent sessions about 55 hours of private Members' time have been devoted to their bills and about 48 hours to their motions.

Since 1982–83, opposition time has consisted of 19 days each session which are available to the Leader of the Opposition to initiate the subject of debate. The Opposition can elect to have up to two of those 19 days on Fridays, at the rate of two Fridays for one whole day. This works out at a little over 100 hours a session of opposition time.

The rest of the sittings are government time which does not, however, preclude both the Opposition and private Members making use of it — seeking, for example, explanations of government conduct and information about their future policy and present administration. For instance, during the debate on the Queen's Speech, which is in government time, the Opposition moves amendments to the general review of government policy. Rather differently, if an issue is serious enough, the Opposition may move a "vote of censure" against the Government, and although it is in government time the motion to debate it is always accepted. With regard to private Members, they normally initiate several short debates during the four holiday adjournment motions, one pre-ceeding each recess, which gives them a chance to raise specific matters, and also during the half-hour adjournment debate at the end of each day's sitting. After the formal second reading of the Consolidated Fund Bills (there are usually three a session) the subsequent adjournment motion, which can last until 9 a.m. the following morning, provides many private Members with time to raise matters which concern them. All this is in government time and demands a response from the Government.

The main purpose of this government time, however, is to ensure that government business passes through Parliament. The following table, mostly based on the session 1980–81, suggests the way it may be divided. Many of the following chapters treat the use of this government time in greater detail.

Table 3
Division of House of Commons Time

Debate on the Address		about 37 hours
Legislation:	2nd reading	196 hours
	Committee stage	57.5 hours
	Report stage	146 hours
	3rd reading	21 hours
	Lords amendment considered	26 hours
Delegated legislation:	Affirmative motions	90 hours
	Negative motions	19.5 hours
Debates:	Government motions	91 hours
	Censure motions	13.5 hours
	Adjournment motions	41.5 hours
	Adjournment motions (holidays)	20 hours
	Adjournment motions (½ hr)	80 hours
	Adjournment motions (SO No. 10)	3.5 hours
	Consolidated Fund Bills	3–4 days
European Community:	Documents motions	43 hours

Naturally there is a shape to the parliamentary session, and the work of Parliament noted in Appendix 1 gives a good idea of the way in which this shape changes during the session both within each House and as between the two Houses of Parliament. The reader is advised to read the introductory note before tackling the Appendix itself.

After the Queen's Speech, both Houses spend nearly a week on the debate on the Address. It is not until this is completed, with its focus on different major subject areas from the third day's debate onwards, that the Government introduces debates on its legislative progamme. Because most select committees of both Houses are now set up for a Parliament, except for the first session of a Parliament they can get down to work very quickly; thus the two columns in Appendix 1 under Commons select committees and Lords select committees show entries from the beginning of the session. The half-hour adjournment debates are also to be found from the beginning of the session but parliamentary questions are not answered in either Chamber until towards the last days of the debate on the address. There are also throughout the session occasional ministerial statements to the House, marking emergencies, accidents and other crises for which the Government may or may not be actually responsible.

The Government's legislative programme is well under way before Christmas and the first bills have been assigned to standing committees where they appear on two or three mornings a week. For a few very important bills the committee stage is taken in the whole House. There is also at this time a considerable amount of delegated legislation being debated. These appear as O for Order or R for Regulation in Appendix 1. This work is interspersed with a number of general motions (both government and opposition) on various subjects in this 1980–81 session, including matters such as forestry policy and the Brandt Commission report. The first events in the financial calendar during the session take place before Christmas, namely the presentation of the Autumn Statement and its debate and the presentation of the Votes on Account and the Winter Supplementary Estimates (see chapter 9). The Christmas Recess adjournment debates were taken on 19 December and both Houses then adjourned for Christmas.

In the middle of January, when Parliament returned, the tempo of work for both Houses including their committees quickened. More standing committees had been set up in the Commons but they did not sit on Mondays and Fridays. (Many Members have considerable distances to travel to and from their constituences at the weekend.) Industrial problems led to further government statements while other ministers reported back to Parliament about their work to the meetings of the Council of Ministers of the European Communities. The House of Lords meeting four days a week meanwhile devoted a great deal of time to the committee stage of the important Wildlife and Countryside Bill. February was one of the busiest months and the House of Commons special standing committee on the Criminal Attempts Bill took evidence on three occasions before starting its normal standing committee examination of the bill. Private Members' bills started on Fridays with the Indecent Displays (Control) Bill second reading on 30 January 1981.

On 10 March the Chancellor introduced his Budget with a review of the economy, together with his proposals for taxation for the following financial year. Although the glamour surrounding the Budget has declined in recent years the set piece of his speech, together with a further three or four days' debate, remain an important fixture in the parliamentary calendar. (It is usual these days for the Main Estimates to be laid before the House on Budget Day.) Standing committees meanwhile were thick with legislation and the select committees, especially the departmental select committees, were keeping their many witnesses on their toes. And the House of Lords continued sitting four days a week, their select committee system also being very busy especially with European Community affairs.

In late April, almost immediately after Parliament reassembled following the Easter Recess, the Finance Bill, introduced by the Government to legalise their budget proposals, started its journey through the committee state, some clauses being taken in committee of the whole House of Commons and some clauses in standing committee. The annual two-day debate on defence was taken just before the Spring Bank Holiday and bills which were introduced in the House of Lords early in the session, including the Wildlife and Countryside Bill, were now being debated in the House of Commons standing committees.

By early June most of the debates in the House of Commons on legislation were taking account of amendments and this was followed by the third reading stage, while the House of Lords itself busily examined legislation which had been introduced in and had passed through the House of Commons. To cope with the flow the House of Lords regularly sat five days a week. A month later the Statutory Instruments Standing Committee was taken up with debates on

Orders and Regulations and the Scottish Committee with Scottish Estimates. Most select committees had come to the end of their evidence sessions and are not mentioned in Appendix 1 because they were holding private deliberative sessions while considering and drafting their reports. The last week before the summer recess was especially busy for backbenchers and departments, with many short debates on the Consolidation (Appropriation) Bill on 21 July and then adjournment debates on 31 July. The Statutory Instruments Standing Committee had meanwhile tidied up the Orders and Regulations needing debates and during that last week the select committee rooms were almost silent, with just the Energy Committee taking further government evidence on energy conservation. But the House of Lords was busy right up to the last moment before rising for the Summer Recess.

On 8 October the House of Lords returned to work mostly on legislation which had been passed to them from the Commons at the end of July. This House of Lords work on legislation continued when both Houses were sitting from 19 October onwards and the House of Commons found itself caught up in completing legislation. But at this stage of the session there was no work for the standing committees and very little for the select committees.

The rhythm of this parliamentary year has to some extent varied over the centuries, although it has always respected the need to be in recess when the harvest is collected. It is a rhythm which clearly affects the civil service, especially those who need continually to be glancing over their shoulder at Westminster. Who better to confirm this fact than Sir William Armstrong who, as then head of the Home Civil Service in 1973, replied to a question from Michael Foot MP asking him whether he thought the House of Commons kept any control over the Executive:

> Oh it certainly exercises some control, certainly a very great influence. Things are quite different when Parliament is not sitting. In a recess, especially the long Summer Recess, the feel in Whitehall is quite different, a certain slackness sets in.[1]

30 October was the last day of the session. The Commission in the House of Lords was read out by the Clerk of the Parliaments and turned the session's final large set of bills into acts and, with the Commons attending, the Lord Chancellor read out the Queen's Speech concluding the session and then prorogued Parliament. The Commons then returned to their Chamber, the Speaker read out the Commission's terms and the Queen's Speech was ordered to be printed in the House of Commons Votes and Proceedings. Then the Speaker left the chair, the session closed, corridors emptied and a quiet long weekend followed. Well, it was quiet for some, but not for those who polished the Robing Room, rolled carpets down the Royal Gallery, dusted the throne and checked the television arc lights. Early in the next week, with the traditional pomp of the Queen's Speech, the parliamentary year started once more.

NOTES

1. This question was asked during a TV programme, the text of which was published as *The State of the Nation: Parliament* (Granada Television, 1973), p.99

PART TWO: PROCEEDINGS

4. The Queen's Speeches

The Queen's Speech opening each session of Parliament is *par excellence* concerned with the theme of this volume. It is also a very splendid occasion when the three parts of Parliament — the Monarch, her Peers and her Commoners come together in a blaze of historic pageantry which today is presented to the people through television. Even on the greyest November day the programme set out below, which is followed with impeccable timing, brings colour and excitement to both citizen and foreign tourist. To this visual effect must be added the sound of military bands, horses with their jingling harness, sharp orders to present arms, with bells and chimes mingling in the background as the elegant Irish coach rolls along the Mall from Buckingham Palace and then carries the Queen down Whitehall to the House of Lords. There she is to deliver her Government's message to Parliament.

HER MAJESTY THE QUEEN, accompanied by His Royal Highness The Prince Philip, Duke of Edinburgh, having proceded from Buckingham Palace, will arrive at 11.15 o'clock at the Royal Entrance to The Palace of Westminster, where Her Majesty will be received by the Great Officers of State and others there assembled and conducted to the Robing Room.

Her Majesty, having put on the Royal Robes and wearing the Imperial Crown, will join the procession awaiting her in the Royal Gallery at 11.27 o'clock and will proceed in State into the Chamber of the House of Lords, the procession moving in the order following:

Fitzalan Pursuivant Extraordinary
J. M. ROBINSON, ESQ.

Rouge Croix Pursuivant H. E. PASTON-BEDINGFELD, ESQ.	Bluemantle Pursuivant T. D. MCCARTHY, ESQ.
Portcullis Pursuivant P. B. SPURRIER, ESQ.	Rouge Dragon Pursuivant P. L. DICKINSON, ESQ.
Arundel Herald Extraordinary R. O. DENNYS, ESQ.	Beaumont Herald Extraordinary F. S. ANDRUS, ESQ.
Wales Herald Extraordinary F. JONES, ESQ.	Norfolk Herald Extraordinary G. D. SQUIBB, ESQ.
Somerset Herald T. WOODCOCK, ESQ.	Lancaster Herald P. L. GWYNN-JONES, ESQ.
Richmond Herald M. MACLAGAN, ESQ.	Windsor Herald T. D. MATHEW, ESQ.
Chester Herald D. H. B. CHESSHYRE, ESQ.	York Herald C. M. J. SWAN, ESQ.

WHITEHALL AND WESTMINSTER

Gentleman Usher to
Her Majesty
LIEUTENANT-COLONEL
SIR JULIAN PAGET, BT.

Gentleman Usher to
Her Majesty
CARRON GREIG, ESQ.

The Treasurer to
H.R.H. The Duke of Edinburgh
RICHARD DAVIES, ESQ.

Equerry in Waiting
to Her Majesty
SQUADRON-LEADER ADAM WISE

The Crown Equerry
LIEUTENANT-COLONEL
SIR JOHN MILLER

Equerry in Waiting
to Her Majesty
LIEUTENANT-COLONEL
BLAIR STEWARD-WILSON

The Comptroller of
Her Majesty's Household
CAROL MATHER, ESQ.

The Treasurer of
Her Majesty's Household
JOHN COPE, ESQ.

The Keeper of
Her Majesty's Privy Purse
PETER MILES, ESQ.

The Private Secretary
to Her Majesty
THE RIGHT HON. SIR PHILIP MOORE

Norroy and Ulster King of Arms
J.P.B. BROOKE-LITTLE, ESQ.

The Lord Privy Seal
THE RIGHT HON. JOHN BIFFEN

The Lord President
of The Council
THE VISCOUNT WHITELAW

The Lord High Chancellor
THE LORD HAILSHAM OF
SAINT MARYLEBONE

The Gentleman Usher of
the Black Rod
LIEUTENANT-GENERAL SIR DAVID HOUSE

Garter King of Arms
LIEUTENANT-COLONEL SIR COLIN COLE

The Earl Marshal
THE DUKE OF NORFOLK

The Lord Great Chamberlain
THE MARQUESS OF CHOLMONDELEY

THE SWORD OF STATE
ADMIRAL OF THE FLEET
THE LORD HILL-NORTON

THE CAP OF MAINTENANCE
THE LORD COCKFIELD

The Queen's Most Excellent Majesty

accompanied by

HIS ROYAL HIGHNESS THE PRINCE PHILIP, DUKE OF EDINBURGH

Pages of Honour

JAMES BASSET, ESQ.
MARQUESS OF LORNE

MARQUESS OF HAMILTON
GUY RUSSELL, ESQ.

THE QUEEN'S SPEECHES

Woman of the Bedchamer	The Mistress of the Robes	Lady of the Bedchamber
HON. MARY MORRISON	THE DUCHESS OF GRAFTON	THE COUNTESS OF CROMER

Gold Stick in Waiting	The Lord Steward	The Master of the Horse
GENERAL SIR DESMOND FITZPATRICK	THE DUKE OF NORTHUMBERLAND	THE EARL OF WESTMORLAND

Lord in Waiting to Her Majesty		The Vice-Admiral of the United Kingdom
THE LORD SOMERLEYTON		ADMIRAL SIR JOHN BUSH

The Captain of the Yeomen of the Guard		The Captain of the Honourable Corps of Gentlemen at Arms
THE EARL OF SWINTON		THE LORD DENHAM

Air Aide-de-Camp to Her Majesty	First and Principal Naval Aide-de-Camp to Her Majesty	Aide-de-Camp General to Her Majesty
AIR CHIEF MARSHAL SIR DOUGLAS LOWE	ADMIRAL SIR JOHN FIELDHOUSE	GENERAL SIR FRANK KITSON

The Comptroller Lord Chamberlain's Office		The Gentleman Usher to the Sword of State
LIEUTENANT-COLONEL SIR JOHN JOHNSTON		AIR CHIEF MARSHAL SIR JOHN BARRACLOUGH

Field Officer in Brigade Waiting		Silver Stick in Waiting
COLONEL ANDREW DUNCAN		COLONEL JAMES HAMILTON-RUSSELL

The Lieutenant of the Yeomen of the Guard		The Lieutenant of the Honourable Corps of Gentlemen at Arms
COLONEL HUGH BRASSEY		COLONEL RICHARD CRICHTON

The Queen being seated on the Throne, the Peer bearing the Cap of Maintenance will stand on the right and the Peer bearing the Sword of State on the left of Her Majesty, on the steps of the Throne.

The Lord High Chancellor, The Lord President of the Council, the Lord Privy Seal and the Earl Marshal will stand on the right of Her Majesty; the Lord Great Chamberlain will stand on the steps of the Throne, on the left of Her Majesty, to receive the Royal Commands. The Officers of Her Majesty's Household will arrange themselves on each side of the steps of the Throne in the rear of the Great Officers of State.

At Her Majesty's Command the Gentleman Usher of the Black Rod will proceed to summon the Speaker and Members of the House of Commons to the Bar of the House of Lords.

DEPARTURE

When Her Majesty retires, the Procession will return in the same order as before to the Robing Room, where Her Majesty will unrobe and be conducted thence to the State Carriage by the Lord Great Chamberlain and the Earl Marshal, preceded by the Officers of Arms.

As soon as Her Majesty has departed, the Crown, the Cap of Maintenance and the Sword of State, will proceed under escort to the Royal Entrance.

Her Majesty's Judges will proceed through the Royal Gallery to the Royal Entrance.

The Gentlemen at Arms, having handed in their Axes, will proceed to the Norman Porch, followed by the Yeoman of the Guard.

10.30	The Honourable Corps of Gentlemen at Arms and The Queen's Bodyguard of the Yeomen of the Guard assemble at the top of the stairs leading from the Norman Porch.
10.45	Doors closed to the Public
10.45	A dismounted party of the Household Cavalry arrive at the Norman Porch and proceed to line the staircase.
10.47	The Queen's Bodyguard of the Yeomen of the Guard enter the Royal Gallery.
10.52	The Honourable Corps of Gentlemen at Arms proceed to the Princes Chamber.
10.52	The Crown, the Cap of Maintenance and the Sword of State, arrive at the Royal Entrance and proceed to the Regalia Room.
10.55	The Crown, the Cap of Maintenance and the Sword of State, arrive under escort in the Royal Gallery.
10.57	The Officers of Arms leave the Princes Chamber and proceed to the stairs leading from the Norman Porch.
11.00	The Members of the Royal Family not in the Procession arrive at the Norman Porch and proceed to the Robing Room.
11.05	The Crown is borne by the Lord Great Chamberlain into the Robing Room.
11.07	The Lord High Chancellor proceeds from the Princes Chamber to the foot of the stairs leading from the Norman Porch.
11.09	The Members of the Royal Family not in the Procession leave the Robing Room and proceed to the Chamber of the House of Lords.
11.15	Her Majesty the Queen arrives at the Royal Entrance and proceeds to the Robing Room.
11.20	The Cap of Maintenance and the Sword of State are handed to the Peers detailed to carry them and join the Procession in the Royal Gallery awaiting Her Majesty The Queen.
11.27	Her Majesty enters the Royal Gallery and the Procession advances into the Chamber of the House of Lords.

DRESS (A Collar Day)

Peers: Robes over Full Ceremonial Day Dress, Full Dress Uniform or Morning Dress. The Master of the Horse, the Captain of the Honourable Corps of Gentlemen at Arms and the Captain of the Yeoman of the Guard: Full Dress Uniform without Robes.

Gold Stick in Waiting, the Gentleman Usher of the Black Rod, the Comptroller Lord Chamberlain's Office, Silver Stick in Waiting, Field Officer in Brigade Waiting, Officers of Arms, Gentlemen at Arms and Yeomen of the Guard: Full Dress Uniform.

Others: Full Ceremonial Day Dress or Morning Dress with which Stars of Orders limited to two in number, a neck Badge, Decorations and Medals may be worn. Knights of the several Orders will wear their respective Collars.

Norfolk.

Earl Marshal

Meanwhile, the House of Lords itself (which is a relatively small chamber) is already packed with people and there is an atmosphere of suppresed expectancy. Peers in full parliamentary robes and peeresses in evening dress crowned with tiaras are greeting each other. Law lords and lords spiritual are crowded onto the benches. Members of the diplomatic corps are present, most in white tie and tails but with occasional flashes of native dress in exotic colours. And then the Queen's trumpeters' fanfares are heard in the distance as, after she has robed and wearing the great imperial crown, she progresses through the Palace of Westminster down the Royal Gallery, which is full of distinguished guests and lined by Beefeaters. As silence falls, the Queen arrives at the House of Lords, her long train borne by and, when she takes her seat on the throne, carefully displayed by young pages. It is a breathtaking scene, completely eclipsing any theatrical production. And of course it is real: the Queen has come to perform her duty of opening the session of Parliament.

Black Rod, an officer of the House of Lords, is despatched to the "other Chamber" and summons the Commons to the royal presence while all in the House of Lords remain waiting in complete silence. It seems a long three or four minutes before the steady tramp is heard of approaching Commoners in a procession two by two led by Mr Speaker, closely followed by the Prime Minister and the Leader of the Opposition. They stand at the bar of the House of Lords and then the Lord Chancellor dressed in black and gold legal robes steps forward and offers the Queen a copy of the speech which she is to deliver from the Throne. It has been written by the Government to inform Parliament.

As an example of a Queen's Speech, on 22 June 1983 she addressed Parliament as follows:

My Lords and Members of the House of Commons

(1) I look forward with great pleasure to receiving the President of Sri Lanka on a state visit in October and to paying visits to Kenya, Bangladesh and India in November. I also look forward to being present on the occasion of the Commonwealth Heads of Government meeting in New Delhi in November.

(2) My Government are determined to sustain Britain's contribution to Western defence. They will play an active and constructive part in the North Atlantic Alliance. They will modernise the existing independent nuclear deterrent with the Trident programme and will maintain adequate conventional forces.

My Government, in co-operation with the United Kingdom's allies, will work vigorously for balanced and verifiable measures of arms control. They strongly support the United States' proposals for reductions in nuclear forces. They stand by the NATO decision to counter existing Soviet systems and to begin the deployment of cruise and Pershing II missiles by the end of 1983. The numbers finally deployed will depend upon the outcome of the Geneva talks.

(3) My Government will work constructively for the development of the European Community. They will continue to seek a lasting solution to the budget problem. They will support negotiations for the accession of Spain and Portugal to the Community.

(4) My Government will continue fully to discharge their obligations to the people of the Falkland Islands. They reaffirm their commitment to the people of Gibraltar. They will continue talks with China on the future of Hong Kong, with the aim of reaching a solution acceptable to this Parliament, to China and to the people of Hong Kong.

(5) My Government will continue their full support for the Commonwealth. They will play an active and constructive role at the United Nations. They will promote increased co-operation and trade with developing nations. They will maintain a substantial aid programme directed especially at the poorer countries and will encourage the flow of British private investment.

My Government will work in close co-operation with governments of other countries and with international institutions to promote international recovery on a non-inflationary basis. They will urge the need to preserve and strengthen an open world trading system.

Members of the House of Commons

(6) Estimates for the Public Service will be laid before you.

My Lords and Members of the House of Commons

(7) My Government will pursue policies designed to increase economic prosperity and to reduce unemployment. They will seek a further reduction in inflation. They will continue to maintain firm control of public expenditure and a responsible financial strategy based upon sound money and lower public borrowing.

My Government will promote growth in output and opportunities for employment by encourging industry to be adaptable and efficient, and to compete successfully. Continued attention will be paid to the development and application of new technology. The improvement in training will be sustained. The special employment measures will continue to assist those out of work.

(8) A bill will be introduced to give trade union members greater control over their unions.

Legislation will be introduced to prepare for the introduction of private finance into nationalised industries, including British Telecommunications, and the Royal Ordnance Factories. Provision will be made for the regulation of telecommunications and the reform of the Telegraph Acts.

Legislation will be introduced to reform the organisation of public transport in London.

Legislation will be brought forward shortly to restore the major tax reductions proposed in the 1983 Budget but not yet enacted.

My Government will encourge the further development of United Kingdom oil and gas resources, and introduce legislation to abolish royalties in new fields. The disposal of the British Gas Corportion's oil assets will be completed.

My Government will pursue policies which sustain our agricultural, food and fishing industries. Legislation will be introduced to make more farming tenancies available in England and Wales.

Legislation will be brought forward to provide a selective scheme to curb excessive rate increases by individual local authorities, and to provide a general power, to be used if necessary, for the limitation of rate increases for all authorities. Measures to improve the rating system will also be laid before you.

Proposals will be prepared for the abolition of the Greater London Council and the metropolitan county councils.

Legislation will be introduced to extend the right of certain public sector and other tenants to buy their homes, and to reform the system of building control in England and Wales.

My Government will remain steadfast in their support for the services which maintain law and order. A bill will be introduced to replace the existing law on the prevention of terrorism. For England and Wales, legislation will be brought forward to modernise the law on police powers and to amend the law of criminal evidence and on police complaints procedures. Proposals will be prepared for the establishment of an independent prosecution service.

Measures will be brought forward to protect personal information held on computers, and to establish a cable authority and provide a framework for the development of cable systems.

A bill will be introduced to improve family law and its administration in England and Wales.

Further action will be taken to ensure that patients receive the best value for the money spent on the National Health Service.

My Government will pursue policies for improving standards of education and widening parental choice and influence in relation to schools. Legislation will be introduced to enable grants to be paid to local education authorities in England and Wales for innovations and improvements in the curriculum.

Measures relating to Scotland will include reforms to the rating system and the reform of the law relating to roads.

(9) In Northern Ireland, my Govenment will continue to give the highest priority to upholding law and order. Through the Northern Ireland Assembly, the people of Northern Ireland will continue to be offered a framework for participation in local democracy and political progress on the basis of widespread acceptance throughout the community.

Other measures will be laid before you.

My Lords and Members of the House of Commons

(10) I pray that the blessing of Almighty God may rest upon your counsels.

The section numbers attached to this Queen's Speech do not appear in the original and have been inserted by the author to suggest the structure of this key document. The speech naturally covers the manifesto of the recently-elected majority party which the Queen had invited to form the Government; but examined more closely it turns out to be a revealing document.

Section 1 is quite personal to the Queen as she is describing her actions as Monarch. These are of course all undertaken with the agreement of Government, because they have political implications, but nevertheless she is welcomed and feted abroad as nothing less than Head of State. Section 2 refers to the most important role of Government, namely national security, and this quickly runs into section 3, the Government's specific commitment to the European Communities. Sections 4 and 5 treat of foreign affairs generally and Britain's ongoing inter-governmental commitments. At this point, in section 6, the Queen pauses a moment. She looks down the Chamber and addresses only members of the House of Commons — in view of its exclusive role in financial matters. Section 7, addressed again to both Houses, turns to the broad domestic problems as Government sees them and then section 8, the largest, brings forward the programme of legislation which has been approved by the Cabinet. Some of the bills are politically charged and may have been in the election manifesto, while others are more routine matters promoted mostly by the departments themselves. Section 9 contains another commitment to an ongoing policy, namely in Northern Ireland, and she concludes with the necessarily open-ended: "Other measures will be laid before you." Section 10 is again quite personal, when the Head of State and indeed the Head of the Church, prays for the success of "your counsels".

When the Queen has ceased reading, the Lord Chancellor steps forward to receive the copy of the speech. Then the royal procession, gathering itself slowly together, exits right while, after a few moments, Members of the House of Commons return down the corridor to their Chamber and the Speaker directs that: "The Gracious Speech from the Throne to both Houses of Parliament be printed at the appropriate place in the Votes and Proceedings."

During the next six sitting days there is debated (from about 2.35 p.m. or later to 10 p.m.) the following motion:

That a humble Address be presented to Her Majesty as follows:

Most Gracious Sovereign, we your Majesty's most dutiful and loyal subjects, the Commons of the United Kingdom of Great Britain and Northern Ireland in Parliament assembled, beg leave to offer our humble thanks to Your Majesty for the Gracious Speech which Your Majesty addressed to both Houses of Parliament.[1]

The motion is not proposed by a minister but by two Members selected by the Prime Minister. They are followed one by one by all of the party leaders. In 1983 during the six days debate on the Address, 116 backbench Members spoke. During the first two days various subjects were debated, but while on the first day no minister responded for the Government, on the second the Home Secretary introduced the day's proceedings and the Secretary of State for the Environment wound up the debate. The third day was the first with a specific subject, industry and privatisation, with the Secretary of State for Trade and Industry opening the debate and the Secretary of State for Energy winding up. On the fourth day the welfare state was debated, with the Secretary of State for Social Services leading for the Government and the Minister of Health concluding. On the fifth and sixth days the Opposition proposed amendments critical of the Government, which means that on the fifth day, which was on foreign affairs and defence, the Foreign Secretary spoke *after* the critical motion was proposed by the Shadow Foreign Secretary but the Secretary of State for Defence wound up the debate for the Government. The sixth and final day was concerned with the economy and employment and again the Shadow Chancellor proposed an amendment to the motion which was critical of the Government and his speech was then followed by a contribution from the Chancellor of the Exchequer. The final winding-up speech on the debate on the Address, or the debate on the Queen's Speech as it is more colloquially known, was made to a crowded and noisy Chamber by the Leader of the House. And as Big Ben started to strike 10 p.m. the Speaker put the question, there was a hearty cry of "No", division bells rang out and then started the first of maybe 200 divisions to be held during the session.

The debate on the Queen's Speech is a chance for backbenchers to display their interests and talents, for ministers to present a *tour d'horizon* of their responsibilities and for shadow spokesmen to measure themselves against their adversaries on the benches opposite. But it is something more than that, because over half the Cabinet will speak during these few days. It is thus a rare chance to measure the attitude and commitment of the Government and the manner in which they are likely to treat the House of Commons during the coming session.

Often forgotten and seldom mentioned by the media or press is the second Queen's Speech of the session, which takes place at the prorogation of Parliament. Once again Members of the House of Commons led by their

Speaker are summoned to the House of Lords, but this time the speech is read by the Lord Chancellor. The Queen's Speech which concluded the session opened on 22 June 1983, was delivered on 31 October 1984 and was really an end-of-term report by the Government to Parliament. The Lord Chancellor said:

My Lords and Members of the House of Commons,

(1) The Duke of Edinburgh and I were pleased to receive the state visits of His Highness the Amir of Bahrain in April and the President of the French Republic and Madame Mitterrand last week.

(2) We look back with much pleasure to the visits we have made over the past year. As Head of the Commonwealth I was in New Delhi on the occasion of the Commonwealth Heads of Government meeting in November. We paid state visits to Kenya, Bangladesh and India in November and Jordan in March. Our thoughts are with the people of India today following the tragedy of Mrs Gandhi's assassination. We visited France in June, to attend the commemoration of the 40th anniversary of D-Day. We were in Canada in September and October for the bicentenary celebrations of New Brunswick and Ontario, and to visit Manitoba.

My Government welcomed the independence of Saint Christopher and Nevis, Brunei's resumption of full responsibility for its own external relations, and the decision of both countries to join the Commonwealth.

(3) My Government have sustained Britain's contribution to Western defence, playing an active part in the Atlantic Alliance. They welcomed Lord Carrington's appointment as its Secretary-General. In the absence of an arms control agreement, my Government fulfilled their undertaking to begin the deployment of cruise missiles by the end of 1983.

My Government, with the United Kingdom's allies, have worked vigorously for balanced and verifiable arms control and disarmament and have sought to improve relations with the Soviet Union and Eastern Europe. They fully supported the United States' efforts to achieve nuclear arms reductions and their readiness to resume the negotiations suspended by the Soviet Union.

(4) My Government agreed with other member states on a fair sharing of the European Community's budget burden and on control of Community spending. They have made proposals for new Community policies.

My Government were hosts to the London Economic Summit in June and welcome its conclusions.

(5) My Government have continued fully to discharge their obligations to the people of the Falkland Islands, while seeking more normal relations between this country and Argentina. They have conducted talks with China on the future of Hong Kong and published the text of a draft agreement. They have been helping with the conversion of the Royal Navy Dockyard in Gibraltar to commerical operation.

My Government have continued to support efforts to restore the independent and non-aligned status of Afghanistan and to settle the tragic conflict between Iran and Iraq. They have welcomed moves to reduce tension in southern Africa, and continue to support peaceful change there and the early independence of Namibia. They supported United Nations efforts to settle the Cyprus question.

Members of the House of Commons,

(6) I thank you for the provision which you have made for the honour and dignity of the Crown and for the Public Services.

My Lords and Members of the House of Commons,

(7) My Government have maintained the policies necessary to reduce inflation and sustain economic recovery. Inflation remains low and the output of the nation

continues to increase. Steps have been taken to increase incentives and to improve the climate for enterprise, the creation of wealth, and adaptability and efficiency in industry and commerce. Measures have been taken to help the unemployed into jobs, to launch a comprehensive foundation training scheme for young people starting working life, and to improve vocational education and adult training.

In order to promote economic efficiency and growth, my Government have continued their policies of exposing state-owned businesses to competition and returning them to the private sector where appropriate. Legislation has been passed to end British Telecom's exclusive privilege of running telecommunications systems, to establish arrangements for the licensing and regulation of telecommunications systems, and to prepare the way for the sale of British Telecom's shares. An act has been passed to enable the introduction of private finance into the Royal Ordnance Factories. The disposal of oil assets of the British Gas Corportion has been successfully completed.

(8) Legislation has been passed to provide for reforms in the tax system, especially for companies, in the interest of greater efficiency, to encourage the further development of United Kingdom oil and gas resources by abolishing royalties for certain new fields, and to provide a framework for the development of cable programme services and direct broadcasting by satellite. An act has been passed to ensure continued funding for the Co-operative Development Agency and to introduce a new scheme of regional development grants.

Legislation has been passed to give trade union members greater democratic control over their unions.

An act has been passed to protect ratepayers by limiting rate increases by high-spending local authorities, and to provide reserve powers for general limitation of rates. Legislation has been passed making interim arrangements for the Greater London Council and the metropolitan county councils pending a decison by Parliament on the abolition of those authorities.

Acts have been passed to extend the right of public sector tenants to buy their homes, to reform the system of building control in England and Wales, and to assist purchases of public sector houses which have proved to be defective. Legislation has been passed to make more farming tenancies available in England and Wales, and to make other improvements in the law relating to agricultural tenancies.

An Act has been passed transferring control of London Transport from the Greater London Council to the Government.

Legislation has been passed to modernise and clarify the law of England and Wales governing the investigation of crime and evidence in criminal proceedings, to strengthen the ties between the police and the community there and to extend powers to prevent acts of terrorism and to increase safeguards for people subject to such powers.

An act has been passed to introduce important new safeguards for individuals about whom information is held on computers.

Legislation has been passed to improve family law and its administration in England and Wales, to clarify the liability of occupiers of premises to persons other than their visitors and to amend the law concerning limitation of actions.

My Government has continued to work for higher standards in education, announcing proposals on the school curriculum, examinations and increasing the influence of parents over their children's schooling. Legislation has been passed to enable grants to be paid to local education authorities in England and Wales for improvements and innovations.

Legislation has been passed to replace non-contributory invalidity pensions with a severe disablement allowance. My Government has also embarked on a series of fundamental reviews of the social security system, seeking to ensure that this large programme operates effectively and in ways suited to present-day needs.

My Government has taken further action to ensure that patients receive the best value for money spent on the National Health Service.

(9) My Government has encourged Northern Ireland's elected representatives to seek arrangements, acceptable across the community, whereby responsibilities can be returned to local administration. A high priority has been given to the maintenance of law and order and support for the Northern Ireland economy.

For Scotland, measures have been passed to extend the right of public sector tenants, and to improve the legislation governing rating and valuation, promotion of tourism overseas, roads and inshore fisheries.

(10) My Lord and Members of the House of Commons, I pray that the blessing of Almighty God may attend you.

The structure of the Queen's Speech at prorogation is the same as the one she delivers herself at the opening of Parliament. It contains quite a full resumé of what the Monarch and the Government have undertaken for the country and of the work that Parliament itself has completed. In this speech section 1 covered the Queen's personal actions and sections 2–5 concerned the Commonwealth, defence, the European Communities and foreign affairs respectively. Section 6 was a message of thanks to the Commons for financial support, section 7 was concerned with domestic matters and section 8 contains quite full references to the most important government legislation passed during the session. After referring to Northern Ireland and Scotland in section 9, the Queen in section 10 again concluded on a personal note. Having delivered the Speech, the Lord Chancellor then concluded the session by proroguing Parliament and announcing the date of the opening of the next session.

The two speeches can be interesting to compare. Opening the session the Queen was able to speculate to only a small extent on foreign affairs. Her prorogation speech in this area has a great deal to report on the uncertainties and surprises of the previous 16 months and the actions to which they had led. In domestic affairs it is different. While there may be some areas of disappointment (Northern Ireland for instance), it is probable that the Government considered the Queen's Speech concerning government legislation passed to be reporting on a satisfactory session.

Meanwhile, after the Speaker and Members of the House of Commons had returned to their Chamber, Mr Speaker rose and said:

I have further to acquaint the House that the Lord High Chancellor, one of the High Commissioners, delivered Her Majesty's Most Gracious Speech to both Houses of Parliament, in pursuance of Her Majesty's Command. For greater accuracy, I have obtained a copy and directed that the terms of the Speech be printed in the Votes and Proceedings. Copies are being made availabe in the Vote Office.

The speech is read into the record of the House of Commons, which record concludes:

Thereafter a Commission for proroguing Parliament was read, after which the Lord Chancellor said:

My Lords and Members of the House of Commons

By virtue of Her Majesty's Commission which has been now read we do, in Her Majesty's name, and in obedience to Her Majesty's Commands, prorogue this parliament to Tuesday the sixth day of November, to be then here holden, and this Parliament is accordingly prorogued to Tuesday the sixth day of November next.

End of the First Session (opened on 15 June 1983) of the Forty-Ninth Parliament of the United Kingdom of Great Britain and Northern Ireland, in the Thirty-Third Year of the Reign of Her Majesty Queen Elizabeth the Second.[2]

NOTES

1. HC Deb. vol. 967, c.52
2. HC Deb. vol. 65, c.1390–92

5. Debates: Government Motions, Opposition Motions, Adjournment Debates

Whenever the House of Commons debates there must be a clear motion before it. There may also be an amendment to the motion. At the end of the debate the Chair puts the question whether the motion is accepted or not; if there is an amendment then this will be put first, and the House arrives at a decision. If clear disagreement is signified when the question is put there follows a division and a vote.

I have taken at random the first 10 sitting days of 1984 to illustrate the pattern of House of Commons debates. Table 4A shows that there were 28 debates in this period and Table 4B gives a break-down of these debates in terms of the type of business conducted.

Table 4A
House of Commons Debates 16.1.1984–27.1.1984: Chronology

Date	Subject and Motion	Ministers and Department	Length	Divisions
16.1.84	1. Ordnance Factories and Military Services Bill Motion for second reading	Min. of State and Under-Sec. of State Defence Procurement	6½ hours	2
	2. Urban Development Corporations Resolved (Financial Limits) Order 1983 be approved	Under-Sec. of State Environment	1¼ hours	–
	3. School Transport Motion to adjourn	Under-Sec. of State Education	25 minutes	–
17.1.84	4. Rates Bill Motion for second reading	Sec. of State and Under-Sec. of State Environment	6¼ hours	2
	5. Rates Bill [Money] Resolved . . . the payment out of moneys . . .	Under-Sec. of State Environment	1 hour	1
	6. New Towns (Borrowing) Resolved (Limit on Borrowing) Order 1983 be approved	Under-Sec. of State Environment	1 hour	–
	7. Health, Wales Motion to adjourn	Under-Sec. of State Wales	30 minutes	–
18.1.84	8. Tenants' Rights etc. (Scotland) Amendment Bill As amended (in standing committee) considered and third reading.	Under-Sec. of State Scotland	5¾ hours	4
	9. Highlands and Islands Shipping Services Draft undertaking between Sec. of State and North Scotland, Orkney and Shetland Shipping Company . . . be approved	Under-Sec. of State Scotland	42 minutes	–

37

Date	Item	Minister	Time	
	10. Swans Motion to adjourn	Under-Sec. of State Environment	30 minutes	–
19.1.84	11. Occupational Pensioners (Housing Benefit) [Fifth Opposition Day] Motion that this House noting . . . urges H.M. Govt. to reconsider this matter at once	Sec. of State Social Services and Minister for Social Security	3 hours	1
	12. Nottingham County Council Bill [Lords] As amended considered	–	2¾ hours	–
	13. Ashfield Skill Centre Motion to adjourn	Minister of State Employment	30 minutes	–
20.1.84	14. Education Motion that this House welcomes the proposals of Govt. in relation to curriculum, examinations & teachers . . .	Sec. of State Education	4 hours 50 minutes	–
	15. Medway Health District (Resources) Motion to adjourn	Under-Sec. of State Health & Social Security	30 minutes	–
23.1.84	16. Local Government Rate Support Grant Report (England) 1984–85 be approved	Sec. of State and Under-Sec. of State Environment	7 hours 50 minutes	1
	17. Leyland Vehicles Motion to adjourn	Under-Sec. of State Trade and Industry	30 minutes	–
24.1.84	18. Scott Lithgow (Britoil Contract) [Sixth Opposition Day] Motion that this House recognising the central importance of Britoil contract . . . demand that immediate steps be taken by Govt. to secure the future of the yard	Sec. of State Scotland and Minister of State Trade and Industry	2 hours 50 minutes	1
	19. British Rail Engineering Ltd [Sixth Opposition Day] Motion that this House being opposed to large scale redundancies . . . urges Govt. to reject the Serpell strategy for BR . . .	Sec. of State and Under-Sec. of State Transport	2 hours 30 minutes	2
	20. Education (Assisted Places) Draft Education (Assisted Places) (Amendment) Regulations 1984 . . . be approved	Under-Sec. of State Education	1 hour 30 minutes	1
	21. Tax Office, Matlock Motion to adjourn	Financial Secretary	27 minutes	–
25.1.84	22. Prevention of Terrorism (Temporary Provisions) Bill As amended (in standing committee) considered and third reading	Min. of State and Home Secretary Home Office	7 hours	6

38

	23. A30 (Cornwall) Motion to adjourn	Minister of State Transport	30 minutes	–
26.1.84	24. European Communities Developments Motion that this House takes note of the Report on EC Developments January–June 1983	Minister of State Foreign & Commonwealth Office Economic Secretary to Treasury	5 hours 10 minutes	1
	25. European Assembly Elections Draft European Assembly Elections Regulations 1983 . . . be approved	Under-Sec. of State Home Office	1 hour	1
	26. British Rail (Southern Region) Motion to adjourn	Under-Sec. of State Transport	22 minutes	–
27.1.84	27. Reuters (Flotation) Motion	Minister of Information Technology	4 hours 52 minutes	–
	28. Teacher Training Motion to adjourn	Under-Sec. of State Education and Science	28 minutes	–

Table 4B
House of Commons Debates 16.1.1984–27.1.1984: Type of Business

Debate number	Parliamentary time	Type of Business
1,4,5	Government time	Legislation, 2nd reading
8,22	Government time	Legislation, report and 3rd reading
2,6,9,16,20,25	Government time	Delegated legislation
12	Government time	Private bill
24	Government time	Report debated
3,7,10,13,15,17, 21,23,26,28	Government time	Half-hour adjournment debate
11,18,19	Opposition time	Opposition motion
14,27	Private Members' time	Private Members' motion

The arrangement of government and opposition time is through the "usual channels", a term used for discussions between the Whips of the government and major opposition parties. The business of the House is announced on Thursday afternoons but only for the following week and the Monday thereafter. As described in chapter 3, the Government control most of the time and they initiate nearly all legislation (debates 1,4,5,8 and 22 in tables 4A and 4B), and all delegated legislation (debates 2,6,9,23 and 25). There was only one government report discussed in this period (debate 24) and that was the six- monthly report on developments in the European Communities. Opposition time used in this fortnight were the fifth and sixth of the 19 opposition days which are allotted each session (debates 11,18 and 19).

The allocation of the third block of time, that of private Members, is not arranged behind the scenes. On a number of days each session, which are specified at the beginning of the session, a register is opened for the 10 or 11 days allotted for private Members' motions. When the book is closed on each designated day, the ballot for private Members' motions takes place in the Chamber. The Clerk Assistant takes a numbered slip from a box, reads out the number and the Speaker then reads out the successful Member's name. Three Members are picked, though often the first debate takes all the available time. The Member must choose his subject 10 days before the debate, thus giving the minister time to prepare his reply. He may delay the actual wording of his motion until the day before the debate. During this particular fortnight debates 14 and 27 were decided upon in this fashion. Finally, at the end of each day the Government moves the adjournment of the House and for up to 30 minutes a Member's particular subject may be debated. The Speaker holds a private ballot to decide which Members may raise matters on this adjournment motion. But for the Thursday adjournment debate, the Speaker himself chooses the Member. In this fortnight debates 3,7,10,13,15,17,21,23,26,28 came into this category.

For all these debates save one the Government was represented by a minister, of secretary of state, minister of state, or under-secretary of state level, depending on the debate's importance in the mind of the secretary of state. Most adjournment debates, for instance, are handled by an under-secretary of state, while the Government's response to the Opposition fifth and sixth days' motions, and indeed to one of the private Members' motions, was at secretary of state level.

Before turning to a few examples of the use made by ministers of these debates, I should say a word about debate 12, since this was unusual. The Nottingham County Council Bill is a private bill promoted by the County Council. It does not concern the Government directly, which is why no minister is directly responsible during the debate. However, in the course of these debates a minister may give the Government's view on the bill. It is very unusual to have such a debate, but although the main procedures for private bills are held outside the Chambers such bills do formally pass through the House. If Members call "Object" when the motion is proposed to give them a reading, and if this is repeated on two or three occasions, then in the end they are debated, as they were in this case.

Debate 1 was concerned with legislation, the second reading of the Ordnance Factories and Military Services Bill. The minister's speech will have been carefully drafted by his civil servants and mentions both the general background and the content of the bill together with the importance of specific clauses:

Minister of State for Defence Procurement (Mr Geoffrey Pattie): I beg to move, that the bill be now read a second time.

The purpose of the bill is to enable the royal ordnance factories, which are at present an integral part of the Ministry of Defence, to become an independent commercial organisation established under the Companies Acts. The royal ordnance factories [ROFs] are a large, closely integrated engineering and chemical production organisation consisting of 13 factories, each of which is expert in particular aspects of the manufacture and supply of defence equipment and munitions.

The present organisation and its antecedents have served this country well for nearly 400 years, through the Napoleonic wars, the two world wars, the recent Falkland Islands conflict, and now, in times of peace, in the development of the most up-to-date equipment to meet an increasingly sophisticated threat. The present product range of the royal ordnance factories stretches from battle tanks to bombs, mines to missiles, and rifles to respirators. Most of those products are designed to meet a specific requirement of our armed forces, but a significant part of the royal ordnance factories' work has been exported, and they are increasingly concerned with products related to the needs of armed forces other than our own. Other countries have taken a keen interest in purchasing the ROFs' high-quality products. We wish this record to continue, subject of course to the control which the Government exercise over all arms sales abroad.

Today, as in the past, the ROFs are staffed by a loyal and dedicated work force numbering just under 18,500. Their efforts have made the organisation a success not only in terms of the quality of its products, which are second to none in the world, but in its trading performance. We are considering a successful organisation and the bill will enable the ROFs to build on that success.

Since the Second World War the royal ordnance factories' organisation has moved progressively towards more commercial disciplines and accountability. The ROF trading fund was the first such fund to be established under the Government Trading Funds Act 1973. It was set up in 1974 and has operated since then with great success, winning the Queen's Award for Exports in 1976 and 1978. . . .

Clauses 2 and 3 supplement the provisions of clause 1 by defining the ambit of the property, rights and liabilities that may be transferred initially and by laying down some general rules regarding the operation of schemes and the publication of their contents. In this last connection, hon. Members will observe that the Secretary of State is bound to report to Parliament on the contents of a scheme. That is in clause 3(9). Clause 4 brings in schedule 2, which contains provisions relating to the transfer of employment.

Those clauses are the heart of the bill. Clauses 5 to 13 deal with incidentals — such things as the acquisition of further securities in a company after its initial establishment; the appointment of nominees to act on behalf of the Secretary of State; the extinguishment of liabilities pertaining to the trading fund after transfer of assets out of the trading fund; the conferring of certain exemptions from stamp duty; and the making of provision incidental to the investment of private capital. The House will not expect me at this stage to go into detail on all those provisions.

Clause 14 deals with International Military Services Ltd. This Clause has an entirely separate purpose from that of the rest of the Bill. International Military Services Ltd is already constituted as a private limited company under the Companies Act and has the same legal responsibilities as any private sector company. The purpose of the clause is to provide statutory authority for the contingent financial liability incurred by the Secretary of State for Defence when he assumed ministerial responsibility for the affairs of International Military Services Ltd and became sole owner of its shares.

In his winding up speech the Under-Secretary of State for Defence Procurement (John Lee) accepts that the Government will have to respond to some of the points raised during this debate on the principle of the Bill:

Mr Robert C. Brown: I accept that the minister cannot give all the answers tonight. Will he therefore assure the House that he will either introduce or accept amendments to the bill which would write into the act the guarantees which the employees are currently seeking?

Mr Lee: The Government will consider that point, but tonight I cannot make guarantees or any specific statement from the dispatch box.

On the next day debate 4 is the second reading of the Rates Bill. Again facts and figures will have been carefully drafted, as this extract shows:

Secretary of State for the Environment (Mr Patrick Jenkin): I should like to give the House a few figures because they tell the story very clearly. Since 1978–79 the average increase in councils' current spending in cash terms has been 86 per cent. But what is one to say about Islington or Greater Manchester where the spending has gone up 105 per cent in the same period?

Mr Reg Freeson (Brent, East): What about grants?

Mr Jenkin: This is spending. This has nothing to do with grants. I should have thought that the right hon. Gentleman would have understood the difference. I am sorry, the right hon. Gentleman's question was not clear.

What is one to think of Greenwich where it has gone up 114 per cent, or Leicester or Camden?

Several Hon. Members *rose——*

Mr Jenkin: Let me get a little further on because it is important that the House hear the case. What is one to think of Hackney, whose expenditure has increased by no less than 154 per cent? And of course top of the league, unrivalled for profligacy, is the GLC whose spending has gone up no less than 185 per cent. Central Government have had to pay the cost of that. [Further figures follow.] While on the subject of business rates, I mention two further changes. Schedule 1 will from 1985–86 give all non-domestic ratepayers the right to pay rates by instalments — domestic ratepayers already have this facility. For next year I have made an order to raise the limits for rateable vaue to £10,000 in London and £5,000 elsewhere. In the following year, the option will be available to all non-domestic ratepayers. I shall make regulations exempting empty industrial pro-perties from rates.

The bill includes also an important provision to increase accountability of councils to domestic ratepayers. Many domestic occupiers of council properties — we have heard this complaint over the years — do not pay their rates direct but have them included in their rents. Such occupiers will, from 1985, receive clear notice of their rating liability and a copy of the information about their council's budget which councils send out. We propose also to issue new rate demand rules for 1985–86.

As in the previous debate Members not only raise issues but ask questions and in the winding up speech a minister with the help of his civil servants will seek to reply to some of these:

Under-Secretary of State for the Environment (Mr William Waldegrave): The Government are proposing to provide reserve powers to protect the citizen and the ratepayer where the system is not protected properly by its own self-righting mechanisms.

The hon. Member for Copeland (Dr Cunningham) asked how much would be saved. . . . Undoubtedly, we shall have a prolonged opportunity to discuss these matters in committee. However, let us say that we were to save £300,000,000 — that is probably the order of magnitude, as my right hon. Friend said — in the first year. It will depend entirely on the criteria that we finally agree. Let us say that the figure is £3,000,000 or £4,000,000. That would be a major contribution to keeping Government finances on an even keel. I have already mentioned the scale of savings that we could make in this connection alongside the kind of savings——

Mr Straw *rose*——

Mr Waldegrave: The hon. Gentleman knows perfectly well that until we have discussed and agreed the criteria it would be foolish to say exactly how much, and what is more, we do not yet know what the effect on local councils' budgeting for next year will be. Of course, many local councils are budgeting sensibly in advance of this bill.

Debates 8 and 22, also on legislation, are rather different as they are con-cerned with a later stage of two bills' passage through the House — the report stage. After the second reading most bills go to a standing committee for examination and are debated clause by clause. They then return to the House for the report stage. During the report stage there are firstly new clauses proposed and then amendments. Many of the new clauses are proposed by the Government and some by the Opposition. The new clauses and the amendments to be debated are selected by the Speaker and they often arise from the earlier debate in standing committee. The following passage from a ministerial contribution — on the Tenants' Rights etc. (Scotland) Amendment Bill — demonstrates the kind of detail that may be involved at this stage:

Under-Secretary of State for Scotland (Mr Michael Ancram): New clause 9 would repeal subsection (10) of section 2 of the Tenants' Rights, Etc. (Scotland) Act 1980, which provides that a tenant who has received an offer to sell, but subsequently withdraws his application, shall not be entitled to make a fresh application for a further period of 12 months. Amendment 1 is a consequential amendment, which would delete subsection (3) from clause 1.

In committee we had a very useful discussion of the transitional provisions in clause 1. Subsection (3) in particular sought to provide that, where a tenant had received but not accepted an offer to sell on the date the bill takes effect, he should be entitled to withdraw his application and submit a fresh one, to take account of the higher levels of discount available, without having to wait the normal period of 12 months which would be required under section 2(10) of the 1980 act.

I took it from the debates that we had in committee that this suggestion would find favour with both sides of the committee. The hon. Member for Glasgow, Garscadden (Mr Dewar) makes faces. I suppose that everybody is entitled to change his mind. I cannot remember whether the hon. Gentleman was still on the committee when we discussed this matter, but my recollection is that there was general support for this suggestion.

If section 2(10) is repealed, then there is nothing to stop a tenant who has a current offer to sell, which he has not yet accepted, at the time the bill takes effect from withdrawing his application and submitting a fresh one immediately, and subsection (3) of clause 1 therefore becomes unnecessary. As a consequence, amendment 1 proposes that this subsection of clause 1 should be omitted.

I hope that the new clause and the amendment find favour with the House.

In these report stages of bills, although the debates on new clauses are formally like second reading debates, they are often at a lower political temperature than are the main second reading debates on the policy of the bill as a whole. Ministers' speeches are always a mixture of information and politics, but at the report stage the politics may be diluted, as shown in the following passage from proceedings on the Scottish tenants' rights bill:

Mr Ancram: I beg to move, that the clause (new clause 11) be read a second time.

The new clause would extend the benefits of the right to repair to tenants of district councils and other housing authorities, who occupy tied houses. Although tenants of tied houses do not have security of tenure, they already enjoy the other rights that make up the tenants' charter under the 1980 act with the exception of those rights that would conflict with their status as service tenants. The right to repair will be in addition to the tenants' charter. It is appropriate that this new right should be extended to tenants of tied houses. An amendment to this effect was brought forward in committee by the hon. Member for Glasgow, Maryhill (Mr Jim Craigen), and while I supported the underlying principle, I said that the amendment's drafting was not entirely acceptable. I seem to recollect that I gave it fairly high marks, on the advice of those who advise me on drafting.

The hon. Gentleman agreed to withdraw his amendment on the understanding that the Government would bring forward a suitable amendment on report with exactly the same intention, to extend the right to repair to tenants of tied houses. That is the purpose of the new clause, and I trust that it will be welcomed by right hon. and hon. Members on both sides of the House.

Mr Craigen: As the Minister pointed out, the Opposition put forward this proposal in committee. I thank him for improving upon our excellent drafting. I trust that the marking range has increased as a result of the Government's draftsmen applying their minds to the problem.

When new clauses have been completed and the report stage moves to amendments, then the debate may be even less politically motivated, as shown in the following passage (relating to clause 3 dealing with the "right to carry out repairs"):

> **Mr Ancram:** I beg to move amendment No. 7, in page 3, line 37, leave out from "be" to " and" in line 38 and insert "determined in such manner as the regulations may specify".
>
> The purpose of this amendment is to make it clear that regulations setting up the right to repair scheme may provide for disputes arising under the scheme to be referred to arbitration, rather than the sheriff court.
>
> When the right to repair was discussed in committee, hon. Members on both sides expressed concern that tenants might be deterred from pursuing disputes before the sheriff because they might find the procedures involved complex or forbidding. It is clear from the wider consultations, that many people who have been asked to comment on the scheme share these concerns.
>
> The majority of disputes arising under the scheme are likely to be of a technical nature — for example over the adequacy of a repair, or the appropriate level of payment. In committee I accepted that there was merit in the suggestion that disputes of a technical nature might be settled by an independent arbiter, for example, a man of skill. I have tabled the amendment in response to representations. I hope that in the light of the acceptance that the suggestion found in committee the amendment will be welcomed and approved.

So much for the Government informing Parliament during debates on legislation. A rather different situation arises when the Opposition puts down the motion for the House to debate. This happened during the fortnight covered in tables 4A and 4B in debates 11,18 and 19. With debate 11 on occupational pensioners (housing benefit) Norman Fowler (Secretary of State for Social Services) proposes, as would be expected, that the Opposition's motion should be replaced by his own and says:

> I beg to move, to leave out from "House" to the end of the question [the text of the opposition critical motion] and to add instead thereof:
>
> "notes that even after the changes in housing benefits announced as a result of the Chancellor's Autumn Statement, expenditure on social security benefits, including housing benefits, will continue to rise in real terms in 1984–85; considers that the greatest help Her Majesty's Government can give occupational pensioners and all social security beneficiaries is to conquer inflation; and congratulates the Government on the substantial progress made in bringing inflation down to the lowest levels for 15 years."
>
> I wish at the outset to make clear the position on the proposed reductions in housing benefit. As the House will know, the proposals made after the Chancellor's Autumn Statement were referred to the Social Security Advisory Committee, to which the hon. Member for Oldham, West (Mr Meacher) referred. That committee has reported to me in the last two weeks and I am currently considering its proposals. Obviously I wish to study carefully what the committee has said, and I shall be publishing the report, together with the Government's response on the matter, in the next few weeks.

I am anxious to make it clear at the outset also that the Government are not inflexible on the proposals. As well as considering the views of the advisory committee, we shall take into account what is being said in this debate about the proposed changes. I thought it right to make that position clear at the beginning of the debate. I shall come shortly to the areas of consideration, but first there are two initial points I should make because they go to the heart of the debate.

First, we must recognise the background against which we are debating housing benefit, and it is not the background as stated by the hon. Member for Oldham, West. It is that social security spending next year is expected to run at about £37,000 million which is 29 per cent of the planned total of public expenditure. We expect it to be almost £1,000 million higher than assumed in last year's Public Expenditure White Paper, and that is even after allowing for the savings that we want to achieve in the social security budget.

The second point I wish to emphasise is that the Government have already announced that provision has been taken within our spending plans for all weekly benefits to be uprated next November in line with prices, not only the pledged benefits but the unpledged ones also, such as supplementary benefit and unemployment benefit. By any standards the Government are spending a vast amount of money on social security provisions. . . .

In the winding up speech for the Government, Dr Rhodes Boyson, the Minister for Social Security, is of course resisting a motion of criticism. First he takes the opportunity briefly to review government policy in general, but as the second passage below shows he concludes by turning to the specific motion before the House:

Reference has been made to the effect that there is no sense of heart, compassion or feeling on this side of the House. Let us look at the record of the Government on social security. Social security expenditure now is 25 per cent up in real terms in four and a half years. Even allowing for increased numbers on unemployment and supplementary benefit and 600,000 more pensioners than there were in 1979, almost every benefit is higher in real terms than it was when we came into office. One-parent benefit is the highest ever, and child benefit is at its peak. On the handicapped, we are spending 21 per cent more in real terms now than when we came in in 1979. With reference to the pensioners, as my right hon. Friend said at the beginning of the debate, between November 1978 and November 1983 the pension has been increased by 74.6 per cent, and the retail price index has gone up by 68.8 per cent. In other words, the purchasing power of the pension is higher than when we came into office.

Reference was also made to heating. Heating additions in 1978–79 were £124,000,000. Heating additions in 1983–84 will be £350,000,000, £100,000,000 more in real terms than when we came into office. It was this Government that made any person on supplementary benefit at the age of 70 automatically eligible for a heating allowance. That was done not by the so-called compassion lobby opposite, but by this Goverment out of the real money with which it was dealing. . . .

My right hon. Friend said that we will look at everything that has been said and that includes all the suggestions put forward on housing benefits. My right hon. Friend and I have read the Social Security Advisory Committee report, and have looked at it carefully. Hon. Members will have the assistance of our comments on it when it is published at the time the regulations are laid.

It is as well to remind the House that, after I met the local authority leaders last October, we announced our intention to bring in about 25 variations to make the scheme easier to carry out, variations that have cost us between £3,000,000 and

£4,000,000, but which we are glad to do at the request of the local authorities. Whatever has been said in the House to day about what local authorities have done on housing benefits, I believe that the vast majority of local authorities have done their best to implement the scheme. The information coming in — and I met the local authorities only three weeks ago — is that it is now largely turning over. Indeed, the Association of Metropolitan Authorities said the housing benefit scheme has recently moved into a more stable position and that local authorities are now generally beginning to cope with the new scheme.

We will take note of what has been said in the debate, and we will consider what has been said by the National Association of Citizens Advice Bureaux.

Delegated legislation is where a statute, called the enabling act, has given a minister power to bring in a regulation and in many cases with the approval of Parliament. This motion is put to the House following a debate of not more than an hour and a half. Debates 2,6,9,20,23 and 25 in tables 4A and 4B are all motions to approve government proposals. They are sometimes concerned with financial limits as is the case with numbers 2,6 and 16. Patrick Jenkin (Secretary of State for the Environment), introducing the motion approving the Rate Support Grant Report (England) 1984–85 (debate 16), included the following:

I come to the settlement for 1984–85. Faced with a budgeted overspend in the current year of £750,000,000 — three-quarters of that overspend comes from no more than just 16 Labour-controlled authorities — I have had to increase the White Paper provision — [*Interruption.*] Penalties are nothing to do with this issue. I am talking about spending and there is no question of any penalties affecting the amount that they decide to spend. . . .

I have had to increase the provision for next year by £540,000,000, to £20,400 million. That is the figure for local authority current spending. Of course, that increase has put pressure on other of the Chancellor of the Exchequer's programmes. The targets that I have set are consistent with that figure of £20,400 million.

In setting targets, I have tried to take account of the representations made to me by local authorities. The big change this year is that I have made a larger distinction than ever before between the majority of authorities which have tried to find savings, and the high-spending minority which have not. But I do not question for one moment that the targets imply real economies across the board even for responsible low-spending councils.

The target for most low-spending authorities — there are 233 in that category — is a cash increase of 3 per cent over the adjusted budget for this year. By contrast, most high-spending authorities have targets representing cash cuts of up to 6 per cent. What those targets will buy will depend crucially on the rate of increase in local government costs, and two-thirds of those costs are wages. A clear message of this settlement is that restraint in manpower costs is needed more than ever this year. If the local government employers concede high pay settlements this year, of course even the maximim 3 per cent increase from budgets will mean even greater cuts elsewhere. The downward trend of manpower numbers must be resumed. Councils simply cannot expect to keep their spending below target if they allow their manpower numbers to rise.

At a later stage in his speech Patrick Jenkin gave the Government's view on the work of a recently established organisation:

Before I sit down, I want to say something about a new factor in the equation — the Audit Commission. Set up under the 1982 Local Government Finance Act, the commission was given a specific remit to look at value for money in local authority spending. The commission really got under way in April of last year, and it has already produced an impressive handbook entitled *Economy, Efficiency, and Effectiveness* explaining how it proposes to tackle this aspect of its work. Copies are in the Library of the House, and I am sure that the commission will be happy to provide a copy to any hon. Member who wishes to have one. Copies have been sent to every local authority, and each local authority has been given an individual profile of its own spending, costs and other data — including demographic data — together with comparisons with the figures of other comparable authorities of the same class. . . .

A rather different regulation requiring approval by the House concerned the 1984 European Assembly election (debate 25). It was proposed by David Mellor (Under-Secretary of State, Home Department) and his lucid brief was most comprehensive, as the following extract shows:

Before I describe the changes in more detail it may be for the convenience of the House if I say something in general about the arrangements being made for the second general European Parliament election in June this year.

As hon. Members wil recall, the first direct elections took place from Thursday 7 to Sunday 10 June 1979, with the United Kingdom voting on the Thursday. Under the Community legislation of 1976, the next elections fell to to be held exactly five years later, from 7 to 10 June 1984. However, the Council of Ministers decided earlier this year that it was not possible to hold the elections during that period, which coincides with the Whitsun holiday in several member states. As my right hon. Friend the Minister of State, Foreign and Commonwealth Office, informed the House on 23 February last year, the Council originally proposed that the election should be held from 17 May to 21 May 1984. After consultation with the Parliament, it was agreed that the period should instead be from 14 to 17 June 1984. My right hon. Friend has accordingly made an order fixing Thursday, 14 June 1984 as the day of election in the United Kingdom.

The other member states voting on Thursday will be Denmark, the Netherlands and the Republic of Ireland. France, Belgium, Germany, Greece, Italy and Luxemburg will vote on the Sunday. As in 1979, the votes cannot be counted until polling has closed in every member state. It is not yet clear at what time on Sunday, 17 June, this will be, but my right hon. and learned Friend will advise the political parties and acting returning officers as soon as the infomation is known. The regulations require the returning officer to begin the count "as soon as practicable" after polling has ended throughout the Community. It is up to him to decide whether it is practicable to begin on the Sunday evening.

In his winding-up speech the minister took full note of some of the contributions made by Members.

The hon. Member for Knowsley, North (Mr Kilroy-Silk) made a more serious contribution to the debate. I shall deal with two of his points before letting my hon. Friends go to their beds. He mentioned an important point about whether the timetable for the European elections and its coincidence with the local elections would cause any difficulties. I have taken some advice on that question, and I can confirm that notice of the European election will be published at least one day before polling day for the ordinary local elections. I am assured that that will have no effect on party political spending on either the local or the European elections. I will check again, and if I am wrong about that I will let the hon. Gentleman know. He raised the point in good faith and I want to deal with it.

The minister's final speech, in response to Robert Kilroy-Silk's second point, included a full summary of the work of the Boundary Commissions, on which it had been the Government's view "for some months . . . that the Boundary Commissions will be able to present to the Home Secretary in time for him, given normal circumstances, to be able to lay the relevant orders before the House — proposals that would enable the June elections to be held on new boundaries". The whole debate contained a great deal of information from the minister who, in commending the motion to the House, concluded:

> I should have liked to commend the regulations to the House in good time, but Liberal Members are up at quite unwarrantedly late time of night for them, and so that they can divide the House, and so prove beyond peradventure to their constituents that they are in the House at this time of night — perhaps for the first time, for some of them, in the whole of their parliamentary careers — and still be at home, tucked up in their beds with cups of Horlicks and improving literature well before midnight, I shall conclude.

Debate number 24 in the tables is one of the regular debates on European Communities affairs which are discussed in chapter 11. The final group of debates during this fortnight were the half-hour adjournment debates which concluded each day's proceedings (debates 3,7,10,13,15,17,21,23,26 and 28). Although these are held in government time they provide many opportunities for Members to bring ministers to the despatch box and respond to their worries. In debate number 10 Jeremy Hansley was worried about swans:

> The number of swans in parts of Britain has declined seriously. It was noticed during the 1970s that flocks in many parts of the country were diminishing and by 1978 the famous flock of swans upon the Avon at Stratford had disappeared. Numbers on the Thames have declined dramatically. During the 1956 annual swan-upping there were found to be 1,311 swans and cygnets on the Thames. Between Putney and Henley in 1982 the figure had droped to 255. Last year, there were 179.
>
> I have figures for the Thames, following counts for the dyers and vintners companies and the Keeper of the Queen's Swans in 1953. Then there were well over 1,000 swans. In 1983 there were well under 200 swans on the main part of the Thames. Of the 19 swans that underwent a post-mortem in 1983, particularly from the Kingston—Richmond stretch, 17 died as a direct result of lead poisoning. Both Mr Cobb of the dyers and vintners companies and Captain John Turk, the Keeper of the Queen's Swans, agree that the main cause of the swan decline is lead poisoning. I stress that it is not the only cause by any means.

The minister (William Waldegrave, Under-Secretary of State for the Environment), in agreeing that lead poisoning was a major cause, indicated the Government's position following a report by Nature Conservancy Council. This report had been made at the express request of the Minister of Agriculture.

> The working group report recommended a number of courses of action, the most important of which were: first, that the code of practice for anglers, developed by the National Anglers Council, should be given maximim publicity; secondly, that the use of split-lead shot by anglers should be phased out within five years; thirdly, that research and development of acceptable non-toxic alternatives to lead should be pursued vigorously; and fourthly, that the Nature Conservancy

Council should review the position in 1984 to establish how far the programme for action had met with success.

My colleague and predecessor in this responsibility, in a written reply to Sir Frederick Burden on 10 December 1981, welcomed the report on behalf of the Government and concluded with these words: "I hope that all bodies who have a concern in these matters will use their best endeavours to implement the report's recommendations and combine to alleviate the suffering of our swan population and to eradicate it causes." [*Official Report*, 10 December 1981; Vol. 14, c. *487*.]

More recently, in April last year, the Royal Commission on Environmental Pollution, in its report on lead in the environemnt agreed with the NCC report. The Royal Commission recommended: "Urgent efforts should be made to develop alternatives to . . . lead fishing weights. . . . As soon as these alternatives are available, the Government should legislate to ban any further use of lead shot and fishing weights . . . where they are irretrievably dispersed in the environment."

The Government have made the following response to the Royal Commission's report: "The Government strongly support the recommendations of the Nature Conservancy Council report on lead poisoning of swans: that urgent efforts should be made to develop alternatives to anglers' lead weights, and that efforts should be directed to the phasing out of lead in angling within 5 years (from 1981). Research into suitable alternatives is well advanced and the Department of the Environment will continue to monitor progress towards the substitution of lead within the timescale suggested by the NCC. The Government hope that a withdrawal of lead can be achieved by voluntary means, but legislation will be considered if necessary." That is still the Government's position. It shows our resolve to remove the major cause of suffering to these beautiful birds.

In conclusion, therefore, I can do no more than repeat the Government's firm commitment to the phasing out of anglers' lead and to confirm that we will not hesitate to legislate if it proves necessary. Nevertheless, I am sure that we all hope that the cessation of the use of lead shot in angling can be achieved voluntarily.

I pay tribute once again to my hon. Friend for bringing up a subject that is important and about which the Government are greatly concerned.

Bearing in mind this promise to legislate, not frequently given in Adjournment debates, we can look at a second adjournment debate — the one on British Rail (Southern Region), debate 26. The Member raising the subject was protesting at the rail service and in his reply the minister (David Mitchell, Under-Secretary of State for Transport) set out his position as minister at the beginning of his response. It is rather different from the situation with regard to swans.

I have listened carefully to what my hon. Friend the Member for Reigate (Mr Gardiner) told the House about the rail services in his constituency. I understand the concern that his constituents and other British Rail passengers feel if the level of service that they have been used to is changed, and I am sure that they will be grateful to my hon. Friend for his concern in their interest and for raising this matter.

However, I should make it clear at the outset that the level of service on routes, and the timetabling of services, are matters entirely for the British Railways Board. Ministers have no power to intervene. Nevertheless, I shall take the opportunity to draw my hon. Friend's remarks to the attention of the chairman of British Rail.

He then gave a full account of proposed improvements in 1984, especially those in the Member's constituency, and the way it fits into "the broader context of the railway passenger business, operated within the framework of the broad stategic objectives set by the Government . . .". The debate was a classic illustration of a minister not responding to aspects of the day-to-day running of British Rail, a nationalised industry, but accepting the Government's responsibility for ultimate policy. And in addition he glances over his shoulder at the chairman of British Rail.

> My hon. Friend may be assured that that [adjustment of services to demand] is a continuing process, and I am sure that in the light of what he has said today BR will continue to consider the points that concern his constituents.

There was nothing unusual about the 28 debates during this fortnight (27 requiring government response), but even selecting a few of them suggests the range of subjects covered and the variety of government replies to the House of Commons. Most of the media gives an unbalanced view of the work done within the House of Commons and no more so than in their treatment of the six to nine hours' debate each day. In conclusion, one can imagine, on the basis of the brief selections above, the work undertaken in departments during the preparation for these ten sitting days.

Not all debates, however, take place in the Chamber of the House. If we exclude the question of the committee stage of bills taken in standing committees together with the work of the Statutory Instruments Standing Committees and the European Community Documents Standing Committees, then debates outside the Chamber may take place in the following ways:

(1) *The Scottish Grand Committee.* This committee is made up of all the elected Members for Scotland. It debates the bills which have been certificated by Mr Speaker as relating to Scotland—on the principle of such bills, that is— and reports to the House whether it recommends or not that they should be read a second time. The second reading of the bill is then a formal matter with no debate. After it has been to one of the two Scottish Standing Committees for the committee stage it can be returned to the Scottish Grand Committee for the report stage. It would then be returned to the Chamber for the third reading. In addition, on not more than six days a session the Scottish Grand Committee debates general matters concerning Scotland which have to be referred to it by a minister. At the end of 1983 for instance, on 12 December and 15 December, the committee debated the state of the National Health Service in Scotland. The first of these meetings was in Edinburgh and the second at Westminster. The motion was: "That the committee do now report to the House that the committee has considered the matter of the National Health Service in Scotland". Finally, the committee debates Scottish Estimates on not less than six days a session. The procedure is the same as for their debates on general matters.

(2) *The Welsh Grand Committee.* This committee is made up of all the elected Members for Wales. When they consider bills the Committee of Selection may add to the Welsh Grand Committee a further five Members. There are very seldom bills which relate only to Wales but in such cases the Welsh Grand Committee debates the principle of the bill and reports to the House whether it should be given a second reading. As with Scottish bills, the second reading is then taken formally. There will then be a special motion to set up a standing committee to consider the bill as there is no Welsh equivalent to the two Scottish Standing Committees.

The Welsh Grand Committee also considers major subjects. For instance, on the same day that the Scottish Grand Committee was considering the National Health Service, the Welsh Grand Committee was considering the "National Health Service in Wales". In early 1984 they debated "Transport and Communications in Wales". The wording of the motion was similar to the wording of the motion before the Scottish Grand Committee.

(3) *The Northern Ireland Committee.* This committee consists of all Northern Ireland Members (there are now 17) together with up to 20 more Members nominated by the Committee of Selection. This committee may consider policy documents, for instance the administration of salmon and inland fisheries, which was debated in July 1983, or energy matters, debated in December 1983 and January 1984. They may also consider draft orders for Northern Ireland. These draft orders are proposals for legislation covering Northern Ireland and the debates on them are tantamount to a second reading debate on the principles of the legislation. (The Northern Ireland Assembly of course has no powers to legislate.) The procedures of the Committee are similar to the Scottish and Welsh Grand Committees.

(4) *Standing Committee on Regional Affairs.* This committee has been used very sparingly indeed. It is concerned with "matters relating to regional affairs in England". It is made up of all Members for constituencies in England together with five Members nominated by the Committee of Selection. As with the committees on Scotland, Wales and on Northern Ireland it can discuss matters referred to it by a Minister of the Crown.

The form of debate of all of the above committees is the same as for debates in the Chamber. A motion is introduced, normally by a minister, and the subject is considered often in the broadest of terms. The debates are published in the same format as debates in the House (although not quite as quickly) and they are important sources of information for the areas and the subjects concerned. The Scottish press, especially when the Scottish Grand Committee meets in Edinburgh, reports the proceedings quite fully. However, many libraries which subscribe to the daily *Hansard* do not take these debates on more specific matters, although they represent important reports by ministers on legislation and its administration.

The spoken word at Westminster takes two public forms: (i) the questioning of ministers in the House and of ministers and others in select committees; and (ii) the speeches of debate. However, debate at Westminster is very different from the hemicyclic harangues more common on the Continent. Frontbench speakers, whether opening the debate or winding up at the end, will normally address the House for about 30 minutes each. Backbench Members will usually speak for about half this time. But it is quite usual, unless a minister is under great pressure of time, for him to "give way" if there is an important intervention by another Member. To a lesser extent points are raised during other Members' speeches. The result is much more of a dialogue and these exchanges are important not only as part of the political quality of debate but also as part of the exchange of ideas and experience between Government and Parliament.

6. Questions and Ministerial Statements

Distributed round the libraries and offices at Westminster and part of the equipment of many Members and their personal staff are pale yellow forms with a text which reads as follows:

PARLIAMENTARY QUESTION

For answer on:..
(DAY)   (DATE)

If ORAL
insert **X**

If for
WRITTEN
ANSWER
leave blank

If for
PRIORITY
WRITTEN
insert **W**
and give
date for
answer

Name..

Constituency (..):

To ask...

....,
(TITLE OF MINISTER)

Signed...

When a Member wishes to table a question to a minister he completes this form and hands it in at the lower Table Office, a small room behind the Speaker's chair. The clerks at the Table Office will check whether the question is acceptable from the procedural point of view and will advise Members if the wording or subject matter is out of order. They will also help him to redraft the question to ensure it is in order and therefore can be tabled. Asking questions is a popular exercise, the number asked in a session having roughly doubled from about 20,000 to about 40,000 or more during the last 20 years.[1] This great growth reflects Members' changing view of their own role. Whether it is their increased select committee work, the greater effort they put into their constituency work helped by their increasing number of paid personal staff, or indeed the growing number of questions they ask, it all illustrates the acceptance by most Members in recent years that their job in the House of Commons is today a full-time one.

Members can ask one of three types of questions. First there is the question

52

actually answered in the House by a minister in person and called an oral question. They are sometimes broadcast and are answered during the 55 minutes or so of question time on Monday to Thursday each sitting week, i.e. about 36 weeks a year. Members are rationed in the number of oral questions they may ask. The restriction is eight questions during any 10 sitting day period; of these, not more than two questions can be asked on any one day, and not more than one can be addressed to any one minister. To table a question for oral answer the Member must put an X in the box on the yellow form.

The demand to ask oral questions is much greater than the supply of time to answer them in the limited question time available, so in practice Members table their questions on the earliest possible day, a fortnight before they will be answered by the minister, and at 4 p.m. each day the questions submitted are shuffled together and then drawn out as in a ballot to form the order of questions a fortnight ahead. As only the first 25–30 questions will be answered in the Chamber, and many more than this are normally tabled even on the first day of the fortnight, this is the only equitable system. To complete the routine for oral questions at this stage, once their order is determined they are sent to the printer, who early next morning has printed the list; this is then one of the papers tackled by the staff of the various departmental parliamentary clerks as soon as they start work. If a question has been addressed to the wrong minister it is at this point that it will be transferred to the correct one and the Table Office and the Member will be informed which department will be replying. One effect of the great demand to table oral questions is that in practice departments have nearly a fortnight to prepare a reply.

It is important that departments themselves should regularly respond to Members in the Chamber; to ensure this, there is a rota which sets down clearly the first department to answer oral questions each day. As there are about four departments under each day, and as it is seldom that more than one department's questions are completed, ministers are likely to face questioning every four weeks. The exception to this is the Prime Minister, who faces 15 minutes of questioning twice a week. On certain days at 3.10 p.m. questions move to another minister in order to include all ministers in a four-weekly cycle. The programme for departments answering questions is shown in table 5.

Ministers are under no obligation to answer questions and there is quite a long list of subjects on which questions have been refused in the past.[2] These include, as you would expect, aspects of defence and security, the detailed workings of certain organisations within the general purview of the minister, commercial information regarded as confidential and personal information on civil servants etc. In addition, ministers will be told by their civil servants if the assembly of the reply is going to cost more than £200. They must then decide whether to reply or not. If there is a tradition of not answering a question, the minister can be asked once a session if that remains the policy. If he has refused to answer a question outside this tradition he may be asked again after three months.

The second type of question is the priority written question. In this case the Member puts a W in the box on the yellow form and he must give 48 hours' notice to the department; there is no restriction on numbers. A third type is the written question, where the Member leaves the box blank and where again there is no restriction on numbers or period of notice.

Table 5
Order of House of Commons Oral Questions

	Monday	**Tuesday**	**Wednesday**	**Thursday**
Week 1	Transport Wales Energy Attorney General[1] Foreign & Commonwealth (overseas development questions)[3]	Defence Employment Social Services Educ. & Science At 3.15 p.m. Prime Minister	Scotland Foreign & Commonwealth Trade & Industry Environment Solicitor General for Scotland[3]	Home Office Northern Ireland Ag., Fish & Food Treasury At 3.15 p.m. Prime Minister
Week 2	Wales Energy Transport Member answering for Church Commissioners[1] Member answering for House of Commons Commission[2] Arts[3]	Employment Social Services Educ. & Science Defence At 3.15 p.m. Prime Minister	Foreign & Commonwealth Foreign & Commonwealth (EEC questions)[1] Trade & Industry Environment Scotland	Northern Ireland Ag., Fish & Food Treasury Home Office At 3.15 p.m. Prime Minister
Week 3	Energy Transport Wales Lord Privy Seal,[1,4] Civil Service[3]	Social Services Educ. & Science Defence Employment At 3.15 p.m Prime Minister	Trade & Industry Environment Scotland Foreign & Commonwealth	Ag., Fish & Food Treasury Home Office Northern Ireland At 3.15 p.m. Prime Minister
Week 4	Transport Wales Energy Attorney General[1] Foreign & Commonwealth (overseas development questions)[3]	Educ. & Science Defence Employment Social Services At 3.15 p.m. Prime Minister	Environment Scotland Foreign & Commonwealth Trade & Industry	Treasury Home Office Northern Ireland Ag., Fish & Food At 3.15 p.m. Prime Minister

1. Starting not later than 3.10 p.m.
2. Starting not later than 3.15 p.m.
3. Starting not later than 3.20 p.m.
4. Also answers as Leader of the House and Chairman of the Select Committee on House of Commons (Services) and on behalf of the Lord President of the Council and the Chancellor of the Duchy of Lancaster.

So much for the mechanics of tabling questions, but why do Members ask them? Not all of them do, of course, but excluding 100 or so ministers who actually do not question their government colleagues, about three-quarters of Members ask questions regularly. Because commentators concentrate so much on the cut and thrust of question time in the House they sometimes forget the most obvious fact that most questions are asked to obtain information from the Government. By far the majority are written questions and there is very little scope for political knock-about in the hundreds of columns of written answers which are bound in at the back of the columns of *Hansard*. It would, however, be foolish for a department or a minister not to be wary of what lies behind an innocent-looking oral parliamentary question, because the initial question as printed on the Order Paper is only setting up a target. It is when the Member is called by the Speaker to ask his supplementary question that he presses his real point. This is in most cases political. From the viewpoint of information, therefore, there is a great distinction between the content and the motive of an oral question and those of a written question.

The question has been tabled, printed overnight among the notices of motion in the Vote Bundle which is delivered early next morning to the parliamentary branch in the relevant department. It is now up to the Government to prepare the answer for the House if it is likely to be answered orally, or for publication in *Hansard* direct if it is to be a written reply.

Once it is firmly decided which department will reply, the relevant parliamentary branch opens a new file for the individual question. Most of these files are highly coloured to avoid their becoming buried in heaps of other papers. The file arrives on the desk of the civil servant responsible, together with a deadline for his draft reply to the parliamentary branch, and he and his staff set out to do three things. First, there is the preparation of a draft reply, which may begin at quite a low grade of civil servant or with a specialist who is working hundreds of miles from London; within a few days the draft reply will arrive on the desk of, say, the assistant secretary in charge of the division responsible for the subject of the question. Secondly, it is often appropriate to prepare a background paper, because replies are kept short and the subject, which may be quite technical or complicated, needs to be explained to the minister. Thirdly, if it is an oral question, there will be prepared draft replies to about a dozen anticipated supplementary questions. It is at this point that the department is interested to work out the real motive of the questioner and a lot of thought goes into these drafts. The draft replies then work their way up through the hierarchy and finally reach the minister. It is unlikely that he will have to spend too long on the written answers; the Oral Answers are of course another matter.

In the case of priority written questions a reply, sometimes just a holding reply, must go out on the day specified by the Member. If it cannot be answered fully, it is normal to reply within a week or to explain why there is further delay. Sometimes, for instance, it may involve getting complicated information from abroad. Other written questions receive replies as soon as they can be made ready and copies of all these written answers are sent to the Member asking the question, the Library of the House of Commons and the press and broadcasting media at about 4 p.m. of the day of reply. In theory they should appear in *Hansard* the next morning, but with the great growth of parliamentary questions there is sometimes a printing bottleneck and they may be held up for a day or two. That explains why there are sometimes issues of *Hansard* which are devoted entirely to written answers, although they are numbered as a part of the whole issue of that particular day.

In a growing number of cases the minister's reply reads along the lines: "I shall write to the honourable Member . . .". In this case it has been arranged from the beginning of the session 1983/84 in the House of Commons and session 1984/85 in the House of Lords that a copy of the minister's letter to the Member is deposited in the Library of the appropriate House. Those letters are kept and made available to Members but the information in them is made available to the public through the House of Commons Public Information Office. The letters are indexed and the letter of reply referred to by date in the Parliamentary On-Line Information System (POLIS). Subsequently the Member sometimes tables a question asking for the information to be printed among written answers in *Hansard* and the Government normally concurs.

With regard to the answering of oral questions, the secretary of state has first to decide on the distribution of replies as between himself and his junior ministers, because in the Chamber they will work as a team. Secondly, there will often be a last-minute meeting of ministers with senior advisers, after the ministers have studied their questions and answers, both to check and update facts and to exchange views on the political aspects — oral questions being very much a blend of both. Ministers will often then take a quiet lunch to hone their replies to possible supplementaries and, accompanied by the parliamentary clerk and their private secretaries and others who will attend in the Official Box, they will all aim to reach the Chamber in plenty of time.

Most replies to oral questions are kept short and simple; where tables and the like are included then the minister will say: "I will, with permission, circulate it [the detail] in the Official Report", i.e. *Hansard*. Depending on the nature of the subject, the Member asking the question and the minister replying, supplementary questions may well result in extra information being given to Parliament. The opportunity may arise for the minister to give information which redounds to the credit of his department or the Government, and of course sometimes questions are tabled by friends of the minister to give him just such an opportunity. Until recently these supplementary questions, which outnumber the original question by about two or three to one, have not been indexed in *Hansard*. From January 1984, however, when the published index became based on the House of Commons Library's computer-based indexing system (POLIS) and compiled by the Libary Department, all these supplementary questions have been included in the *Hansard* published indexes (see chapter 14).

While ministers normally only have to answer oral questions once a month, the Prime Minister answers questions in the House twice a week. Since 1961 there has been a reserved 15-minute period on Tuesdays and Thursdays. In order to avoid the question being transferred to a minister with specific responsibilities, most of these questions refer to the Prime Minister's engagements etc. and offer an opportunity for a supplementary which can in practice be thought up on the spur of the moment, thus giving the Member the possibility of putting a question without notice, such as is done, for instance, in the Australian House of Representatives. No Prime Minister reaches that office without a great deal of practice at thinking and speaking on his or her feet, so most of them welcome the challenge of question time, which may well give them an extra chance to make or reaffirm a statement of policy or offer a governmental reaction to a new situation. As an example of what happens, the following exchange took place on the afternoon of 28 February 1984, just 24 hours after a major debate on the GCHQ (Cheltenham) affair at the end of which the Government had achieved a handsome majority.

Mr Peter Bruinvels asked the Prime Minister if she will list her official engagements for 28 February.

The Prime Minister (Mrs Margaret Thatcher): This morning I had meetings with ministerial colleagues and others, including one with the Premier of Bermuda. In addition to my duties in the House I shall be having further meetings later today, including one with Chancellor Kohl. This evening I hope to have an audience of Her Majesty the Queen.

Mr Bruinvels: Will my right hon. Friend find time today to comment on the secondary action being taken by trade union members all over the country — action that is illegal and totally irresponsible? Is it not true that from 1979 to 1981 there was disruption at Cheltenham, with national union leaders interfering with the workers there because of disputes elsewhere?

The Prime Minister: Yes. The action that has been taken by the trade unions today to encourage breaches of contract is further justification for the action that the Government took to protect national security at GCHQ.

Mr David Steel: As the Leader of the Opposition has taken action against two members of his party for voting against the Government last night, what action does the right hon. Lady propose to take against members of her party who refused to support her? Does she accept that yesterday's debate revealed widespread unease in all parts of the House about her continued intransigence on the issue of GCHQ, and has she anything fresh to say to the House?

The Prime Minister: No. A majority of 176 is good enough for me, and I am grateful to the right hon. Gentleman for providing the opportunity.

Mr John Page: Is my right hon. Friend aware, as a north London Member, of the gross inconvenience that has already been caused to her constituents, mine and others by the bus and underground strike? Will she take every opportunity to point out the uselessness and selfishness of that action?

The Prime Minister: Yes. Action of this kind hits ordinary people and is greatly to be deplored and condemned.

Mr Merlyn Rees: Does the Prime Minister care very much whether the TUC co-operates with her Government or not?

The Prime Minister: Yes, and an example of that co-operation is the voluntary agreement reached over the political levy recently.

Sometimes other departments are involved in the elaborate preparations required to brief the Prime Minister. There can be few systems of government where its leader is exposed to the regular examination which takes place in the House of Commons either answering specific questions on his or her responsibilities, security for instance, or more frequently offering a general defence of the Government's policy.

A quite distinct type of parliamentary question is the private notice question (PNQ). This is where a Member may wish to ask a minister a question as a matter of urgency and concerning a matter of public importance. The exception to needing these requirements is the Leader of the Opposition, who does not table questions but only asks them through the PNQ procedure. The most regular use of this procedure is at 3.30 p.m. on Thursdays, when he regularly asks the Leader of the House what is to be the business of the House from the following Tuesday to the following Monday week inclusive. It is only then that most Members learn from the Government what work Parliament will under-take during the coming 10 days. For private notice questions there is no question of using the services of the Table Office. The Member applies to the Speaker before noon, and at the business meeting which the Speaker holds each day at that hour with his senior advisers he decides whether to allow it or not. He gives no reasons for his decision.

Meanwhile, the department involved will have been informed immediately by the Speaker's Office and if the question is allowed then it is likely that a few lunches will be cancelled in order to provide a full brief for the minister in time for him to study it, ask his officials questions and get ready to give his answer at 3.30 p.m. Within the House of Commons the television annunciators which indicate the business being transacted in the Chamber will show, from the time of the Speaker's agreement, that a PNQ on a certain subject is to be answered. The question has not of course appeared on the printed Notices of Motion section of the "Vote" for the day so at 3.30 p.m., the end of question time proper, the Speaker rises, reads out the question and calls on the minister to reply. There then generally follows about 10 to 15 minutes of time for supplementary questions. Private notice questions can be a useful method for the Government to give up-to-the-minute information on disasters, acts of terrorism, problems of industrial relations affecting the general public etc. Also useful is the fact that on Fridays it is possible for a Member to ask the Speaker for permission to ask a private notice question if he does so before 10 a.m. even though oral questions are not normally answered on Fridays. It is seldom that there are more than two or three private notice questions in a month and sometimes they are rather less frequent.

Not every parliamentary question demands a response from the Government. Members may table questions on domestic matters concerning the House of Commons itself, such as the provision of facilities which may be the res-ponsibility of one of the sub-committees of the House of Commons (Services) Committee; there are also regularly a small number of questions to the House of Commons Commission especially concerning House of Commons staff and estimates. Occasionally the questions can be very domestic. The following question was answered on the afternoon of 12 March 1984; it shows how well the responding Member was briefed:

Members Dining Room

Mr Harry Greenway asked the Lord Privy Seal whether the catering sub-committee is consulted about the menu in the Members Dining Room and cafeteria; and if he will make a statement.

Mr Fergus Montgomery: I have been asked to reply to this question. The catering sub-committee is not consulted about menus, which are the responsibility of the head of the refreshment department and the executive chef. I hope the House will agree that the choice is admirably varied and the value excellent.

Mr Greenway: I am sure that the House agrees with my hon. Friend, but does he share my regret at the decline of the traditional British pudding? Does he agree that Parliament has a role to play in preserving good rice pudding, summer pudding, plum pie and similar delights by placing them even more regularly on our menus? Does he not think that schools and housewives would then follow the example set by the House and keep the traditional pudding alive?

Mr Montgomery: I remind my hon. Friend that there is a wide range of puddings on offer. In a 37-week parliamentary year rice pudding was on the menu more than 40 times, summer pudding 10 times — in view of our summer, that seems reasonable — and plum pudding 50 times around Christmas and 10 times in other periods of the year. I admire the way in which my hon. Friend has managed to keep his figure — he perhaps feels that he should be built up — but most hon. Members need to be built down because we have dietary problems. Therefore, we try to avoid fatty puds whenever we can. If my hon. Friend had been in the House at lunchtime today, however, instead of in his constituency, where I know that he is most diligent, he would have noticed that both plum pudding and custard and creamy rice with blackcurrants were on the menu.

Finally in this chapter, which treats of proceedings in the House when there is no actual motion before it to debate, there is the ministerial statement. In many ways these statements, which generally follow question time or occasionally a private notice question, are the most direct method of Government informing Parliament. The minister must inform the Speaker in advance that he is going to make a statement; he does not need his permission nor the leave of the House, and he must, via the parliamentary branch of his department, get clearance from 10 Downing Street, the Government Chief Whips and the Leaders of both Houses. It is normal for the statement to be made in both Houses, but if the House of Lords is not sitting the text is added to the issue of the House of Lords *Hansard* for the next sitting day. Statements are sometimes quite long, 10 to 15 minutes, and they may be followed by up to another 30 minutes of questioning, although as there is no motion before the House there can be no debate.

One problem for the Opposition in preparing their response to a ministerial statement is that they are likely to see the proposed text only about half an hour before the statement is made. As these statements are often elaborate in the information they give and since the resources of the Opposition are limited, if the shadow minister sees the text of the statement sufficiently early there may again be some lunches cut short in order to prepare suitable questions.

An example of a major regular statement is when the Prime Minister reports to the House after a meeting of the European Council or the Foreign Secretary after a meeting of the Council of Ministers of the European Communities. In a quite different category the Government may decide to make a policy statement to scotch a provocative rumour. Whatever the reason, and again there are seldom more than two or three statements a month, the Government are assured of a crowded House and their information is in plenty of time to reach the evening's broadcasts and the following morning's papers.

Oral questions, private notice questions, statements — which between them fill the House of Commons from 2.35 p.m. to 3.30 p.m. and sometimes later, on Mondays to Thursdays — are important both to the Government and to Parliament. The timing and the style of the events mean that the Government is addressing the electorate beyond the Chamber, and Members asking the questions are equally aware of this; but for sheer information it is often the written answers which should be studied. The columns of questions and answers are made up of those oral questions which were not reached by the end of question time on a particular day (the majority), the priority written questions and the ordinary written questions — in total something like 35,000 a session.[4]

The Government use written answers for distributing a great deal of information. Ministers and their departments bring statistics up to date, for instance, or arrange them in different patterns in response to Members' individual enquiries. They have long lists of data tabulated and sometimes use written answers to give important replies concerning reports, even occasionally select committee reports in the form possibly of a minister's letter to the committee's chairman. Sometimes they slip in statements of policy which must be made public but not too obviously public.

Questions are asked mostly for information but they are also a weathervane of concern felt by Members. The information given is not only often of real value to the backbencher, but answering them is part of the education of a minister and helps him to reflect on problems. This is followed sometimes by action on the part of his department.

NOTES

1. The number of questions tabled for written answer for sessions 1977/78 to 1983/84 inclusive is set out in HC Deb. vol. 67, c.349w
2. Such a list was published by Peter Hennessy in *The Times* of 4 May 1978, but the list is subject to change.
3. The position before 1961 was described in the Fifth Report of the Select Committee on Procedure (Sessional Committee) — *Questions to the Prime Minister* (1976–77 HC 320 p.xi) — as follows: "From 1904 until 1960 the Prime Minister was liable to answer questions not later than No. 45 on Mondays, Tuesdays, Wednesdays and Thursdays. From the early 1950s, however, it became less usual for the Prime Minister to attend the House for questions on Mondays and Wednesdays: if questions were addressed to him on those days another minister was likely to be asked to reply to them. Prime Minister's questions therefore tended to be concentrated on Tuesdays and Thursdays, when it was understood that the Prime Minister would be present."
4. From 18 July 1984 oral questions to the Prime Minister which are not reached are no longer printed among written answers.

7. Legislation and Delegated Legislation

"Be it enacted by the Queen's most Excellent Majesty, by and with the advice and consent of the Lords Spiritual and Temporal and Commons, in this present Parliament assembled, and by the authority of the same, as follows. . . ." This is the resounding opening paragraph of each public and general act of Parliament and in its constitutional clarity it takes us back to the setting of the Queen's Speech as described in chapter 4 and especially section 8 of that speech where the Queen details the Government's legislative programme to both Houses of Parliament. Passed by this small group of men and women, 650 in the House of Commons and not many more who are active in the House of Lords, the final text of an act is promulgated for the Judiciary to interpret and all citizens to obey.

This particular Queen's Speech was opening not just a session but a newly-elected Parliament, so that in it are included a number of bills preshadowed in the election manifesto on which the voters had just given their verdict. The origin of these policies, wrapped up in legal language as bills, may be grass-roots belief within a party, translated into party conference resolutions, and are sometimes the result of strong lobbying of, and later by, Members. Whatever the pressure, it is essentially a political one, a wish to turn certain priorities into legislation. A different source of legislative proposals are the government departments which consider them necessary to administer agreed policies more efficiently. These will have a lower political profile, but they too may arise partly through the work of pressure groups and also all the apparatus of Parliament informing the Government of ways in which the present legislative shoe pinches, whether it is expressed through parliamentary questions, debate, letters to ministers, reports from the Parliamentary Commissioner etc. A third group of bills, which by definition will not have appeared in the Queen's Speech, may include a number of emergency measures needed to deal with unpredictable problems.

Except for these emergencies, before a bill is drafted to any effect it has to secure a position in the Government's legislative programme. Normally in November, about 12 months before the next Queen's Speech is to be delivered, the Cabinet Office will circularise government departments asking them if they have any bids to make for parliamentary time for legislating during the following session. There are about 500 hours or 65 days a session available for debating legislation in the House of Commons, which breaks down roughly as follows:

Second Reading	..	..	..	200 hours
Committee Stage (Whole House)	..	..	..	50 hours
Consideration on Report		..	..	200 hours
Third Reading	..	..	..	25 hours
Lords Amendments	..	..	..	25 hours

The departments in their reply to the Cabinet Office will need to indicate whether it is an essential technical bill which needs to be passed by a certain date; whether it is highly important politically; or whether it is a non-controversial bill. The department should also indicate how long a bill it would be and also how long it would take to prepare. Views would also be required on whether it was suitable for its second reading to be taken in a second reading standing committee or for being considered in a special standing committee of the House of Commons.

The information is collected by the Cabinet Office, consisting of staff on attachment from other departments. This helps to keep them neutral as between the demands of different departments, as it is quickly learnt that there are more bills proposed than there is parliamentary time to consider them. The information goes to a cabinet committee which decides the first question, namely which bills will be in the next session's legislative programme. This will be agreed by the early spring.

As the bill takes shape the department will liaise if need be with other departments and also if appropriate with outside specialists, interest groups, lobbies etc. in order that possible snags have at least been reviewed. All of this work involves an accurate balancing of interests. In addition the civil servants' antennae will be sensitive to political implications as seen from their minister's point of view and will be taking into account possible problems when the bill is introduced into Parliament.

The next stage is for the civil servants responsible for policy and the legal staff of their department to prepare instructions to enable staff of Parliamentary Counsel actually to draft the Bill. The instructions, which can only be prepared after the policy civil servants have completed all their internal and external consultations, are very much like a legal brief and the staff of Parliamentary Counsel are mostly barristers: there are only 20–25 of them. They are strictly legal professionals who translate the department's requirements into the draft text of the bill. There will be many numbered and printed drafts of the bill going backwards and forwards between Parliamentary Counsel and the department promoting the bill, and other interested departments will be consulted. The process may take months. Finally the draft bill will be considered by a different cabinet committee, which judges its political implications and in this context how it might be handled in Parliament. Judgments for instance have to be made concerning into which House it should be introduced and, depending on its length and complexity, when in the session it should be given a first reading.

All this work goes on behind closed doors and so far Parliament has not been involved in the legislative process. Members see the text for the first time when, following the first reading, i.e. just of its short title, the bill is ordered by the House to be printed and appears in the Printed Paper Office of the House of Lords and the Vote Office of the House of Commons, which are responsible for the distribution of papers to Members in their respective Houses. Long before the bill is published the Government may have trailed its coat regarding its policy by producing a Green Paper or consultation document, but there is great inconsistency in the way in which these are published. There seems to be no inter-departmental policy, indeed sometimes no clear policy within a single department, as to the status and form of publication of these papers. Sometimes they have been Command papers, sometimes produced by

HMSO, sometimes not, and they have varied from being documents of general circulation to being those of restricted circulation. All those that come to Parliament are listed in the House of Commons *Weekly Information Bulletin* and Members among others would be able to comment on the proposals by the department's deadline. The Government may then have published a White Paper with their proposals spelt out, but these are laid before Parliament, published as command papers by HMSO and are available to all. Such papers may help Members to understand the background to the bill before they pick up the text for the first time. It is not unusual for the department to issue a quite lengthy press notice when a bill is first published and this will be available in the Library for Members to consult.

Let us consider at this stage a particular bill. Section 8 of the Queen's Speech (see p. 30) starts: "A bill will be introduced to give trade union members greater control over their unions." On 26 October 1983 the Secretary of State for employment (Tom King) introduced into the House of Commons the Trade Union Bill (its short title) — "A bill to make provision for election to certain positions in trade unions and with respect to ballots held in connection with strikes or other forms of industrial action; and to amend the law, relating to expenditure by trade unions on political objects" (its long title). The wording of the long title defines the scope of the bill. The text appeared after the first reading as [Bill 43] of session 1983–84 and went on sale to the public for £2.70. It ran to 17 clauses on 17 pages. In front of the actual text of the bill, which has been drafted by Parliamentary Counsel, there is an explanatory and financial memorandum which has been written by the department to explain the contents to Parliament and others and which in this case ran to four closely printed pages. This explanatory memorandum is not part of the bill but is designed to give information only and may not include any argument in favour of the bill. To ensure this impartiality the text is checked by clerks in the Public Bill Office of the House of Commons. The memorandum must include, if it is relevant, a note about the financial effects of the bill and any effects it may have on public service manpower.

At the end of the bill there is its short title by which the act will be cited and details about when the act will come into force. In this case part I was to come into force through the Secretary of State making a statutory instrument and parts II and III "on the expiry of the period of two months beginning with the day on which this act is passed".

On 8 November 1983 the bill had its second reading in the House of Commons. The second reading of a bill is not just the debate on the principle but the occasion when the bill as a whole is accepted or rejected by the House. The minister's speech introducing the bill will have been drafted with great care by his civil servants, while he himself will contribute the politics: quotations from such speeches are to be found in chapter 5. That chapter, however, is concerned mostly with debates that take place in the Chamber; in the House of Commons second reading debates are sometimes taken in a second reading committee. Under Standing Order 69 a minister may propose that a bill is referred to such a second reading standing committee, provided more than 20 Members do not object. After debating the issues, this standing committee reports back to the House, where the second reading of the bill is taken formally. From the viewpoint of the civil service there is little difference in the minister's second reading speech introducing the bill, except that in the more intimate atmosphere of a standing committee there may be more occasion for Members to ask for information from the Government front-bench. This situation may also affect his winding-up speech at the end of the debate.

This second reading committee system is not used very often. Standing Order 69 dates from November 1967, but in 1979 it was extended so that private Members promoting public bills could make us of it. It is used normally for bills "which are not measures involving large questions of policy nor likely to give rise to differences on party lines". As indicated in chapter 5, if a bill concerns only Scotland its second reading may be similarly debated in the Scottish Grand Committee. Because of its distinct system of law, special legislation for Scotland is quite usual. Very occasionally there is a bill relating just to Wales, when it similarly could be debated at the second reading stage in the Welsh Grand Committee.

Since 1980–81 there has been on a few occasions a modification to the usual procedure outlined above. The minister presenting the bill may move, immediately following its second reading, that it be committed to a special standing committee. This committee may meet once in private and three times in public, in order to take evidence in the manner of a select committee, including the taking of evidence from civil servants. These evidence sessions are limited to two and half hours at each meeting. In 1980/81 this procedure was used with three bills, in 1981/82 with one bill and once in session 1983/84. Its use has been limited to non-controversial bills but clearly it is an interesting way of combining select committee techniques with current procedures on legislation and it enables the House of Commons to secure more background information on a bill at an early stage of its journey through Parliament.

In most cases the committee stage of bills in the House of Commons is taken in standing committees of between 16 and 50 Members, which are arranged and follow procedures as in the House of Comons in miniature (see plan 1). Bills are divided into parts, within these into clauses, within clauses into sections and within sections into sub-sections. The Trade Union Bill 1983 was divided into four parts, within these into 17 clauses and within these clauses into 100 sections. It went into Standing Committee F on 22 November 1983 and the committee had 37 sittings between that day and its last meeting on 1 March 1984. The order in which a bill is examined in committee is clauses, new clauses, schedules, new schedules, preamble and title. The breakdown of these meetings was as follows:

Committee Meeting(s)	considered clause(s)	Committee meeting(s)	considered clause(s)
1–9	1	23–24	5
10	1 & 2	25–28	6
11–18 pt.1	2	29–30	7
18 pt.2	3	31–32	8
19	4	33	8 & 9
20	3	34	10–14
21	3 & 4	35–36	14
22	4 & 5	37	14–17
			& new clause 4

Clauses 1–6 were Part I of the bill and concerned with "secret ballots for trade union elections" and clearly merited and got the most detailed examination.

Plan 1: Standing Committee

The layout of a standing committee (to consider bills clause by clause) is shown below. Standing committees do not call evidence or hear witnesses; they are a microcosm of the Chamber of the House of Commons during a debate, and the room layout reflects this.

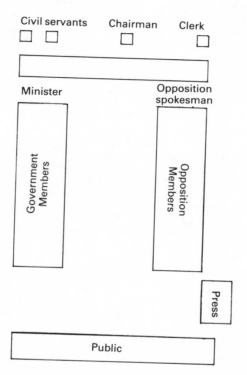

The committee stage of a bill is when, from the viewpoint of Whitehall, the real work begins. Government amendments and amendments from Members which are endorsed by the Government are drafted like the main bill by Parliamentary Counsel. The team of civil servants formed to support the minister as he pilots his bill through Parliament will undertake all the necessary liaison with other departments and other outside interests and ensure that any necessary support is available to the minister in the committee room itself. There were some 305 amendments tabled to the Trade Union Bill, together with four new clauses of which the fourth, tabled by the minister, was added to the bill at the committee stage.

Some years ago a three-part Granada TV series on Parliament gave a good idea, in its first programme, of the preoccupations of the civil service at this stage of a bill.[2] The bill was the Fair Trading Bill 1973 and the following quotations are taken from actual filmed meetings of the civil service team formed to support the minister, Sir Geoffrey Howe, who had introduced the bill. The tensions and context of their work are clear. In addition to conversations such as these, they were having ministerial briefing meetings, liaising with other departments, lobbies etc. The team in order of appearance were:

Elizabeth Llewellyn-Smith	..	..	Assistant Secretary in charge of co-ordination of civil servants on the bill
Cyril Coffin	..	..	..	..	Under-Secretary in charge of the bill
Michael Casey	..	..	..	..	Assistant Secretary in charge of consumer affairs in the bill
Michael Ware	..	..	..	..	Assistant Solicitor in charge of drafting instructions to Parliamentary Counsel for the bill

2 February 1973

Llewellyn-Smith [*dictating to secretary*]: Just do it as a draft and head it "Amendment number 68: Resist" and then can you put in brackets after "resist", but indicate willingness to look again at the structure of the consumer trade practice provisions. [*Picture fades. . . .*] This amendment is probably inspired by a suggestion circulated to certain members of the standing committee by the Consumers' Association, stop. [*Picture fades . . .*] And ministers may like to take the line that they will listen sympathetically to constructive suggestions put forward in the committee as to the powers the director should have. Full stop." That's the end. Put "resist" again at the bottom and the date. I'll do a covering minute later on, but I'm not quite sure who I'll send it to.

6 February 1973

Cyril Coffin: They broke off [the standing committee debate] on those drafting amendments of Mr Hamilton's about "from time to time"?

Llewellyn-Smith: We did. I'm going to put up a rather tough little thing on this. I mean, again, Mr Emery [the minister] was saying that "I'll think about it and take further advice" and so on, but we really will wreck our relationship with the Parliamentary Counsel and also store up an awful lot of trouble if we start accepting. . . .

Coffin: Was he inclined to accept it?

Llewellyn-Smith: Oh yes. Mr Lyons [Member for Bradford East] leapt to his feet and said that it wouldn't make any difference to a court if these words were in or out and. . . .

Coffin: So why didn't they accept them?

Llewellyn-Smith: But I mean, once you start accepting them [Michael Casey enters]. . . . I say, I think I'm going to put up a tough little piece, if Michael Ware approves of it, on "from time to time". I think if we begin by crumbling on these things there's no end to the trouble.

16 February 1973

Llewellyn-Smith: What she wants [Mrs Oppenheim, government backbencher] is for him [the director] to look at actual quality, not whether the quality is misrepresented or. . . .

Casey: I know what she wants, but it's rather difficult to cope with the amendment without discussing the philosophy behind the bill; and saying that the only way to deal with quality is to deal with the rules of the game within which people make their bargain about quality.

Llewellyn-Smith: Well, when Mr Luce says that Mrs Oppenheim is expected to press this amendment very hard, this could mean that like Mr Taylor this week she was prepared to actually *vote* for it; in which case obviously the

Opposition will vote for it too. . . . This is why I'm trying to think of how one can make absolutely clear the other ways. I mean this is not the right way, perhaps, to deal with improving standards of quality. But what are the ways that the director will pursue?

Casey: I think we can. . . . Look, we've got two courses of action. One is to rehearse all these arguments which explain why we don't think this is a sensible amendment, that it pre-empts really what we hope to do at report stage when we've had a chance to deal with the thing as a whole, and therefore we think that it's undesirable. Or to get hold of Mrs Oppenheim behind the scenes and explain there, and say "Now this is our view, we're going to be tough on this. Do you really want to press it?"

Llewellyn-Smith: Yes. Well, if we're going to suggest that, the sooner we suggest it on Monday the better. I'd be in favour of doing that. I think probably on her part there's no misunderstanding. She knows what the bill is intended to do and just thinks it should do something else.

Casey: Well, if you think it's a silly amendment, you've got to say it's a silly amendment, or say that you'll consider the silly amendment, and consider it and deal with it at report stage.

2 March 1973

Michael Ware [reading his notes on the discussion so far]: In essence, you want him [the director] to be able to look at the acts and omissions of manufacturers, wholesalers and retailers which adversely affect the interests of consumers.

Llewellyn-Smith: In the UK.

Casey: I think that is exactly what Parliament wants. So how do we give him a discretion? It was the minister who suggested we give him a discretion as to the scope of his duties. I'm not sure what this means or how it should be done.

Ware: "It shall be the duty in any case in which the director considers is appropriate. . . ."

Llewellyn-Smith: These sort of general duty provisions are really pretty meaningless anyway. It's just an indication of what Parliament expects the chap to spend money on. I mean the difference now is that we are deliberately bringing in these things where you have these advisory committees that you wrote your paper about — food and drugs and so on. I mean, what is the director's relationship to be with them? Is he to go through them, and let them take the thing up directly with their own minister, or is he to go straight to the secretary of state, sort of bypassing them?

Casey: In committee, Geoffrey Howe's approach to this was to say that it would be sensible if the director-general had power to react to information coming to him, for the purposes of informing or possibly advising other ministers. It would be going too far, I think, that he should make *recommendations* to other ministers because they have their own committees charged with recommending action. I mean, the Minister of Agriculture will not want the director-general to make recommendations that Marks and Spencers shouldn't put cyclamates in orange juice, because he's already got a committee doing this. So we've got to cut out that. . . .

No, it can be made perfectly clear, can't it, in debate, that we widen the fields of review to meet the point that Members made that where he gathers information on these matters, he should be able to react to them and pass information on? But we don't want him swamped, and we don't expect that he's going to duplicate the other bodies who are in this field. And that's it. It can be quite easily explained, can't it? That we envisage his role in this way. And no-one can then turn round and say that they expected him to do a lot of things that Parliament have been told he won't do.

Llewellyn-Smith: That's the object we want to achieve, and I mean what it's going to look like, how it's worded, is nothing to do with us.

Ware: It looks politically about right, doesn't it?

Casey: What procedures do we have to run through now to get this settled? There's inter-departmental clearance and the question of instructions. And then clearance with ministers.

Coffin: Well, I wonder whether Michael had better not have a shot at draft instructions, if he feels able to, on the basis of this rather desultory conversation. And then. . . .

Llewellyn-Smith: Yes, yes. And then at that stage it goes to the other departments before the instructions are actually delivered. . . .

Narrator: One month later the reactions have arrived from other government departments concerned with consumer protection. The Ministry of Agriculture, Food and Fisheries, known as MAFF, objects to the director-general having powers to review in its area of expertise — health and safety. So after another long meeting, the civil servants at Trade and Industry have worked out a more cautious wording. It allows the director-general to actively review economic matters but only to "take note of" complaints coming in about health and safety. Now this formula must go again through ministerial channels to be approved.

An important word in the first quotation above is "resist". The civil service in preparing their brief for their minister will set down the agreed policy with regard to an amendment in terms such as "resist", "accept in principle" and of course "government amendment". Full briefings and arguments for the minister are then drafted. During the committee stage in bills in recent years, however, it has become more usual, with the agreement of course of the minister, for Whitehall to supply Members with more information. This comes in the form of Notes on Clauses which are unpublished but made available through the Vote Office. They do not contain arguments — that is confined to the Minister's brief — but they set out to explain the meaning of the amendment or new clause. A recent set of Notes on Clauses on the Northern Ireland Bill 1984, which was made available to Members, ran to some 20 pages.

The committee stage completed, the Trade Union Bill was reprinted [Bill 112] with a new clause 4 so that it ran to 18 clauses and a commencement date was inserted for Part III. The bill was then considered in the Chamber of the House of Commons (the report stage) in the order new clauses, amendments to the bill, new schedules and amendments to the schedules. This debate on the report stage [3] lasted two days (26 March and 2 April 1984) and resulted in some further amendments; the bill was then reprinted [Bill 130]. The third reading was held on 25 April.

Three weeks later the bill had its second reading in the House of Lords, where it arrived as HL 206 and this was followed by three days in committee of the whole House, where the breakdown of work was as follows:

Meetings	Clauses
1	1–2
2	2–7, 9–15
3	15–18

On 12 July the report stage was taken in the House of Lords, the bill was reprinted as amended as HL 284 and received its third reading on 18 July. The

bill returned to the Commons and was reported as amended by the Lords [Bill 221] and their amendments were considered and agreed to on 24 July 1984. Two days later it received the Royal Assent. It had taken just nine months of intense departmental work, much of it with Parliament, to pass the 20-page bill.

The achievement of Parliament in legislating is not to be measured necessarily in the number of amendments made nor in it thwarting the will of the Government, which has after all been sent to Westminster by the electorate. Both Houses of course need to pass the bill, but in doing so they have the chance to insist that the minister, and the Whitehall machinery behind him, must think hard about what they are doing and how they are doing it, must stand up and justify their proposals in detail in a public forum and do those two things conscious that they are fully reported to the electorate. In doing this the Government are required to pass a great deal of information to Parliament and this in turn makes it available to the country. The quantity of legislation passed during recent years is set out in table 6A. Preparing and drafting this legislation must have kept Whitehall and Parliamentary Counsel very busy. But this impressive quantity is also reflected in the consequent delegated legislation, the text of the more important of which must be laid before Parliament. This is set down in table 6B.

Table 6A
Legislation: Acts

	Volumes	Pages
1963	1	1505
1968	2	2532
1973	3	2248
1978	3	1534
1983	3	1541

Table 6B
Delegated Legislation: Statutory Instruments

	Volumes	Pages
1963	3	4900
1968	6	4952
1973	8	7290
1978	6	5885
1982	6	5540
1983	6	6439

The requirement to lay delegated legislation depends on the wording of the parent act under which the Government presents it to Parliament. The term being "laid" means that the instrument is delivered by the responsible government department to the Votes and Proceedings Office in the Clerks' Department, listed for the next day's published Votes and Proceedings, passed to the Library for the use of Members and at least 50 copies supplied to the Vote Office so that interested Members may have their own copy. The House of Lords follows a similar pattern.

This delegated legislation will normally have been drafted by a legal adviser of the department responsible for administering the parent act or occasionally by Parliamentary Counsel. Practically every instrument carries an explanatory note, which is not part of the instrument but explains its main effects without going into the underlying motives. Instruments are of various classes. Some require an affirmative resolution authorising them to be made or, if already made, to remain in force. The resolution will be moved by a minister from the responsible department and may be debated for an hour and a half or occasionally longer. Very many others are subject to a negative resolution, i.e. a motion to annul them after they have been made which can be moved by any member of the House. Such a motion cannot be moved or, if moved, debated after 11.30 p.m. Other instruments are simply laid before the House and some are not even laid, and neither of these classes are subject to parliamentary control. Both an affirmative and a negative instrument may be referred to and debated in a standing committee, who take no decision on the motion but simply report that the committee have considered the instrument. But whether an instrument is debated in the House or a standing committee the Government will be required to explain the reason for and the meaning of the instrument. For this reason a negative resolution is often tabled to secure information about the Government's intentions or the meaning of the instrument. It should be added that it is impossible to amend instruments under post-war acts on motions to approve or annul them. Some information about an instrument can be quickly ascertained from headnotes, for instance whether it is a draft instrument and requires approval by resolution of each House and, where applicable, the dates of making, laying and coming into operation.

Before instruments are considered by the House or a standing committee they are almost invariably considered by the Joint Committee on Statutory Instruments. This was set up in 1973 and consists of seven Members of the House of Lords and seven Members of the House of Commons. One of the House of Commons Members who is in the opposition party is the chairman. The committee examines "every instrument laid before each House of Parliament" —they number nearly 2,000 a session — to check whether the instrument has been delayed regarding its laying or publication, is *ultra vires* the parent act, is defective or unclear in its drafting or needs to be brought to the attention of Parliament "on any other ground which does not impinge on its merits or on the policy behind it". The Committee has the help of two legal experts, namely the Counsel to the Lord Chairman of Committees in the House of Lords and the Speaker's Counsel in the House of Commons. Before it considers reporting to Parliament the Joint Committee on Statutory Instruments calls for evidence from the department sponsoring it.

Initially the committee asks for written evidence which the department submits as a memorandum. Sometimes this is not adequate and the committee will ask for a further memorandum or for oral evidence. This latter will be taken from departmental officials, both administrative staff and those from the legal section. All this evidence whether written or oral is published in the usual select committee fashion as a House of Commons paper. The committee reports back to the two Houses that it has examined a particular instrument and this appears in a weekly report they make to the House during the session. This report groups instruments which have been examined in the following lists:

Draft Instruments requiring Affirmative approval
Instruments subject to Annulment
General Instruments, laid
General Instruments, not laid
Orders subject to Special Parliamentary Procedure
(Northern Ireland Instruments are grouped separately)

If an instrument involves public finance (e.g. the imposition of taxes, expenditure or an increase in borrowing powers), the parent act normally requires that it be subject to parliamentary control in the House of Commons only. In that case it goes through exactly the same procedure but this time before the House of Commons Select Committee on Statutory Instruments. The membership of this House of Commons committee is the seven House of Commons Members of the joint committee.

As a coda to this chapter mention must be made of the situation of legislation for Northern Ireland. Before 1972 Northern Ireland legislation was a matter for the Northern Ireland Parliament sitting in the great classical building at Stormont outside Belfast. Since direct rule from Westminster was introduced, legislation for the province has been through a system of Orders in Council. The Order may start with the minister issuing a proposal for a draft Order in Council for approval by resolution of each House of Parliament. It includes the words:

> Her Majesty, in exercise of the powers conferred by paragraph 1 of schedule 1 to the Northern Ireland Act 1974 and of all other powers enabling her in that behalf, is pleased, by and with the advice of her Privy Council, to order . . . .

As with statutory instruments there is an explanatory note. There is also in the case of proposals for draft Orders an explanatory document which is more detailed than the explanatory note and which invites comment by a particular date in the same way as consultative documents. The explanatory document comments on the financial and staffing implications of the proposal in the same way as the explanatory and financial memorandum attached to a bill. The next stage is for a draft Order in Council to be laid by the minister. Very occasionally it is referred to one of the statutory instruments standing committees but normally it is debated in the House of Commons itself. In either case a full explanation of the Order will be given to the House by one of the ministers of the Northern Ireland Office. It is finally published after being approved by both Houses of Parliament, with two references. First it has "the title" followed by (NI) Order and a serial number. In addition it has a statutory instrument serial number. The Orders are not however published among the statutory instruments but in volumes of Northern Ireland Statutes.

Legislation, together with its consequent delegated legislation, takes up over half the time of the House of Commons and nearly all of the time of its standing committees. Appendix 1 suggests the balance of work during the session. Although the House of Commons traditionally has a number of lawyers, especially barristers among its number, most Members are generalists in the law not professionals. For this reason in the course of passing laws Parliament seeks information and arguments from Government which are of direct relevance not only to the legislators themselves but also to those who subsequently will administer the law and the citizen to whom it will apply. The explanations and discussions in Parliament remain important in this connection, although once the legislators have completed their task in many cases the department responsible for promoting the bill produces a straightforward guide to its working.

NOTES

1. First Report of the Select Committee on Procedure 1964–65, HC 149 para. 3
2. This was published as *The State of the Nation: Parliament* (Granada Television, 1973). Quotations are from Part I — "A law in the making: four months inside a ministry".
3. Under Standing Order 78, if a bill has been considered by a second reading committee or by the Scottish Grand Committee, it may be referred back to one of these committees at report stage.

8. Select Committee Work

A great deal of Parliament's work, as with many large organisations, takes place in committees. Select committees are groups of Members chosen to form a committee and appointed by the House to investigate a subject. They take oral and written evidence from witnesses and then report back to the House, normally setting down their conclusions and recommendations. They have been part of the parliamentary scene at least since Tudor times and remain the most formal and often the most rigorous method of Parliament obtaining information from government witnesses and others. Most select committee work is undertaken by regularly appointed committees and table 7 lists those of the House of Commons.[1]

The committees on domestic matters need not detain us. As their designation suggests, most of their evidence is taken from Members or parliamentary staff and government departmental evidence is normally limited to subjects such as accommodation, construction work, etc., which have a direct impact on the working of Parliament. The three committees under "Other Committees" in the table are noted in the relevant chapters: European Legislation in chapter 10, Parliamentary Commissioner for Administration in chapter 12, and Public Accounts in chapter 9. We are then left with the 14 departmental committees which since 1979 have been a vital method of Parliament seeking government information and checking on the performance of the main departments of state.[2]

Members of these departmental select committees are all backbenchers; there are no ministers or opposition spokesmen on them and they are chosen by the Committee of Selection. At their first meeting they choose one of their members as chairman. Their terms of reference are: "to examine the expenditure, administration and policy of the principal government departments and associated public bodies and similar matters within the responsibilities of the Secretary of State for Northern Ireland".

The physical arrangement of a select committee, as shown in plan 2 (on page 75), reflects the nature of its work. Through arranging the members round a horseshoe and their sitting in no particular order, with a chairman in the centre leading the questioning, there is little sense of a group of political adversaries but much more one of a parliamentary enquiry. There are two types of committee meetings, namely evidence-taking sessions normally in public and frequently broadcast, and deliberative sessions when the committee discusses matters including their draft report to the House; the latter are always in private and therefore never broadcast. If the committee is on the air, and it is up to the committee to decide, then there is a red light on indicating this fact. The oral evidence is normally published day by day while the written evidence is usually published at the end of the enquiry with the report.

Before turning to the impact on Government of this system, it is important to note the parliamentary staffing of these committees. All committees have a clerk, a secretary, two or three support staff and in a few cases an assistant clerk.

Table 7
House of Commons Select Committees*

These Committees are appointed for a Parliament unless marked* in which case they are appointed for just the session.

Domestic Matters Committees

House of Commons (Services) (20)
With Sub-Committees on
  Accommodation & Administration (7)
  Catering (4)
  Computer (5)
  Library (4)
  New Building (6)
Liaison (Committee Chairman) (23)
Members' Interests (13)
Privileges (17)
Procedure (16)
Selection (9)
Sound Broadcasting (5)
*Standing Orders (11)

Departmental Committees

Agriculture (11)
Defence (11)
Education, Science and Arts (11)
Employment (11)
Energy (11)
Environment (11)
+Foreign Affairs (11)
+Home Affairs (11)
Scottish Affairs (13)
Social Services (11)
Trade and Industry (11)
Transport (11)
+Treasury and Civil Service (11)
Welsh Affairs (11)

Other Committees

European Legislation (16)
Parliamentary Commissioner for
  Administration (8)
Public Accounts (15)
Statutory Instruments (7)
Joint Committees with the
  House of Lords
Consolidation etc. Bills (11)
Statutory Instruments (7)

* excluding ad hoc select committees
( ) = number of members
+ has power to appoint sub-committees

Plan 2: Select Committee

These are permanent staff and in addition about a third of the committees have one, occasionally more, committee assistants doing research work. Finally committees may hire specialist advisers who are paid on a per diem basis. These are experienced specialists, often academics, and apart from giving advice on specific matters, they may often act as the antennae of the committee and keep a watching brief on specific areas of committee interest.[3] They help to keep their information sharp and up-to-date. Finally, with regard to those internal information sources, the committee as a whole and its Members as individuals use the services of the House of Commons Library, especially its research staff.

The procedural methods of each of these committees are the same but their particular style of working differs, just as the style or culture of government departments differs. With regard to the committees, this variation depends firstly on the chairman but also to some extent on the subject area of the committee. The chairman is the key figure with regard to the nature of his committee's work and his job may take up a third or more of his time. He negotiates with his colleagues, chairs the meetings (which may sometimes involve rescuing witnesses who get themselves into difficulties), leads the questioning, sits on the Liaison Committee (made up of the chairmen of all committees) as the representative of his committee and acts as its spokesman in the House. He normally represents the committee in its relationships with the media and certainly when it travels in the United Kingdom or abroad. Finally he works closely with the clerk of the committee, who is there not only to give procedural advice but also to provide and run all the supporting services, to co-ordinate the committee's work with his colleagues and to act as the liaising official between the committee and the outside world, including of course government departments. The subject area of the committee also causes variety in its style and working methods because their work in connection with some departments, for instance social services or education, results in a great deal of lobbying and evidence from many organisations outside Government, while in other areas such as defence, and to a considerable degree foreign affairs, most of the evidence will come from government departments.

Let us assume that a committee, after considering six or eight possible subjects within its terms of reference, decides to run a major enquiry and a quite short one. The committee through its clerk will issue a press notice and immediately get in touch with the departmental liaison officer who is the committee's point of contact in the department they are shadowing. In some departments the liaison officer is the parliamentary clerk and in a few it is the minister's private office; however, it is becoming increasingly usual to have a departmental liaison officer playing the role for select committee work that parliamentary clerks play for other parliamentary matters. In the choosing of a subject, the department may on occasion offer a suggestion and conversely the committee might informally check the lie of the land with the department to see whether a question that interests them is about to be overtaken by events. An enquiry when the situation is changing quickly might be a waste of everybody's time. But the final decision as to what subject to consider rests entirely with the committee. The committee will often start by calling for a preliminary paper from the department and this will help to set the scene.[4] Sometimes the departmental liaison officer will have to co-ordinate the response from more than one department if the subject looks like crossing departmental boundaries; sometimes it is necessary for more than one department to respond with a preliminary paper. The various liaison officers in this case will obviously ensure that the Government is giving a consistent and co-ordinated reply to Parliament.

With regard to witnesses, committees sometimes concentrate on inviting ministers; at other times they want to question permanent and deputy secretaries and civil servants of a lower grade. By questioning ministers the committee both test them as individuals — the committee of course see the minister as responsible for the policy but also as a fellow Member of the House — and get their opinion down on the record. By questioning the most senior civil servants they examine the administration of government policies and if they want greater detail on a subject it may be best to question someone at about assistant secretary level.[5] Officials may pass questions on policy to ministers, as in pure constitutional terms the minister is responsible to Parliament for policy and the official to the minister for its execution. With increasing experience both committees and officials have become more relaxed about these relationships; yet it remains a fact that it is the minister and his department who are under scrutiny by the select committee, which is required to report back to the House of Commons.

In order to reduce the lengthy and expensive business of briefing departmental witnesses the committee may informally suggest the line of questioning they are likely to pursue; but as always with Members of Parliament, who act very much as individuals, witnesses may frequently be tested by the unexpected.

There are a number of areas where witnesses will decline to give evidence. These include the private affairs of individuals and organisations: negotiations including those concerned with commercial contracts etc., cases where the minister is acting in a judicial role, advice to ministers and the mechanics of decision-making. The reason for such reticence is to enable the Government to conduct negotiations, accept or reject advice, and argue and come to a decision in an uninhibited manner — uninhibited, that is, because the preliminary stages to such decisions are not going to be public information for 30 years at least.

Many ministers and some officials quite welcome the opportunity to appear before these committees. Apart from helping them to concentrate the mind, this particular strand of Government informing Parliament gives them a public forum to explain and justify their present policy and suggest possibilities for the future. The meetings are quite well reported by the national press and the specialist journals, while the BBC compile a weekly programme from the taped proceedings offering an interesting contrast to sound broadcasts from the Chamber. Two attempts to introduce a bill to televise the work of the committees have been made and this suggests a further line of development.

The government department giving evidence may be one of quite a large number of witnesses. Once evidence of any type is given to a committee it is their property and liable to publication. In other words, it is information in the public domain and may not be published by the witness without the committee's agreement before it is printed by the House of Commons. The department will be sent the evidence of other witnesses and may well be recalled for a further evidence session if the committee wishes to follow up any points. With the close of evidence sessions the department and its liaison officer have a short break while the report is drafted. It is then examined by the committee clause by clause. The committee must also decide how much written evidence it wishes to publish. Normally all government evidence would be published, but if on grounds of economy some is not, then this is noted in the report and a set of unprinted evidence is sent to the House of Commons Library for Members to consult and a set to the House of Lords Record Office for the public to consult, with the agreement of the committee clerk.

When the report and evidence are published it is usual for the committee to issue a press notice and hold a press conference. It is also usual for the Government to decide on their response. The Government seek to respond to the report in two months, but frequently that is too short a time, especially if the reply requires inter-departmental consultation; with the agreement of the committee the time for reply may accordingly be extended to six months. The actual government reply may come in a number of forms. First, if the committee's report has raised policy matters and the Government wish to reply and set out their policy, then they will generally reply in the form of a command paper. Alternatively, they may reply in a memorandum to the committee. The committee will then include it in one of their special reports, sometimes with their comments, and this will be published as a House of Commons paper. An answer with a lower profile is where the minister replies by letter to the chairman of the committee. This may be published by the Leader of the House as a written answer in *Hansard*. It is also of course open to the committee to publish it as a special report. Finally and very rarely, the minister might make a statement in the House, in which case the chairman will be informed in advance, or a reply from the minister may be included in a debate. The committee if it is dissatisfied is always free to say so and return to the subject.

Part of the responsibility of these committees is to cover departmental expenditure. The Public Accounts Committee examines such expenditure retrospectively, whereas departmental select committees may examine the estimates of future expenditure. So far it cannot be said that this area of their work has been very effective. Some have examined departmental estimates and taken evidence fairly regularly; other committees have found themselves short of time. For instance, the Defence Committee did not examine the defence estimates either in 1982, because they were busy with the Falklands enquiry, or in 1983, because of the general election. Protagonists of the new committees have been aware of this shortcoming and recently it has been decided to allocate three days' debate a session for the discussion of committee reports on departmental estimates. The debates are selected by the Liaison Committee — in other words by the chairmen of the select committees — and the first one was held in 1983. With three days on which it is possible to draw ministers to the despatch box so that they can explain and justify their expenditure to the House of Commons, it is likely that these committees will concentrate to a greater degree than hitherto on this aspect of their work during the second Parliament of their existence.

Mention of debating reports on estimates brings up the whole question of the importance of these select committees. In a reply to a parliamentary question the Leader of the House indicated that during the 1979–83 Parliament 3 per cent of the departmental select committee reports had been debated and a further 7 per cent had been brought to the attention of Members as of direct relevance to a debate — a total of about 20 reports altogether. On these occasions the Government were again required to justify their stance in the face of the committee's original report and to update information given in their earlier evidence. Taken at its face value this tally may not represent a very impressive achievement. The real importance of their work is, however, far more difficult to estimate. The committees are popular with Members, among whom there was a considerable demand for places in late 1983, from both those re-elected in June of that year and those elected for the first time. There is at Westminster a reasurring belief that the committees strike a balance between being exacting and yet constructive. When membership of the committees for the 1983 Parliament was finally decided a number of ex-ministers had joined their ranks, which suggests that already there was some cross-fertilisation through Members with experience in government supporting this parliamentary work. Also difficult to measure is the importance of committee evidence and reports in educating Members and thus improving their performance vis-à-vis the Government, of concentrating minds and bolstering justifications within departments and of informing the media, and through them the public, about the complex problems of our society.

Perhaps it is best to conclude with the Whitehall view of this achievement in the words of Sir Douglas Wass in his fourth Reith lecture of 1983:

> The existence of the committees has had a number of what I regard as beneficial effects on policy making. Some of these I had frankly not foreseen. The first has been the impact on the thinking of ministers and civil servants: the knowledge that your department is going to be examined *in detail* on the background to a policy statement is a great encouragement to be rigorous in formulating your justification for them. . . . I have seen the effect of this discipline on the Treasury. . . . A further beneficial effect has been to oblige Whitehall to publish more information. . . . To take another benefit, I think that whenever ministerial decisions are plainly questionable their weakness is now more likely to be exposed by the committees than was possible when the debate and questioning were largely confined to the floor of the House.[6]

Obviously a report on these committees soon after the end of their first Parliament, rather like a report at the end of a first term, is a preliminary assessment only; but it does suggest an organised renaissance of select committee work, having a very real role to play in Government informing Parliament.

NOTES

1. About 25 per cent of the House are members of departmental select committees and up to about 20 per cent are members of other select committees. For a list of House of Lords select committees, see table 15 on p.108.
2. For a preliminary assessment by practitioners see D. Englefield (ed.), *Commons Select Committees: Catalysts for Progress?* (Longman, 1984).
3. For a list of specialist advisers used by the committees during the 1979–83 Parliament see HC Deb. vol.46, c.640–42w. This is reproduced in *Commons Select Committees*, pp. 133–135.
4. For the number of departmental memoranda during the 1979–83 Parliament see HC Deb. vol.46, c.637w. This is reproduced in *Commons Select Committees*, p.125.
5. A 24-page "Memorandum of Guidance for Officials appearing before Select Committees" is available as General Notice Gen.80/38. The part concerning civil servants is reproduced in Appendix 2 of this book.
6. First published in *The Listener* (8 December 1983), p.25; subsequently in *Government and the Governed* (Routledge and Kegan Paul, 1984), pp.69–70.

9. Financial Matters

When the Queen during her speech opening Parliament says "Members of the House of Commons, estimates for the Public Service will be laid before you", she is making two essential points about the relationship of Parliament and Government regarding financial matters. Firstly, only Government can initiate demands for Parliament to provide money; secondly, this request concerns only the House of Commons. The third essential in this relationship is that money can only be authorised through resolution of the House of Commons, normally confirmed by legislation.

In order to provide a cogent background to Parliament's work in this field the Government must provide a small library of information, which appears at various times during the year.[1] But this last sentence raises a problem. Which year are we talking about — the parliamentary year (or session) or the financial year? Table 8 (on page 82) is designed to elucidate the fact that during any one session Parliament is considering activities concerning three different financial years. The table also shows the different roles that Parliament plays vis-à-vis the Government's financial proposals and economic policy.

During any one session, which normally runs from November to October, Parliament is considering financial matters of the last financial year, the current financial year and the forthcoming financial year. It is considering them in different ways. First, it examines estimates for the public service. This consists of supplementary estimates for the current year; statement of excess where there has been overspending in the previous year; and finally the vote on account and main estimates for the forthcoming year. Secondly, it is authorising expenditure of these estimates through legislation (Consolidated Fund and Appropriation Acts). Thirdly, it is authorising taxation through legislation (Finance Act) to raise money to pay for this authorised expenditure. Fourthly it is examining the expenditure of these estimates after they have been audited. This is the work of the National Audit Office and the Public Accounts Committee. In addition to these four specific tasks, Parliament is concerned with the Government's economic policy as a whole, which is where we start.

If we turn to the table and read it from left to right, the story is as follows:

Economic policy. Shortly after the new session of Parliament opens, the Government supply an Autumn Statement which is concerned with the economic prospects of the following year and public expenditure plans for the next financial year. It includes a review of the Government's medium-term financial strategy. This is a House of Commons paper of about 30 pages laid as a Return to an Order of the House of Commons by the Chancellor of the Exchequer. It is examined by the Treasury and Civil Service Select Committee which reports to the House. The Autumn Statement is usually debated in the House for one day before the House rises for the Christmas recess.

The second economic policy paper to be laid before Parliament is the Public Expenditure White Paper. This appears in January or February and is con-

80

cerned not just with the next financial year but with the two following years. It is a much larger publication than the Autumn Statement, often running to some 200 pages in two volumes and it is a Command Paper. This also is examined by the Treasury and Civil Service Select Committee and is debated in the House for one day. The paper gives firstly a brief overview with charts, etc. This is much used by the press and media. But it also gives fuller information on the main government programmes, including financial figures over several years, a readable text on the Government's aims and the specific remit of the programme and details of the level of departmental staff. Each programme has a relevant bibliography of mostly official publications.

The third occasion when the Government give detailed information on their economic policy is when the Budget[2] is introduced in March or April. The most important paper then presented is the Financial Statement and Budget Report, which includes a further assessment of the Government's medium-term financial strategy. In addition, there is also published on Budget Day the main civil and defence Estimates, together with the memorandum by the Financial Secretary to the Treasury. Ten minutes after the Chancellor sat down having delivered his Budget speech on 13 March 1984, the following information arrived on my desk (all of it made available to Members and of course beyond Parliament):

Financial Statement and Budget Report 1984–85 (see above).

Resolutions to be moved by the Chancellor of the Exchequer. These were the tax changes which needed to be agreed immediately under the Provisional Collection of Taxes Act 1968.

26 press notices from the Inland Revenue describing tax changes.

8 press notices from the Customs and Excise including tax changes.

9 press notices from the Treasury.

1 press notice from the Department of Transport.

1 press notice from the Bank of England.

1 press notice from the Department of National Savings.

The Next Ten Years: Public Expenditure and Taxation into the 1990s Treasury Green Paper (Command Paper).

Memorandum from the Financial Secretary to the Treasury (Command Paper).

Immediately after the Chancellor introduces his Budget there is a four- or five-day debate which provides ample opportunity for the Government to explain and the House of Commons to examine the former's economic policy.

Authorisation of taxation. Taxation must be authorised through legislation, so following the general debate on the Budget proposals the Government introduces the Finance Bill. The one day second reading debate is generally taken as a further occasion for a wide-ranging consideration of the Government's economic policy (for which purpose the Treasury and Civil Service Committee presents a report); the clauses of the bill are then examined in detail, some in a standing committee and some in a committee of the whole House of Commons. This Finance Bill must receive the Royal Assent before 6 August or the Government could not continue to raise any newly proposed taxes.

Estimates and authorisation of expenditure. The Government must supply Parliament with clear estimates of the money they need for their different programmes. In the course of the session a number of papers are submitted concerned with estimates of expenditure during the three different financial

Table 8
Financial Business

Financial year A Ended 31 March	Financial Year B: 1 April – 31 March			Financial Year C: 1 April – 31 March		
	November – December	January	February – March	March – April	June – July	August
Economic Policy	Autumn Statement[4] on Financial Year C (HC Paper) Examined and reported on by the Treasury & Civil Service Committee Debated 1 day	The Government's Expenditure Plans Financial Year C and following two years (Command Paper) Examined and reported on by the Treasury & Civil Service Committee Debated 1 day		Budget and Taxation Proposals for Financial Year C including Financial Statement and Budget Report (HC Paper)[4] Budget — Debated 4 or 5 days		
Authorisation of Taxation		Debated 1 day		Finance Bill 2nd Reading – Debated 1 day	Finance Bill continues with some clauses in Committee of the whole House and some in Standing Committee	Finance Act for Financial Year C
Estimates of Expenditure[2]	Winter Supplementary Estimates for Financial Year B (HC Paper) Note by the Financial Secretary to the Treasury (not printed) →		Ministry of Defence Votes A for Financial Year C (HC Paper) Spring Supplementary Estimates for Financial Year B (HC Paper) →	Main Civil and Defence Estimates for Financial Year C (HC Paper) Memorandum[5] by the Chief Secretary to the Treasury on these Estimates. →	Summer Supplementary Estimates for Financial Year C Note by the Financial Secretary to the Treasury (not printed) →	

Authorisation of Expenditure	Through the Consolidated Fund Bill[1]	Civil Vote on Account[3] for Financial Year C (HC Paper) / Defence Vote on Account[3] for Financial Year C (HC Paper)	Through the Consolidated Fund (No. 2) Bill[1]	Note by the Financial Secretary to the Treasury (not printed) / Statement of Excesses for Financial Year A (HC Paper)	Through the Consolidated Fund Appropriation Bill[1]	Includes index to Main Estimates[6] (Command Paper)	Through the Consolidated Fund Appropriation Bill[1]	Appropriation Act for Financial Year C
Accounts and Audit	Appropriation Accounts (audited by Comptroller and Auditor General) for Financial Year A are laid before the House	Reports prepared by the Public Accounts Committee mostly during January to June on both the Appropriation Accounts and any Excess Votes for Finanancial Year A (HC Papers)						
		Government replies to these reports are called Treasury Minutes (HC Papers)						
		Both reports and replies are Debated 1 day early in the next session						

1. The proceedings on these bills are purely formal. After second and third reading there are, following a motion for the adjournment, a series of private Members' motions which are related to the scope of the particular bill, which may be debated until 9 a.m. the next morning (or 8 a.m. if the motion was moved on a Thursday). Proceedings on these bills in the House of Lords are also purely formal. Northern Ireland Appropriations are not covered by Consolidated Fund Bills but by Appropriation (Northern Ireland) Orders.

2. Three days a session are alloted for consideration of these Estimates: (i) one before 6 February to consider winter Supplementary Estimates for Financial Year B and the Vote on Account for Financial Year C; (ii) one before 18 March to consider Excess Votes (if any) for Financial Year A following a report by the Public Accounts Committee, Spring Supplementary Estimates for Financial Year B and Defence Votes A for Financial Year C; and one before 5 August to consider outstanding votes. The subjects and lengths of these debates are chosen by the Liaison Committee, following examination of the work of and the information provided by the Public Accounts Committee and the departmental select committees.

3. A Vote on Account is money which has to be approved by the House of Commons before the end of Financial Year B, through the Consolidated Fund Bill, in order to finance payments in the early months of Financial Year C before the Appropriation Act has been passed.

4. This paper includes the Government's medium-term financial strategy.

5. From the 1985 Budget this has been recast and simplified as Supply Estimates: Summary and Guide.

6. From 1985 this index is published as a House of Commons paper with the same number as the Main Estimates.

years already mentioned. They are all published as House of Commons papers. Early in the session the Vote on Account appears. This is requesting money to pay for the public services from the beginning of the *next* financial year (April) to bridge the period until the Appropriation Act for the *next* financial year has been passed (August). In other words, it is asking for 45 per cent of the year's estimates "on account". The other paper to appear at this time contains the winter supplementary estimates, asking for extra money for the *current* year. The Financial Secretary to the Treasury accompanies these supplementary estimates with an explanatory note which is a Command Paper but not published. Both these requests are authorised through the Consolidated Fund Bill.

Next, in February–March the spring supplementary estimates appear for the *current* year. Again there is an unpublished note by the Financial Secretary to the Treasury explaining why they are required in terms such as:

Class XVI, Vote 8. Environmental services etc, other education, libraries and arts, and other health and personal social services, Wales   £7,162,000
Additional provision is sought mainly for the increases in the remuneration of doctors and dentists following the 13th report of their Pay Review Body, for more doctors and for an increase in the number of prescriptions dispensed together with the higher cost of drugs. Additional provision is also sought for EC medical costs and welfare food because of increased numbers of beneficiaries. These increases are partly offset by higher dental charges and additional income from national health service contributions.

At the same time, if necessary, a paper is laid requesting further sums of money in order to close the books of the *previous* financial year. This is called the "statement of excesses" and is designed to deal with overspending after the granting of the original estimate, the opportunity having passed for requesting money in the three main supplementary estimates (summer, winter and spring). The House will not vote this money for an "excess vote" until the department's accounts have been checked by the Comptroller and Auditor General, he has reported to Parliament and the Public Accounts Committee has stated that it "sees no objection to the sums necessary being provided by excess vote". The Comptroller sets out to explain to Parliament what went wrong in terms such as:

Class VIII, Vote 4. Royal palaces, royal parks, historic buildings, ancient monuments and the national heritage (Department of the Environment).
This vote was subject to a cash limit which was overspent. Although expenditure fell short of the revised gross estimate (HC 430 of 1981/82), as increased by the supplementary estimate presented in February 1983 (HC 186 of 1982/83), £936,258.22, receipts of classes authorised to be used as appropriations in aid also fell short by £1,125,626.13 of the estimate, as increased by the supplementary estimate, of £10,216,000. The deficiency was mainly due to shortfall in receipts from admission fees, licences etc. for royal palaces and royal parks and from admission fees, sales of publications etc. for ancient monuments, England. The authority of Parliament is sought to provide for the net excess of expenditure over the net estimate, amounting to £189,367.91, by an excess vote.

Both the spring supplementary estimates and the statement of excesses are authorised through the Consolidated Fund (No. 2) Bill. (At this time too a paper is laid by the Ministry of Defence concerned not with money but with manpower. It is Ministry of Defence Votes A, seeking parliamentary authority for the maximum numbers of personnel to be maintained for service with the Armed Forces during the *next* financial year.)

The main Civil and Defence Estimates are published at the time of the Budget. As shown in table 9, they were divided into 17 main classes and within these for 1984/85 it was further divided into 183 votes. Table 10 shows the breakdown of individual "votes" within the largest class, namely that covering defence expenditure.

Table 9
Main Classes of Civil and Defence Estimates 1984/85
(£million)

	Class/Main Programme	Public expenditure element in Estimates	to other main programmes	from other main programmes	Total by main programmes	In Cmnd. 9143 1983/85 Plan
I.	Defence	16,828	1	231	17,060	17,059
II.	Overseas aid and other overseas services	1,867	–	−1,375	492	270
III.	Agriculture, fisheries, food and forestry	898	943	5	1,846	1,916
IV.	Industry, energy, trade and employment	6,206	−54	−1	6,151	6,019
V.	Arts and libraries	229	–	29	258	255
VI .	Transport	2,048	20	16	2,085	2,093
VII.	Housing	1,227	−1	30	1,256	1,162
VIII .	Other environmental services	439	−5	5	438	439
IX.	Law, order and protective services	1,403	–	75	1,477	1,500
X.	Education and science	2,271	–	5	2,275	2,275
XI.	Health and personal social services	13,066	−2	98	13,162	13,137
XII.	Social security	13,236	−87	150	13,299	13,292
XIII.	Other public services	1,716				
XIIIA.	House of Commons: administration	17	2	13	1,759	1,766
XIIIB.	National Audit Office	10				
XIV.	Common services	2,195	−379	–	1,816	1,916
XV.	Scotland	2,919	65	56	3,041	3,036
XVI.	Wales	1,175	36	37	1,247	1,254
XVII.	Northern Ireland	67	82	6	155	150
	Total	67,817	621	−621	67,817	67,539

Table 10
Votes of Class I (Defence) Estimates 1984/85
(£million rounded)

Class I: Defence	1982–83	1983–84		1984–85		
Vote Service	Outturn	Total provision	Forecast outturn	Public expenditure element	Other provision	Total provision
*1. Defence: pay, etc. of the armed forces and civilians, stores, supplies and miscellaneous services	5,908	6,135	6,043	6,395	−10	6,385
*2. Defence procurement	6,505	7,558	7,112	8,083	−2	8,031
*3. Defence: armed forces retired pay, pensions etc.	680	775	775	831	–	831
*4. Defence accommodation services, etc.	740	933	933	1,058	1.3	1,059
*5. Defence: dockyard services	427	428	422	462	–	462
Class I total	14,260	15,828	15,284	16,828	−10	16,818

*Vote subject to a cash limit

Accompanying these main estimates is the memorandum by the Chief Secretary to the Treasury.[3] This includes an introduction to the procedure covering estimates, a basic glossary of terms, and a summary of figures under class and vote. In addition, other tables include pay and pension costs of central government staff as well as the Armed Forces and National Health Service, numbers of staff under each department and receipts from European Community institutions relating to particular main classes. Finally there is an index to the main estimates. The memorandum is published as a Command Paper. This is unfortunate, as it means that the Main Estimates (which are House of Commons papers) are in a different numbered series from their index.[4] The main estimates are authorised by the Appropriation Act passed about the end of July.

Although these main estimates are published in March or even the beginning of April, already by June or July the Government presents the summer supplementary estimates and revised estimates for that same financial year. If this seems to suggest inaccurate estimating, two facts must be remembered. First, the main features of the estimates will in many cases have been decided on as early as the previous summer, so that the summer supplementary estimates are really amending decisions on estimates nearly a year previously. Secondly with Parliament not sitting for nearly three months during the summer it is wise for the Government to ensure that the first adjustments to estimates come before Parliament quite early in the financial year. These summer supplementary estimates and revised estimates are also authorised through the Appropriation Act shortly before the summer recess. The Government then no longer has to live off the Vote on Account authorised by the Consolidated Fund Bill just before the previous Christmas; its estimates and first supplementary estimates for the current year have been formally authorised by Parliament.

In recent years the House of Commons has grown very concerned about the difficulties of examining and expressing views on these various estimates. Debates on the Consolidated Fund Bills had proved to be quite an inadequate method. Since 1982/83 a new procedure has been in force. First, the proceedings on the three Consolidated Fund Bills have become quite formal. These three days have been used for a series of debates initiated by private Members — debates (on a motion for the adjournment) which usually continue through the night until about breakfast time. Secondly, three days a session are now devoted to debating the estimates and it is the Liaison Committee (made up of the chairmen of the select committees) which chooses the subjects to be debated. The object is to tie in the work of the departmental select committees examining departmental estimates with the House of Commons' calendar of financial business as a whole. These departmental select committees often get copies of the different relevant estimates in proof, in order to increase the time they have in which to examine them. It is normal therefore for the House to have before it on these three days the reports of the relevant departmental select committees on the estimates under discussion. Session 1983/84 saw the start of this system on a full scale.

We have considered papers and debates on economic policy, the authorisation of taxation, the presenting of estimates and the authorisation of expenditure. But after this work, there is a ruling of lines and totalling of sums in order to balance the books.

Accounts and audit. The acts by which Parliament appropriates money for the Government to spend are very specific in stating that the money issued from the Consolidated Fund must be spent within the financial year. If it is not, it is returned to the Exchequer. For this reason, with the close of the financial year, the appropriation accounts are made up by the departments, signed by the departmental accounting officer, normally the permanent secretary running the department, and then passed to the Comptroller and Auditor General for audit. The Comptroller has a staff of over 800 to do this job. The National Audit Act 1983 was passed "to strengthen parliamentary control and supervision of expenditure of public money . . .". It states that "the Comptroller and Auditor General shall by virtue of his office be an officer of the House of Commons". He not only checks the figures but "may carry out examinations into the economy, efficiency and effectiveness with which any department . . . used its resources in discharging its functions".

To achieve this the Comptroller will periodically report on areas where he can suggest improvement in the use of public funds. His ideas are then examined by the Public Accounts Committee, which reports to the House. An example of one such report is the Fourth Report from the Committee of Public Accounts 1983–84: *Department of Employment Manpower Services Commission — Special Employment Measures*. The whole working of the special employment measures since 1975 was examined and 11 conclusions and recommendations were offered to the House.

When the accounts have been audited the Comptroller and Auditor General lays them before the House — generally towards the end of the calendar year. The arrangement of these appropriation accounts, which are published as a House of Commons paper, mirrors the main estimates. It is the job of the Public Accounts Committee, on the basis of the Comptroller's reports, to examine these accounts and to make reports to the House. The committee is generally chaired by a senior opposition Member, preferably an ex-Financial Secretary, who will know the system from the inside. The Public Accounts Committee uses the same procedures as other select committees. The committee has up to 15 members. It is not concerned with the merits of policy nor just with the figures, but with administration and ensuring that the policy has been carried through "efficiently, effectively and economically".[5]

The Government gives both oral and written evidence to the Public Accounts Committee, through civil servants and if appropriate through the relevant individual accounting officers who have a personal responsibility for expenditure. These sessions can be demanding for witnesses, partly because they cover a wide field, partly because witnesses are explaining to an exacting committee what may have gone wrong and partly because under modern practice the proceedings are in public and may even be broadcast. In his recent Reith lectures, Sir Douglas Wass (a Treasury civil servant of very wide experience) gave his comment on the working of this method by which Parliament questions the Government:

> The Public Accounts Committee has a formidable reputation in Whitehall, and it commands great respect from civil servants. It is well briefed and fully equipped to examine witnesses. I can assure you that few permanent secretaries who have to go before the Public Accounts Committee will allow themselves any private engagements in the immediate run-up to an appearance.[6]

The Public Accounts Committee reports to the House of Commons and the Government's response to this report is called a Treasury Minute. Both the select committee report and the government response are published as House of Commons papers and at least one day each session is set aside for debating them.

So far we have been talking about the way in which each year the Government recommends and Parliament authorises necessary expenditure and then checks the auditing. There is one further matter to look at, namely the way in which authority in principle is given for *new* forms of expenditure. This is done through the House passing a financial (money) resolution and it usually arises in connection with new legislation.

Once again it is the Government which recommends the expenditure to the House and although it forms no part of the proceedings on the bill this money resolution is normally considered immediately after the second reading policy debate. The resolution is not always debated but debate No. 5 in table 4A (see page 37) is an example of where it was debated. Of course, where an actual amount is proposed (which is not normally the case with a money resolution), Parliament has no power to increase the figure proposed; it can only accept, reject or reduce the figure. In order to supply background information the Government attaches to the Bill a financial memorandum which sets down the implication of the bill for public expenditure. When this bill moves into its committee and later stages only the Government may propose any amendment which results in a different form of or higher expenditure — and then only after the passing of a further financial resolution. If the bill becomes an act, this expenditure will quickly find its way into the estimates, often a supplementary estimate initially and the main estimates thereafter.

There have been a number of major changes in financial procedures in recent years reflecting the fact that the House is not happy with arrangements. These changes have been included in this account. But there are still matters which concern the House, of which the most important is probably the problem of overseeing government borrowing and long-term expenditure. This has been examined by a Procedure Select Committee,[7] but although the report was debated on 6 December 1983 no action on its main proposals has yet been taken.[8] Part VIII of this report, paras. 159–166, is entitled Provision of Financial Information, and the Procedure Select Committee had a number of criticisms to make regarding the way the Government presented this information to Parliament. These included:

(1) In presenting supply estimates "there is not more than an occasional reference to the level of services and no information on targets and outputs" (para. 159).

(2) After examining the information given on individual votes and their subheads, the committee comments: "These are but a few of the many examples of the glaring discrepancies in the amount of detailed information available which bears little relation to what the House and its committees require" (para. 160).

The committee noted evidence given to it by the Chief Secretary to the Treasury concerning the newly introduced "financial management initiative" in government departments. He said that "when this initiative does get off the ground fully it will lead to changes in the presentation and structure of the departments' public expenditure programmes or votes, which will mean more and clearer information for Parliament" (para. 164). At the end of this section of their report the Procedure Select Committee recommended:

> The Treasury and Civil Service Committee and the Public Accounts Committee should between them carry out a full inquiry into the format, structure and content of the financial information for the House and its committees in the light of the outcome of the financial management initiative and the implementation of our recommendations (para. 166).

The Treasury and Civil Service Committee started their work by examing the paper prepared by Andrew Likierman and Peter Vass (see note 1 to this chapter), inviting the Treasury to comment on it in writing and then taking oral evidence both from the Treasury and the twó authors, Likierman and Vass. Then at the end of 1984 they reported making a number of recommendations[9] as follows:

(1) The autumn statement should be further developed, be more up-do-date and "the timescale of the expenditure plans should be extended from one to three years" (para. 9).

(2) The Public Expenditure White Paper should, at the Treasury's suggestion, "be presented primarily on a departmental basis". If departmental annual reports were established the select committee saw most of the material in Part II of the Public Expenditure White Paper being published there (para. 12). The committee also recommended "more consistent treatment of the geographical coverage of expenditure within the UK" (para. 13).

(3) The financial statement and budget report might be replaced by a document "UK Budget" which would include a second volume of technical special analysis including the information in the present budget press notices listed on page 81 (para. 17).

(4) The supply estimates "should be redesigned and should become documents mainly for parliamentary use perhaps available only in type-written form". Departmental reports might then be linked to the estimates and Public

Expenditure White Paper. Such a method could not be applied to supplementary estimates, which need explanations telling Parliament why they are needed, to be published very swiftly (para. 20).

(5) The idea of there being departmental annual reports was supprted by the select committee: "Naturally a prime purpose of the Reports would be to enable Departments to explain their policies." However, they saw the reports also as including "material linked to the estimates and Public Expenditure White Paper" and felt that they should be the starting point for the work of the new departmental select committees (see chapter 8) (para. 25).

(6) The financial management initiative annual reports[10] were seen by the select committee as embryonic departmental annual reports. The committee proposed they should be published at the time of the Budget (para. 26).

Finally, the select committee proposed the following timetable during which their proposed changes should be introduced:

1985	Consultation and agreement on the lines of the reforms.
	Extension of time-scale of the autumn statement.
1986	Conversion of the Public Expenditure White Paper onto a departmental basis.
	Introduction of a new budget document. Reform of the estimates and production of a linked expenditure document.
1987	A common system of annual reports to Parliament from all departments (para. 33).

In March 1985 there was a government response accepting some of these proposed changes, but the Treasury and Civil Service Committee confirmed that it intended to keep the format and presentation of financial documents under review.[11] The Public Accounts Committee also referred to in the Procedure Committee's recommendation has not yet carried out any "full inquiry into the format, structure and content of the financial information for the House . . .".

Financial procedures of the House of Commons are a complicated matter and they take up nearly 100 pages in the current (20th) edition of Erskine May's *Treatise on the Law, Privileges, Proceedings and Usage of Parliament* (1983). This chapter simply sets out to indicate Parliament's main responsibilities regarding government expenditure and the most important information that is necessarily submitted to Parliament.

NOTES

1. For an evaluation of these papers see A. Likierman & P. Vass, *Structure and Form of Government Expenditure Reports: Proposals for Reform* (Certified Accountant Publications Limited, 1984)
2. For some of the build-up to the Budget see Hugo Young & Anne Sloman *But Chancellor* (BBC, 1984), pp.65–83
3. See note 5 to table 8 on page 83
4. See note 6 to table 8 on page 83
5. Erskine May, *Treatise on the Law, Privileges, Proceedings and Usage of Parliament* (20th ed., 1983), p.728
6. Sir Douglas Wass, *Government and the Governed* (BBC Reith Lectures 1983; Routledge and Kegan Paul, 1984), p.66
7. First Report from the Select Committee on Procedure (Finance), 1982/83 (HC 24-I-III)

8. HC Deb. vol. 50, cc.245–91
9. Second Report from the Treasury and Civil Service Committee: *The Structure and Form of Financial Documents presented to Parliament* (1984/85), (HC 110)
10. The first two of these to be published are *Financial Management in Government Departments* (Cmnd.9058, 1983) and *Progress in Financial Management in Government Departments* (Cmnd.9297, 1984)
11. Seventh Report from the Treasury and Civil Service Committee (1984/85) (HC 323) pp.viii–xi is the government response to the Report detailed in note 9 above

10. Foreign and European Communities Affairs

The opening sections of the Queen's Speech (see page 29) are concerned with her actions as head of state and with the Government's responsibilities with regard to defence and foreign affairs. They are a reminder that in this area it is the Queen and her ministers who are all-important. Parliament, with little relevant legislation to consider, is on the sidelines, since foreign affairs is a matter of negotiation, of Government speaking to Government. However, Parliament clearly has an interest in foreign affairs and as external problems often draw a united response, even from opposing political parties, a skilful Government can sometimes use this united parliamentary opinion to support its negotiating position. (Where this cohesion does not happen, as during the Suez Affair of 1956, more mature readers will recall not just a vigorously divided Parliament and nation but also, possibly more uncomfortable, divided families; on this foreign affairs occasion few were able just to sit on the fence.) Negotiations between Governments nearly always take place behind closed doors so that there are indeed problems regarding the Government informing Parliament on these matters.

Although the main focus of Members' parliamentary interest is on domestic matters, their work at Westminster does bring them into an interntional context in a number of ways. The majority of them are members of the Commonwealth Parliamentary Association, under whose auspices they travel abroad and also meet Commonwealth leaders visiting the United Kingdom. Many are members of the Inter-Parliamentary Union, which meets regularly in different cities throughout the world. In the case of both these bodies the areas of their interest is much wider than their title suggests. Then Westminster sends 18 representatives to the Parliamentary Assembly of the Council of Europe at Strasbourg and 18 substitutes are nominated in case of their absence. These same representatives and substitutes attend the Assembly of the Western European Union, which usually meets in Paris and is concerned with international defence matters, though again this is very broadly interpreted. Both these are consultative bodies only, but clearly are part of the foreign affairs context of Members' work. So also is their attendance at the North Atlantic Assembly, where the United Kingdom has a voting strength of 18 (there being no limit on the number of delegates) and which watches the work of NATO, meeting in a different country each year. These are regular international parliamentary commitments, concerning which Members may approach the Foreign Office for a briefing about the Government's standpoint. In addition there are over 100 informal parliamentary groups, each concerned with a different individual country or region. If to this we add invitations from overseas Governments and organisations and occasional visits supported by our Government, we can see that any Member keenly interested in foreign affairs should be able to extend his experience and add to his knowledge.

Because responsibility for foreign affairs rests so clearly with the Government, so also, whatever the difficulties in timing, does the task of informing Parliament. All the traditional methods are used: the command paper, the parliamentary question, the ministerial statement, the debate and, more recently, ministers and civil servants responding to select committee investigations. But first we must look at the treaty series of papers which are solely concerned with foreign affairs.

Negotiations with foreign countries or inter-governmental organsations, if successful, lead to an "agreement" (generally bilateral) or a "convention" (generally multilateral) or an "exchange of notes" or, most formal of all, to a "treaty". It is only after negotiations are completed that the text is published and laid before the House. It is usual for the Government then to wait 21 days before ratifying it. Of course if legislation has to be passed in order to fulfil an agreement, as happened for instance when we joined the European Communities, then ratification has to wait until Parliament has legislated as required. Before ratification the agreement is published (in English only) either in the "country" series (bilateral) or "miscellaneous" series (multilateral). Once it has been ratified and is in force, it is published in the languages of all the signatories and appears in the "treaty" series. In all cases they are published as Command Papers. Lists of ratifications, accessions, withdrawals etc. are published every few months. They are arranged by subject. A slim index to the treaty series is published each year arranged by number and equipped with a subject and country index. Detailed general indexes to the treaty series used to appear every three years or so, but this series has now ceased (the last such index, covering documents up to 1979, having been published in 1983).

For much of this century there has been sporadic discussion about Parliament's need for a foreign affairs select committee. In 1968–69, following a procedure report of 1964 and as part of the so-called "Crossman reforms", a number of "subject" and "departmental" select committees were established. One of the latter was set up "to consider the activities of the Ministry of Overseas Development". In 1971, when the Expenditure Committee replaced the former Estimates Committee, having been granted wider terms of reference than its predecessor, one of its six sub-committees was concerned with defence and external affairs. Finally, when in 1979 the Expenditure Committee was in turn replaced by the current comprehensive system of departmental select committees, there was nominated both a Defence Committee to monitor the Ministry of Defence and a Foreign Affairs Committee to cover the Foreign and Commonwealth Office. The latter committee has the power to appoint a sub-committee, and did so, on overseas development.

During its first Parliament, 1979–83, the Foreign Affairs Committee regularly took evidence from the Foreign Secretary on foreign affairs in general and this dialogue took place on the following dates:

3.12.1980	25.11.1981	10.5.1982
3.11.1981	19.2.1982	20.12.1982

These discussions contrast with the Government's more usual way of informing Parliament through parliamentary question and debate. The committee also issued 21 reports during this period covering subjects as diverse as the Olympic Games, Afghanistan, the British North America Acts and the role of Parliament, and finally, the Mexico Summit and the Brandt Commission report.

Not surprisingly in view of what has been said of the Government's role earlier in this chapter, a majority of the witnesses questioned were ministers or civil servants. The Falklands clearly dominated the interest of the committee in the latter part of the 1979–83 Parliament and early in 1984, when the Foreign Affairs Committee had been re-established after the 1983 general election, it returned to examining this subject.

In chapter 6 there was explained the way in which government departments are on a rota to answer parliamentary questions. The Foreign Office answers questions in the House normally every fourth Wednesday beginning about 2.35 p.m. with general questions on foreign affairs and continuing, not later than 3.10 p.m., by answering questions on European Communities matters. The question session concludes at 3.30 p.m. On one particularly day in early 1984 the question period covered Turkey, Indonesia, international terrorism, Argentina, USSR (human rights), the Gulf War, nuclear disarmament and Syria. Such a list gives a good idea of the range of the Foreign Secretary's responsibility. There then followed a number of questions on European Communities' matters, which included relations between the United States and the EC, the meetings of the Council of Ministers and finally the UK budget rebate. Each of these individual questions lasted about five minutes. However, in the last 20 years the amount of time available for answering foreign affairs questions has halved, despite our joining the European Communities.[1]

The great speed-up in communications means that as never before the Government is required to react instantly to foreign news. Members of Parliament see the same television pictures of events abroad as ministers, and although the latter have a very sophisticated system of telegrams being sent to Whitehall day and night from all over the world, Parliament is always impatient to know the Government's view. For this reason statements in the House are made by the Foreign Secretary or his junior ministers quite frequently. These may be oral statements, often in response to a private notice question, although if the situation is less urgent statements may be found in written answers at the back of *Hansard*. Attendance at meetings in Europe by ministers — other than the Foreign Secretary or of course the Prime Minister attending the European Council — often fall into the latter group.

Finally there are the actual debates. It is usual for one of the days of the debate on the Queen's Speech to be focused on foreign affairs. In addition, at least one full day's debate takes place each session. However, the sheer unpredictability of the subject makes this assertion, although true, of little real value. Much of foreign affairs is concerned not with routine administration but rather with long-term policy (Gibraltar, Hong Kong), short-term responses (Afghanistan, Argentina), and negotiations in private. Such constraints naturally do not make for an easy sustained relationship with Parliament.

European Communities

When Prime Minister Heath signed our treaty of accession to the European Communities in January 1972, it was necessary to introduce a bill in order that we could carry out our obligations. The European Communites Bill, a short bill which took a very long time to be passed by Parliament, empowered the Government to carry out existing and future Community directives through delegated legislation; to apply all existing Community regulations; and to legalise future EC regulations. This last, which was "acceptance in advance as part of the law of the UK of provisions to be made in the future by instruments issued by the Community institutions", was described as "a situation for which there is no precedent in this country".[2] Such a sentence in a government document laid before Parliament was for some almost provocative. It certainly led Parliament to reflect on procedures to ensure that the Government would keep it well-informed on EC matters, and the Government accepted this responsibility. Information from the Government covers two main areas, namely general EC developments (including the budget) and EC legislation.

The chief ways in which Parliament is kept up to date with these general developments can be summarised as follows:

(1) About the 26th day of each month a paper entitled "Estimates of subject headings likely to come up for discussion" is delivered by the Cabinet Office to the House of Commons Vote Office and this is accompanied by a ministerial statement in the House. The paper covers the meetings of the Council of Ministers in the coming month.

(2) After these meetings the minister who attended reports back to the House, making an oral statement if it was an especially important meeting or a written answer in *Hansard* if it is more routine. As already mentioned, when the Prime Minister attends one of the regular meetings of the European Council she reports back to the House in person.

(3) Every six months the Government lays a Command Paper before Parliament called "Developments in the European Communities". This contains a lot of information including summaries of developments under major subject-headings, lists of meetings and ministers attending them, major proposals adopted by the Council and major treaties and agreements made by the EC. It sometimes includes the texts of the more important speeches of ministers in Brussels and elsewhere. A day is set aside to debate each of these papers.

(4) A further day is set aside to debate the European Communities' budget, when the Government can be asked to develop its policies for Members to consider. When the budget for 1984 was being considered (on 20 February 1984) an exchange took place between the minister and a number of Members which illustrates quite clearly the tug of war which can sometimes exist between Government and Parliament when it comes to information. The minister was being taxed about the rebate which was expected by 31 March 1984, when a Member from his own side of the House asked:

Mr Teddy Taylor (Southend, East): What will be done about the default of £42,000,000 which happened on 31 December in relation to the 1982 rebate? The minister kindly told me that my right hon. and learned Friend the Secretary of State for Foreign and Commonwealth Affairs sent a letter to the Commission on 3 January. When I asked about it last week I was told that no reply had yet been received. How can the continentals accept that the Government are firm, because when they defaulted by £42,000,000 all that we did was to send them a letter to which we have not yet had a reply?

Mr Ian Stewart: My right hon. and learned Friend the Foreign Secretary wrote to the Commission. I understand that he received a reply over the weekend, although I have not yet seen it. I have no doubt that the reply will be considered and that we shall take whatever steps are necessary over the 1982 risk-sharing refund. . . .

Dr Oonagh McDonald (Thurrock): The hon. Member for Southend, East (Mr Taylor) has rightly questioned the minister about the letter. It is astonishing that the minister has not seen a copy of the reply. Since the debate will continue until 10 o'clock, will the minister send a message so that the letter is brought here and read out, since it is an important part of the debate?

Mr Stewart: I am sure that my hon. Friend the Minister of State has heard that request. I understand that the letter is addressed to my right hon. and learned Friend [the Foreign Secretary], who is in Brussels — [*Interruption*.] That might be a matter for mirth to opposition Members, but fortunatley the Government treat such communications seriously and do not deliver judgements before they have had time to consider them.

Mr Tony Marlow: On a point of order, Mr Speaker. As the letter is obviously of importance to the debate, is it possible to ensure that somehow a copy of it is put on the Table of the House so that hon. Members who wish to participate in the debate may be made aware of its contents?

Mr Speaker: That would be possible, but I do not think that I can accept such a motion. Laying the letter on the Table of the House is a matter for the Government. . . .

Mr Robin Cook (Livingston): . . . The Economic Secretary cannot expect the House to accept that, because the only copy is in the Foreign Secretary's vanity case in Brussels, it is not possible to produce the letter. There are such things as photocopies and teler. We are not still living in the days of the pigeon post.

Some hours later when the minister was winding up the debate a final exchange took place.

Mr Teddy Taylor: While the House is greatly reassured to hear about the strong action that will be taken if the Common Market defaults on 31 March, will my hon. Friend say what strong action was taken following the default on 31 December last by the Community over the £42,000,000 which should have been paid but was not, bearing in mind that the Foreign Secretary sent a letter on 3 January and that, we understand, a reply has just been received? I hope that the minister will be able to tell us what that reply from the Common Market says.

Minister of State, Foreign and Commonwealth Office (Mr Rifkind): My hon. Friend the Member for Southend, East (Mr Taylor) has referred to correspondence between the President of the Commission and Her Majesty's Government. I am not at liberty to indicate the contents of correspondence of that kind. In saying that, I am not saying anything new; it is a position with which the House is familiar. But the Commission agrees with the United Kingdom that the sum which has not been paid arises out of a political decision by the Council of Ministers and does not arise out of any legal entitlement or disentitlement that the Commission recognises. Therefore, this is a matter which now has to be dealt with within the context of the inter-governmental negotiations now taking place, and it is clearly an issue which will be raised in that context.

This sets out quite neatly Parliament's limited role in the heady world of negotiation. It does not mean, however, that Sir Geoffrey Howe, the Foreign Secretary who had received the letter and was that day in Brussels, might not, at the appropriate moment, make use of Parliament's annoyance. Finally, in connection with EC general developments there is a regular 20 minutes of question time every fourth Wednesday.

When it came to Parliament's decision as to how they should consider EC draft legislation, both Houses set up select committees to examine the procedures which should be introduced to deal with this situation "for which there is no precedent". Both of these committees made reports to their House and full responsibility for keeping Parliament informed was placed squarely on the Government.[3] The new constitutional position was quite clear. The UK Parliament could not play any direct part in EC legislation, which was a matter for Ministers; but Members could make their views clear to the UK Minister who was responsible to Westminster and who through membership of the Council of Ministers was part of the EC legislative process. Both Houses decided to set up "Scrutiny Committees", which are required to examine draft EC legislation and other documents. The following general arrangements were laid down:

(1) When the Commission proposes legislation to the Council, at which stage the opinion of the European Parliament is asked and sometimes the Economic and Social Committee, then the Government must ensure that copies of the proposal are sent to both Houses at Westminster — normally within 48 hours.

(2) Each House has a Scrutiny Committee[4] and in order to help them examine these proposals the government department responsible for the area affected by the proposed legislation must forward to Parliament a departmental memorandum commenting on its legal and political implications. This memorandum must be signed by a minister. In turn the House of Commons committee must report to the House on "why it considered the particular proposal of importance" and point out "the matter of principle or policy which it affects and the changes in UK law involved".[5] Both these committees are assisted by legal staff who are officers of Parliament.

(3) The Scrutiny Committee of the House of Commons meets weekly. It publishes a report after each meeting, the first part of which recommends proposals that its Members believe should be considered by the House. The House of Commons Scrutiny Committee very seldom takes oral evidence from the Government or anyone else.

(4) The Scrutiny Committee of the House of Lords plays a similar role, though through a more elaborate committee system. The chairman sifts proposals into list "A" not requiring further examination and list "B", about one-third of the draft proposals, which should be examined by one of a series of sub-committees covering:

A. Finance, economics and regional policy
B. External relations, trade and industry
C. Education, employment and social affairs
D. Agriculture, food and consumer affairs
E. Law
F. Energy, transport, technology and research
G. Environment

Apart from considering the departmental memoranda, these sub-committees will, if they find an important subject, take oral and written evidence and publish it together with a substantial report; some of this evidence may well be taken from the Government. In short, they work in a traditional select committee way and their reports are read and respected widely.

(5) The final government responsibility is to provide time to debate these documents. Occasionally this is in a standing Committee, but more usually it is in the Chamber. This debate is so that Members may listen to ministers' pre-negotiation views and express Parliament's opinion on the proposal to the

minister before he travels to Brussels, where the Council will legislate. In October 1980 the House passed a resolution requiring the Government, save in exceptional circumstances, to find time for a debate on these proposals before the Council meeting.[6]

The working of the procedures connected with these Scrutiny Committees, especially that of the House of Commons, have been examined from time to time and have not been found to be entirely satisfactory. The extent of the work of the Commons Committee in recent sessions is set out in Table 11.[7]

Table 11
House of Commons Select Committee on European Legislation: Work 1979/80 to 1983/84

	1979–80[1]	1980–81	1981–82	1982–83[2]	1983–84[3]
Consideration of Instruments					
Meetings of the Committee	46	32	30	18	30
Oral evidence	5	2	4	1	4
Instruments reported on	963	745	723	461	761
Instruments reported as raising questions of legal or political importance	340	208	163	161	256
Instruments recommended for debate	138	81	53	59	123
Instruments deposited during session, but not yet reported on	42	78	32	31	36
of which preliminary consideration given to	15	8	9	—	7
Debates held					
Instruments undebated at start of session which had been recommended for further consideration by the House	67	61	49	57	77
Instruments added during session to list of recommendations for debate	138	81	53	60	123
Instruments withdrawn from list	42	20	10	7	12
Total of instruments accumulated for debate during session	163	122	92	110	188
Instruments debated in Chamber	102	66	23	33	64
Debates held in Chamber	27	22	9	12	16
Instruments debated in Standing Committee	—	7	12	—	30
Debates in Standing Committee	—	5	10	—	10
Balance of instruments still awaiting debate at end of session	61	49	57	77	94

[1] 9 May 1979–13 November 1980.
[2] 3 November 1982–13 May 1983.
[3] Figures corrected to 27 June 1984.

Although the Government is now adept at ensuring that the text of this draft legislation and other documents come to Westminster very quickly, the committee found that during 1983 141 out of 672 documents considered by the committee had already been adopted in Brussels. Subsequently two of these were recommended to the House for further consideration. It was proving difficult to mesh in the work at Westminster with that at Brussels. It was also proving difficult to find time to debate these matters, as Table 12 makes clear.[8]

Table 12
Debates recommended by the Select Committee on European Legislation 1981–83

	1983	1982	1981
Documents considered by the Committee	672	717	781
of which, recommended for debate	107	64	71
Documents debated			
on Floor of the House	69	9	34
in Standing Committee	3	21	10
Total	72	30	44
Debates held			
on Floor of the House	18	9	15
in Standing Committee	1	8	7
Total	19	17	22

The Scrutiny Committee decided to take evidence from the Lord Privy Seal/ Leader of the House on the whole question; although much of the questioning was necessarily on rather specific points, the following exchange suggests the balance as between Whitehall and Westminster concerning these EC drafts etc.[9]

Mr Soames: Lord Privy Seal, do you think as Leader of the House and as a considerable House of Commons man that Parliament in its own right as a sovereign body deals effectively with these very complex matters?

Mr Biffen: I think I have to give a generalised answer which I fear is full of potential misunderstanding and misrepresentation, but I think that we have a situation where, of course, Parliament ultimately controls the Executive, the Executive draws its life blood from Parliament, but the truth is that in the day-to-day exercise of authority the Executive really runs without too much constraint from Parliament and in the circumstances of our relationship with the European Community government has retained its sphere of authority, I believe, more effectively than has Parliament.

There could be a further development in House of Commons select committee work with regard to European Communities' affairs. The Procedure Committee of 1977/78[10] recommended that, if any of the new departmental select committees wished to examine EC draft documents to set their work in a Community context, they should do so. Although this idea has not yet been followed up with great enthusiasm, it might well lead to the House of Commons more frequently questioning government witnesses on EC matters. There have, however, been recent enquiries on dairy farming in Wales, acid rain and the Fontainebleau Summit.

Our joining the European Communities has obviously put a new strain on the relations of Government with Parliament. Tensions in the triangle of Whitehall, Brussels and Westminster are more likely than with the simpler axis of Whitehall and Westminster. So far Parliament has been content to use traditional methods, which after 10 years have now settled down and since 1979 have been able to absorb the added constitutional dimension of a directly elected European Parliament.

NOTES

1. Second Report from the Foreign Affairs Committee 1979/80 (HC 511, Appendices 4–5)

2. *Legal and Constitutional Implications of UK Membership of the European Communities* (Cmnd. 3301, 1967, para. 22)
3. House of Commons: First Report from the Select Committee on European Secondary Legislation (1972/73, HC 143); Second Report (1972/73, HC 463 I–II). House of Lords: First Report by the Select Committee on Procedures for Scrutiny of proposals for European Instruments (1972/73, HL 67); Second Report (1972/73, HL 194)
4. The House of Lords has the Select Committee on the European Communities. The House of Commons has the Select Committee on European Legislation.
5. Second Report from the Select Committee on European Community Secondary Legislation (1972/73, HC 463 I–II, para.69)
6. HC Deb.vol.991, c.838
7. First Special Report from the Select Committee on European Legislation (1983/84, HC 527 p.xiii)
8. *Ibid.* p.5
9. *Ibid.* pp.13–14
10. First Report from the Select Committee on Procedure (1977/78, HC 588 I, paras.4.4 and 4.5)

11. The House of Lords

The curtain is rung up on each session of Parliament by the Queen's Speech. Once it is delivered and her procession has retired, once Mr Speaker has led the Members of the House of Commons back to their Chamber and the robed Peers have dispersed for luncheon, there is a moment to reflect, on this first day of the session before the debate on the Address starts on the same afternoon, on the House of Lords.

Looking down from the Strangers Gallery across at the throne, the visitor sees before him the Chamber — the apogee of Victorian self-confident riches and decoration. The government and bishops' benches are on his left with beyond them a small area for the civil servants supporting the government spokesmen on the front benches. The opposition benches are on his right; the front rows on each side are kept apart not just by seating for the staff (the clerks and the *Hansard* reporters) but by the Woolsack in front of the throne and the cross-benches near the bar of the House. Cross-benches are important in the House of Lords and in recent years the number of Peers not opting to support a political party and take a party whip has grown greatly. The Chamber's detail and colour are uninhibited: it seems a long way from the representation of constituency problems and of course it is. Members of the House of Lords represent their own views.

At the beginning of 1985 there were 1,180 members of the House of Lords including 1,154 Peers and Peeresses and 26 archbishops and bishops. Of these 764 were Peers and Peeresses who had succeeded to their title, 30 were hereditary of first creation, 19 were Life Peers appointed as salaried Lords of Appeal and finally 296 were simply Life Peers and 45 Life Peeresses. Within this total 148 had leave of absence from the House not to attend and 100 were without writs summoning them to Westminster. The party breakdown of active Peers was roughly 400 Conservatives, 210 independents (cross-benchers), 130 Labour, 40 Liberals and 40 Social Democrats. Attendance, which is slowly rising, averages well over 300 a day and, as one would expect, Life Peers and Peeresses are proportionally more regular attenders.

The House of Lords sits about 150 days a session but these are often spread over two or three more weeks of the year than are the 170 or so days that the House of Commons sits. Early in the session the House of Lords often sits only on Tuesday to Thursday inclusive but soon it adds Monday sittings and later in the session, when its load of work becomes still heavier, it also sits on Fridays. This changing pattern during the session is shown in appendix 1. Mondays to Wednesdays, like the House of Commons, it sits at 2.30 p.m, Thursdays at 3 p.m. and on Fridays at 11 a.m. The average length of daily sittings has grown in recent years to over 6½ hours, so that in a typical parliamentary session the House of Lords is now sitting about 1,000 hours.

The organisation of the Government in the House of Lords is quite different from its organisation in the House of Commons. There are only about 14 of the ministerial team in the Lords, as opposed to about 90 in the Commons, so this results firstly in government spokesmen there having to answer on a wide range of subjects and secondly in a number of Peers, who are members of the Royal Household, having to respond on certain departmental subjects. Four members of the House of Lords are in the Cabinet, namely the Lord Chancellor, the Lord President of the Council (Leader of the House of Lords), the Chancellor of the Duchy of Lancaster and, a recent inclusion, one Minister without Portfolio. The distribution of government spokesmen regarding departmental responsibilities is set out in table 13.

Table 13
Departments of State and their Government Spokesmen
HOUSE OF LORDS

Agriculture, Fisheries and Food
  Minister of State
  Captain, Yeomen of the Guard
  Lord in Waiting

Arts
  Minister of State

Defence
  Under-Secretary of State
  Under-Secretary of State (Energy)
  Under-Secretary of State (DHSS)

Education and Science
  Minister of State (Foreign and Commonwealth Office)
  Captain, Yeomen of the Guard

Employment
  Minister of State (Privy Council Office)
  Minister of State (Scottish Office)
  Lord in Waiting

Energy
  Under-Secretary of State
  Lord in Waiting

Environment
  Minister of State
  Lord in Waiting
  Lord in Waiting

Foreign and Commonwealth Office
  Minister of State
  Under-Secretary of State (Defence)
  Lord in Waiting

Health and Social Security
  Under-Secretary of State
  Baroness in Waiting

Home Office
  Under-Secretary of State
  Baroness in Waiting

Lord Advocate's Department
  Lord Advocate

Lord Chancellor's Department
  Lord Chancellor

Northern Ireland
  Minister of State

Scottish Office
  Minister of State
  Lord in Waiting

Trade and Industry
  Chancellor of the Duchy of Lancaster
  Minister of State (Agriculture, Fisheries and Food)
  Lord in Waiting

Transport
  Under-Secretary of State (Defence—Aviation)
  Lord in Waiting (all other matters)

Treasury
  Chancellor of the Duchy of Lancaster
  Minister of State (Privy Council)
  Under-Secretary of State (DHSS)

Welsh Office
  Minister of State (Foreign and Commonwealth Office)

The procedure and work of the House of Lords are broadly similar to the House of Commons. Examination of their work in Appendix 1 shows them debating general motions, examining, debating and amending legislation, debating select committee reports, listening to government statements, dealing with delegated legislation and asking questions. An approximate breakdown of time is shown in table 14.

Table 14
Division of House of Lords Time

					per cent
Starred questions	..	..	..	..	6
Debates: general motions	..	..	..		25
select committee reports		..	..		4.6
legislation	..	..	..	..	42.5
delegated legislation		..	..	..	5.7
Statements	..	..	..	..	3.8
Unstarred questions	..	..	..	..	8.4
					96.0

The House of Lords, like the Commons, uses select committees to examine matters and report back to the House, but they hardly ever use standing committees for the committee stage of legislation (they are called Public Bill Committees when they are used). That partly explains the high percentage of time spent on legislation in the Chamber as opposed to the House of Commons, and in general the distribution of House of Lords time is rather different from that of the House of Commons. For instance, the House of Lords spends very little time on financial matters and quite a lot of time on European Communities' affairs.

The work of the House of Lords has increased steadily and substantially during the last three decades. Since World War II the first session when the average sitting reached four hours a day was 1958/59, increasing to five hours a day in 1962/63 and six hours a day in 1970/71. The sittings have averaged over six hours a day for the last five sessions. Attendance during the 1950s was 100 to 150 Peers a day, while for many sessions in the 1980s it has been double that number. Starred or oral questions, which used to be 200–300 a session, are now over 500; written questions did not reach 100 a session until 1969/70 and are now often more than 1,000. If to this is added the Lords' increasing select committee work, it is clear that there is plenty of vitality in the south end of the Palace of Westminster and that the House of Lords is far more demanding of government time and energy than used to be the case.

So much for the facts about the House of Lords; but what is distinctive about its role, especially in relation to the theme of this book? The House of Lords accepts that the House of Commons is preponderant in its political role. This reflects the fact that Peers arrive at Westminster either through inheriting their seats or through being appointed. They do not have to campaign at the hustings, nor do they represent electors or worry about constituents. They live and work at a lower political temperature and this results not only in the courtesies which they express to each other as they work together, but also in the fact that they do not need the discipline of a Speaker. Theirs is not the world of "Order! Order!", despite the fact that quite a large number of the active Peers have previously survived two or three decades of political struggle in the House of Commons down the corridor.

For essentially the same reason, the House of Lords does not usually divide at the end of the second reading of a government bill; indeed, as shown in Appendix 1, a growing number of politically uncontroversial bills are being introduced there first. One result of this politically lower temperature is that Peers have a considerable interest in information, i.e. in being well informed, including being well informed by the Government. And as they are less likely to need this information for the purposes of broad political persuasion and certainly not frequently to make a sharp political point, it is easier for them to examine a subject more impartially.

Not only may their demands for and use of information be more impartial, but also Peers bring to debate a range of experience which is distinct and often different from that of Members of the House of Commons. Most Peers have often satisfied a number of personal ambitions before they reach Westminster; their average age is of course older than the House of Commons; and at most debates there is a distillation of experience that is worth listening to. Let us take two debates, neither of which would be likely to quicken significantly the elector's pulse. First, on 22 February 1984 the Lords discussed "Industrial Resources — Redeployment: EC Coal Policy", the specific subject being "the need to transfer resources from heavy industries with high-cost output and surplus capacity, particularly in the field of energy, into others whose future offers prospects of continuing demand, of profitability and of jobs".[1] The speakers included the following:

Earl of Lauderdale	Former Chairman of the House of Lords European Communities Committee — Sub-Committee F (Energy, Transport and Research)
Lord Kearton	Part-time member of the Atomic Energy Authority, 1955–81; Chairman of the Electricity Supply Research Council, 1960–77; Chairman of BNOC, 1975–79
Lord Stoddart	Member of the House of Commons Select Committee on Energy, 1979/80 to 1982/83
Lord Ezra	Chairman of the National Coal Board, 1971–82
Duke of Portland	Co-opted Member of House of Lords European Communities Committee — Sub-Committee F (Energy, Transport and Research)
Lord Kaldor	Adviser to Labour Governments and to the Chancellor of the Exchequer, 1964–68, 1974–76; Professor of Economics at Cambridge, 1966–75
Lord McAlpine	Deputy Chairman, British Nuclear Associates, 1973–

Earl of Halsbury	Managing Director of National Research Development Corporation, 1949–59; President of Institution of Production Engineers, 1957–59; Nationalised Transport Advisory Council, 1963–67; Chancellor of Brunel University, 1966–
Viscount Torrington	Managing Director, Attock Petroleum plc, 1976–
Lord Dean	Former Shop Steward AUEW
Viscount Hood	Career Diplomat, 1936–69
Lord Bowden	Physicist, Principal of the Manchester College of Science and Technology, 1953–64
Lord Pennock	Deputy Chairman ICI, 1975–; Deputy President of the CBI, 1979–80
Lord Bruce	Chartered Accountant; MP 1945–50; MEP 1975–79

By any standards I believe it would be accepted that the 15 or so people who spoke in this 3½-hour debate drew together experience and exchanged information of a range which would be very difficult to collect in any other forum. Just a week before that debate, the Lords had a short (2½ hours) debate on the Law of the Sea.[2] The speakers included:

Lord Caradon	Colonial Service, 1929–60; Ambassador, later Permanent Representative at the UN, 1961–62, 1964–70
Lord Kennet	Delegate to Council of Europe and WEU, 1962–65; Editor of *Disarmament and Arms Control* 1962–65; Chairman of the Advisory Committee on Oil Pollution of the Sea, 1970–74; MEP 1978–79
Lord Elwyn-Jones	Lord Chancellor, 1974–79
Viscount Hood	Member of British Waterways Board, 1963–73
Viscount Buckmaster	Diplomatic Service, 1946–81
Lord Denning	Master of the Rolls, 1962–82

In this debate too there was a sharp focus of intellect and experience. In both cases I have not mentioned the government spokesmen who replied to the debate, namely the Earl of Avon to the debate on EC coal policy and Baroness Young to the debate on the Law of the Sea. They each spoke for about 20 minutes and, while they responded in some detail to specific points which had been made during the course of the debate, they will have received considerable general briefing from their civil servants.

The quality of active membership of the House of Lords means that Peers are often demanding in terms of securing information from the Government. And in turn the background and contacts which many of them have means that they can arrive at the House of Lords often very well briefed indeed. In addition their smaller responsibilities often give them greater time to probe the Government's performance, although always with the rapier rather than the broad-sword. What are the distinctive aspects of their work?

If we start with oral questions, they are limited to four a day but the length of question time is up to about 30 minutes. If you add to this that it would be unusual for the House of Lords to lose any time bringing itself to order, the result is that individual questions often have longer and more supplementary questions and demand more information than those in the House of Commons. Civil servants will therefore often have to brief the government spokesman very carefully. For instance, on 31 October 1984 a question on the waste of water through leakage took 10 minutes to answer because it resulted in 11 supplementary questions and 10 responses from the spokesman. The very next question was on the future development of the coal-mining industry and lasted even longer, some 15 minutes. In the House of Commons there would be no time for such leisurely probing which can sometimes result in a very real exchange of information.

With regard to government statements made to Parliament, if the House of Lords is sitting they generally interrupt their proceedings so that the government spokesman can synchronise his statement in the House of Lords with an identical one being made by a minister in the Commons. Subsequent questions in the House of Lords on the statement may often illuminate the subject in a way quite different from the questioning in the House of Commons. If the House of Lords is not sitting, then the text of any statement made in the Commons is often printed in the next issue of the House of Lords *Hansard*. Sometimes it is the House of Lords that is sitting, not the House of Commons, and occasionally a matter is of such importance that the Government communicates it to the House of Lords before the House of Commons. This happened in October 1984 when Lord Whitelaw made the first government statement to Parliament concerning the recent bomb attack on the Grand Hotel in Brighton.

When it comes to debates the House of Lords again has more time than the House of Commons to discuss more general matters. One day a week, usually a Wednesday, is set aside for these debates, which are limited to five hours. There may be 20 to 25 such debates a session taking 10–15 per cent of the time of the House. Quite distinct from these are the two short debates (2½-hour limit) which back-benchers and cross-benchers can ballot for and which take place on Wednesdays from the beginning of the session, i.e. from after completion of the five-day debate on the Queen's Speech until the Whitsun Recess. There may be about 20 such debates a session taking up about five per cent of the time of the House.

The range of subjects which may interest the House of Lords is a broad and often a forward-looking one. This is important because one common criticism of both Government and Parliament is that they seldom take a careful long look at a subject and that there is too much reacting to immediate situations, too little making of considered assessments. There is the additional fact that with 26 archbishops and bishops there is a very direct contribution to the debating of society's moral issues from the established Church — a unique fact among world parliaments? — and illustrated by the House of Lords holding an early debate

106

on the Warnock report. That the House of Lords debates subjects such as these often compels government spokesmen and civil servants to think the subject through and to respond.

In the early spring of 1984 the following debates of matters took place:

Date	Matter
15.2.1984	Administration of metropolitan areas
29.2.1984	Foreign affairs and disarmament
7.3.1984	Barriers to women at work and at home
	Nation's assets and current spending
14.3.1984	Higher and further education
21.3.1984	Nuclear holocaust
	Future of the prison service

These two groups of general debates can impose a considerable burden on the Government and civil service, because the Peer raising the question is often moved as much by interest in and conviction about the importance of the subject as by any wish to make political points; in addition he or she may well be widely accepted as experienced in and knowledgeable about the topic. If to this we add the obvious fact that members of the House of Lords are not troubling Whitehall with constituency matters it is clear that the issues they raise and the context within which they see them are frequently wider than the same debate in the House of Commons would be, assuming that the House had time to discuss such questions at all. In a very real sense, therefore, debates are a complement to the work of the elected Chamber and as already suggested often require the Government to step back and consider wider and more long-term problems.

The idea of the House of Lords complementing the House of Commons is not confined to these debates and to its accepted role of being a "revising Chamber" for legislation. In recent years there have been changes in its select committee system which to a considerable degree now complements the work of Commons select committees. Table 15 sets out the select committees of the House of Lords. From the viewpoint of this book, column 1 need not detain us, as most of the evidence taken by these committees is not of general interest; moreover, where civil servants are called as witnesses it is normally because they are providing a direct service to Parliament, e.g. accommodation or printing parliamentary papers. At the foot of column 3, however, there is mentioned the Science and Technology Select Committee. From 1966–79 there was a Science and Technology Select Committee in the House of Commons. It was established at a time when phrases such as "the white heat of technology" were on the lips of Whitehall and Westminster. The committee disappeared, despite a formidable rearguard action to keep it, when the new departmental select committees were set up in session 1979/80. The House of Lords promptly set up their own Science and Technology Select Committee. In recent years this committee, often after taking evidence from civil servants, has issued a number of important reports. As in some of the House of Lords debates, a rather longer view of matters has been taken than either the Government or the House of Commons can usually achieve. But such select committee work can prompt the Government to reflect more deeply in order to prepare their evidence.

In column 2 of table 15 there is listed the European Communities Select Committee together with details of its elaborate system of subject-oriented sub-committees. When we joined the European Communities in 1973 and each

Table 15
House of Lords Select Committees*

1.
Domestic Matters Committee

House of Lords' Offices
With sub-committees on
administration
computers
finance
Library
refreshment department
staff of the House
works of art
Leave of absence and Lords' expenses
Privileges
Procedure
Selection
Sound broadcasting
Standing orders (private bills)

2.
European Communities Committee
with Sub-Committees

European Communities
with sub-committees on
A. finance, economics and regional policy
B. external relations, trade and industry
C. education, employment and social affairs
D. agriculture, food and consumer affairs
E. law
F. energy, transport, technology and research
G. environment

3.
Other Committees

Ecclesiastical
Hybrid instruments
Joint committees with the
  House of Commons
consolidation bills
statutory instruments
Personal bills
Science and technology
  with sub-committees on
agricultural research
environment
new technologies
general purposes

* These committees are appointed for a session; judicial and ad hoc select committees are excluded.

House set up a select committee to consider what procedural changes were needed to tackle the new and unprecedented situation at Westminster, the House of Lords first proposed that there should be a joint committee of both Houses to examine EC draft legislation and other matters, a proposal based presumably on the example of the Joint Committee on Statutory Instruments. This proposal was not acceptable to the House of Commons; since 1973, therefore, each House has had its own scrutiny committee. This gave the House of Lords the opportunity to develop its own distinctive role with the result that it has always been the more important with regard to taking evidence, both oral and written, from a broad range of witnesses, including government departments, and to publishing this information for Parliament and a wider public. Indeed, their reports are often quite long and genuine contributions to the study of the subjects they examine and are regarded in the EC, in information terms, as the most important contributed by any house of any member parliament. As the House of Commons committee does not often take oral evidence, most published government information on these EC matters made available through these traditional select committee techniques results from the work of the House of Lords.

Before leaving this select committee work it is worth remembering that the departmental select committees system in the House of Commons uses up so much of the energy of that House — with regard, that is, to select committee work — that the likelihood of their setting up an ad hoc select committee other than those concerning purely domestic matters has greatly diminished. This is not the case with the House of Lords, which at the beginning of session 1984/85 decided to set up a new ad hoc Select Committee on Overseas Trade. They decided to probe the broad subject of "the causes and implications of the deficit in the UK's balance of trade in manufactured goods". As they call for departmental memoranda, the machinery of Government will once again need to set to and prepare its information for Parliament.

While the methods of work used by the House of Lords are the traditional Westminster ones, as an institution the Upper Chamber has a quite distinct ingredient to add to the relationship of Government and Parliament. The range of experience assembled in its membership, the lack of constituency concerns, the consequent lack of media exposure, the longer-term thinking that it is possible for it to follow are all ways in which it adds to the total picture of Parliament's work. They are important because of the very difficult situation for today's legislators in knowing what role to play. Are parliamentarians generalists questioning and discussing on behalf of the man in the street — the elector — problems of a society where professionalism and specialisation are the order of the day? Are they specialists at examining and passing legislation and in checking on its administration? Aren't they a system for warning the Government, which itself finds difficulty in keeping in touch, where the shoe of policy is pinching the people? They are, of course, all these things and more. The work of the House of Lords dovetails into that of the House of Commons at many levels: in joint committees, as a revising Chamber for legislation; in its emphasis on European Community matters; in its longer-range debates; and of course in the area not touched in this book, namely its judicial work. But above all it is made up of a wide range of people, most of whom have achieved their immediate ambitions before arriving at Westminster and who are therefore in a position to contribute to the national debate from an experienced yet singularly detached viewpoint. A luxury in our value for money age? If so, it is not one we should lightly set aside. The recently authorised experiment of televising its debates may help more adequately to judge its contribution.

NOTES

1. HL Deb. vol.448, c.768–76, 782–832 (22.2.1984)
2. HL Deb. vol.448, c.317–46 (15.2.1984)

12. Parliamentary and Other Commissioners

With the spread of government influence and regulation during the 19th century, a new brand of officials grew up whose job it was to check that citizens and their organisations were living within the law. They were termed "inspectors". Today we still have school inspectors, factory inspectors and, most familiar, inspectors of taxes. The other side of this coin has been the institution in recent years of "commissioners" who are there to take up cases of complaints against the bureaucracy, and thus give citizens in their turn the opportunity to protest about maladministration. Today there are the following such commissioners:

	Name	*Statutory Authority*
(1)	The Parliamentary Commissioner	Parliamentary Commissioner Act, 1967
(2)	The Health Service Commissioner for England	National Health Service Reorganisation Act, 1973
(3)	The Health Service Commissioner for Wales	National Health Service Reorganisation Act, 1973
(4)	The Health Service Commissioner for Scotland	National Health Services (Scotland) Act, 1972
(5)	The Northern Ireland Commissioner for Administration	Parliamentary Commissioner (Northern Ireland) Act, 1969
(6)	The Northern Ireland Commissioner for Complaints	Commissioner for Complaints (Northern Ireland) Act, 1969
(7–9)	The Commissioners (three) for Local Administration in England	Local Government Act, 1974
(10)	The Commissioner for Local Administration in Wales	Local Government Act, 1974
(11)	The Commissioner for Local Administration in Scotland	Local Government (Scotland) Act, 1975

Posts 1–4 are held by the same person, as are posts 5–6, while posts 7–11 are five individuals, making in total seven individual commissioners. This chapter is concerned only with the role of the first six commissioners on the list, as they have a direct responsibility to Parliament. The Commissioners for Local Administration concern themselves with and work through local government.

The role of the Parliamentary Commissioner established in 1967 was consciously based on the role of the Comptroller and Auditor General, who assists the Public Accounts Committee. That is, he was to be an officer of the House of Commons who worked independently of Government and who reported to Parliament in general and to a select committee in particular. To emphasise this relationship the first Parliamentary Commissioner, appointed in 1967, was the then Comptroller and Auditor General. However, most of his staff are civil servants on secondment, usually for three years, and this has sometimes led to some criticism both by the Parliamentary Commissioner himself and the House of Commons Select Committee on the Parliamentary Commissioner for Administration. A distinctive aspect of the British system is that cases of maladministration which are raised by citizens can only be investigated by the Parliamentary Commissioner if they are referred to him by a Member of Parliament. That is because:

> In Britain, Parliament is the place for ventilating the grievances of the citizen — by history, tradition and past and present practice. It is one of the functions of the elected Member of Parliament to try to secure that his constituents do not suffer injustice at the hand of the Government.[1]

This quotation not only describes the thinking behind the post and its relationship with Parliament but also why this chapter is written. The Parliamentary Commissioner in a distinctive way is extracting government information for Parliament.

Enquiries referred to the Parliamentary Commissioner by Members of Parliament must concern the work of central government departments or other bodies listed in schedule 2 of the 1967 Act. They number between 800 and 1,000 a year and during 1982 these were spread among 389 Members who requested investigations — well over half the total membership of the House of Commons. Over 70 per cent of these referred cases were rejected by the Parliamentary Commissioner, and of those which were pursued the citizen turned out to be right in his charge of maladministration about 50 per cent of the time.

In his investigations the Commissioner has quite formidable powers of seeking information from departments. He has access to departmental papers and is able to interview staff. With these powers, civil service staff, together with an experienced inquisitor in charge, the Parliamentary Commissioner's Office backed by a select committee, is a very real check on government maladministration.

The Parliamentary Commissioner communicates formally with Parliament in three ways. First he is required to report annually on his work and his department. This report is examined by the select committee, which takes evidence from the Commissioner and then reports to the House of Commons. Secondly, the Commissioner reports quarterly to Parliament a selection of his reports during the previous three months. Typically they would be about one-third of all his reports, something like 15 out of 45. These summaries are comprehensive ones and give a meticulous and detailed insight into the work going on inside government departments.

First is set down the complaint, then the statutory and administrative background; a detailed narrative of the investigation follows which unveils with singular clarity the working of departments; then there is a report on the findings and finally the conclusion. The Commissioner's report is always passed to the department to check its factual accuracy before it is sent to the Member who raised the matter.

Not surprisingly the Department of Health and Social Security and the Inland Revenue — those government departments which give to or take from the citizen — are the subject of nearly half the charges of maladministration. Most of the complaints are small in themselves but very important from the complainant's viewpoint and sometimes in terms of achieving justice. The examination is of course concerned with the administration of the case rather than its merits, although the two can be closely entwined. A few examples of these cases will give the flavour of the more routine work. They show how the Parliamentary Commissioner has comprehensive and high level access to government information on its administration and if he upholds a claim he sometimes proposes a simple apology and sometimes a remedy in the form of an ex-gratia payment.

Case No. C 457/82: Incorrect advice on mortgage relief to a resident in the Channel Islands

Result: The deputy chairman of the Board of Inland Revenue offered the complainant his apologies for the fact that the department's acceptance of the mistaken claim in 1980 had led to the abortive re-arrangement of his mortgage. And by way of compensation he said that his department were prepared to meet reasonable costs arising from the loan switch and to pay a modest amount in respect of accountants' fees involved in dealing with correspondence up to the end of October 1981. The deputy chairman's offer struck me as fair and reasonable and I provided the department with copies of the papers which had been sent to me in support of the claim for reimbursement. I suggested that an ex-gratia payment of £400 would represent an appropriate sum in respect of the period September 1980 to October 1981 and I am glad to report that the chairman has agreed to pay this amount. I regard this payment, together with the apologies tendered and the remission of £40 tax, as a satisfactory outcome of a justified complaint.[2]

Case No. C 672/82: Mishandling of claim to unemployment benefit

When I invited the principal officer of the Department of Employment to comment on the complaint, he said that the clerk who had accepted the complainant's claim appeared to have assumed from the information given that he was working as a social researcher for two days a week. Acting on this belief the clerk had asked the complainant to complete an inappropriate form (UB 567D) and, without consulting a supervisor, had decided that the complainant's claim should be suspended indefinitely. But the clerk had not then sent a form UB 48, as he should have done, telling the complainant that his claim had been suspended and giving the reason for the suspension. The clerk had also failed to refer the claim to an insurance officer for a decision, as required by standing instructions. The principal officer acknowledged that many of the complainant's subsequent difficulties stemmed from these errors and from the fact that when the unemployment benefit office belatedly passed the details of the complainant's claim to the computer centre on 5 January 1982, the suspension which the clerk had erroneously applied to the claim was also fed into the computer the following day. As a result no payment was made to the complainant and matters hung in suspense until, for some unexplained reason, the unemployment benefit office sent another form UB 567D to him in February 1982.

Although the complainant returned this form on 15 February, the unemployment benefit office did nothing to pursue his claim and were prodded into action only when he wrote to them again on 24 March. The supervisor then examined the complainant's casepapers but failed to refer the claim to the insurance officer. The supervisor has told my officer that he noticed at this stage that there had been unnecessary delays and errors in dealing with the complainant's claim. It is evident, however, that he failed to appreciate that the complainant should be asked to complete a form UB 672 and instead sent him another form UB 567D and the questionnaire for completion. The supervisor has said that he might have written an apology for the delay on the compliments slip which he sent with these forms but that he could not be certain that he had taken such action. It seems to me, however, that by this time the complainant was entitled to no less than a full letter of explanation and apology in view of the delay which had already occurred.[3]

The saga of mistakes in the second of the above cases was to continue for some time yet and drew sharp comment from the Parliamentary Commissioner in his conclusion:

> The catalogue of mistakes made by the unemployment benefit office in their handling of the complainant's claim and correspondence was quite appalling. The principal officer of the Department of Employment has said that he could find no excuse for his department's failure to give the complainant the standard of service to which he was entitled and he has asked me to pass on his sincere apologies for the considerable inconvenience which he has suffered. This I gladly do. Following his successful appeal the complainant received his full entitlement to unemployment benefit.[4]

A final example is taken from a department, that of the Environment, which is less frequently involved with the Parliamentary Commissioner. This summary runs to no less than 23 pages and illuminates the working of the Highways Act 1980, Section 119, Subsection 1. The case was made more complicated because it involved local government as well as central government. The investigation seems to have left little untouched:

Case No. C 876/81: Delay and errors in confirmation of bridleway order

> On 16 July [1980] the file was passed to the officer authorised to sign the decision letter. However he returned it to his subordinate officer on 1 August with a minute saying "I am not happy about the interpretation of 'efficient' use as applied. Can we discuss pl. [please]?" The next entry on the file is dated 15 October 1980 and made by the subordinate officer who noted that the discussion had been delayed because of "our respective annual and sick leaves".[5]

The conclusion suggests, as is often the case with the Parliamentary Commissioner's work, that steps have been put in hand to improve administration. It includes:

> My investigation has shown that there were a number of administrative shortcomings in the way in which the department handled the complainant's case. The inspecting officer's report contained a material error of fact, and omitted comment on a specific aspect of the case which was of some significance. These, while not major errors in themselves, nevertheless contributed — together with the council's incomplete statement — to the formation of an incorrect interpretation by the decision-making officers on which the decision to modify the order was based. The department have accepted that there were undue delays in the consideration of this case and have apologised for them. They have also made improvements in their monitoring arrangements which I hope will be sufficient to avoid such delays in future. They have additionally undertaken a review of the relative priorities given to public path orders and planning appeals. And they have reprimanded one of the officers involved in this case.[6]

So much for the Commissioner's more routine work.

The third formal relationship between the Commissioner and Parliament is where he decides to lay a full report before the House because he considers "the findings and conclusion of my investigation to be of general interest".[7] A recent such report, which generally number one or two a session, is an "Investigation of a complaint about delay in reviewing a conviction for murder", published in January 1984. It received considerable publicity because it concerned an alleged murderer convicted partly on the evidence of Dr Clift, the chief biologist working at the forensic science laboratory at Chorley who was suspended from duty in September 1977. It is impractical to compress a 26-page report which, within the impersonal covers of an HMSO publication, is quite a vivid story, but it does reveal a number of aspects of the work of civil servants. The chief of these in relation to this book is their awareness that their actions may need to be accounted for in some public forum, as they were in this case, and that therefore elaborate minutes, carefully maintained records and files of docketed information are necessary for good administration. In this case, as the Parliamentary Commissioner shows, such system in the Forensic Science Service (FSS) was lacking. Dr Clift took some files home and some of his earlier work was found firstly not to exist and then later was recovered. However, a second and more serious matter was that the Home Office did not show initiative in thinking through the implications for those convicted on Dr Clift's evidence, once he had been suspended for incompetence. The Commissioner set down the issue very clearly in his report:

A miscarriage of justice by which a man or woman loses his or her liberty is one of the gravest matters which can occupy the attention of a civilised society. And it seems to me that when an unprecedented pollution of justice at its source is discovered, quite an exceptional effort to identify and remedy its consequences is called for. My overall impression of the way the Home Office administrators responded to the discovery of Dr Clift's serious shortcomings is that they failed fully to grasp or face the implications. As my investigation has shown, their response was in some respects prompt and efficient; but in others they seem to have been content to adopt a passive and reactive role rather than a positive one. They maintained this while the investigation for the DPP [Director of Public Prosecutions] was in progress and it remained substantially unchanged until after Mr Preece's conviction had been quashed and records of past cases came to light. Following the release to the press in September 1977 of the news of Dr Clift's suspension from duty, media coverage was extensive. And I find it surprising that those members of senior management responsible for the Criminal Justice Department, the Establishment Division and the FSS were not spurred by such publicity into taking a more active interest in the way in which the department as a whole intended to deal with the consequences of Dr Clift's incompetence.[8]

On 14 February 1984, just three weeks after the report was laid before the House, the Select Committee examined the Home Secretary (Leon Brittan), the permanent secretary of the Home Office (Sir Brian Cubbon) and other civil servants on the matter. The Home Secretary in his opening statement said that "the report raises very serious issues about the standards and practice of the Home Office Forensic Science Service and the handling by the Home Office of the cases where there might have been a miscarriage of justice".[9] The permanent secretary was invited to tell the committee the steps which had been taken by the department to prevent a recurrence and he gave a detailed reply, to which the chairman of the committee responded:

We are grateful for that. It is in marked contrast to the attitude shown if one looks at paragraph 19 on page 10 of the Commissioner's report where the Home Office attitude as put forward by the assistant under-secretary is: "We have taken the line that there is no onus on us to take the initiative in trawling through cases handled by Clift that have not been examined by [the police officer]." Here it seems to me — and I am glad of it — there is a marked change between the attitude expressed in the view put forward to the Commissioner and repeated in his report and what you have been kind enough to say to us just now, Sir Brian — a marked change in attitude.[10]

Sir Brian Cubbon. Yes Mr. Chairman.

The next question concluded: "I have not heard anything yet that suggests the department is looking at the onus."[11] This drew from the Home Secretary the following:

As far as I was concerned, one of the major reactions to the report was to accept that, in circumstances where evidence that was tendered by a Home Office employee is rendered suspect, it is now regarded as an onus upon the department to investigate and pursue as vigorously as possible the circumstances in which that evidence came to be given and to scrutinise its reliability. That is a policy statement which I stress to this committee dealing, as I have to, with the future rather than the past.[12]

Whilst this was the nub of the matter, trenchant questioning continued on more detailed aspects, this time by Ken Weetch (Labour):

Mr Weetch. Mr Chairman, I would like to bring up one or two matters. The first is about the Forensic Science Service. It strikes me when anything goes wrong and you need to investigate it, the first task you have to set yourself is to assemble the materials so that you could look into it. Reading through this report, much of the material was not available in the sense that many people did not know where it was. Secondly, they did not know whether it existed or not, whether it had been destroyed; they did not know whether it was in the possession of Dr Clift or not; they did not know whether, if it was in Dr Clift's possession, that it was correct or not that it should be. In fact, it strikes me, reading the report, that the Forensic Science Service and its records, which everyone knows you may have to look at again in a serious case, were in the most incredible mess. Now, do we have your assurance, Home Secretary, that a fundamental examination has now been undertaken of the record-keeping, that if anything goes wrong again someone can put their hands on this and that, someone can say "Well, I know where it is and here is where we look at it" and we can examine it? Have we your assurance that this has been done in the most thorough way so that we can prevent a repetition of what has occurred?

Mr Brittan. The changes that have been made in the Forensic Science Service in the form of, for example, improving the quality assurance system since this affair came to light, go very much further than merely ensuring adequate handling of records. I can assure Mr Weetch and the committee that we have looked very earnestly at the implications for the Forensic Science Service of the matters disclosed in the report, including the questions of record-keeping. I personally have satisfied myself that this is now being done properly.[13]

The Select Committee having taken evidence turned to its report. They knew from the very first words of evidence given them by the permanent secretary of the Home Office that there were lessons which had been learnt from the case:

Sir Brian Cubbon. The first point, Mr Chairman, I should like to make is that the details of this exceptional and serious matter are now very sharply etched in the collective memory of Home Office officials. It will certainly be one of the cautionary cases that will always be brought to the attention of officials engaged in the area of work concerned with possible miscarriages of justice. I am quite sure that the case itself, the Commissioner's report and this committee's examination of it, will be very clearly embedded in the minds of Home Office officials for the future.[14]

And the Select Committee concluded its own report to the House of Commons in equally sober manner:

> The whole Preece affair, and the events surrounding it, were rightly described by the PCA [the Commissioner] as a "sorry saga". It is a disgrace to a civilised society that but for the efforts of a prison chaplain and a Member of Parliament the injustice to Mr Preece and possibly to others might have gone unremedied. And it took a lengthy investigation by the PCA to bring the failings of the Home Office to the department's attention. Only then would they accept that their treatment of the Preece/Clift case had not been "wholly satisfactory". However, we trust that the lessons have been learned and the chances of a recurrence reduced.[15]

Only 20 years ago the Parliamentary Commissioner did not exist and these few examples show that in the overall relationship of Whitehall and Westminster he is able in a manner quite different from any other to ensure that if a question of maladministration is raised via a Member of Parliament he will on behalf of Parliament get at the facts.

The Health Service Commissioners for England, Scotland and Wales — the posts are held by one person who is also the Parliamentary Commissioner — received in 1982–83 some 798 complaints, a figure very close to the number he received from Members as Parliamentary Commissioner; 71 per cent of these were rejected. These and other facts are found in the annual report of the Health Service Commissioners which he is required to make to Parliament and which is subject to scrutiny by the Select Committee on the Parliamentary Commissioner for Administration which reports to the House. The Health Service Commissioners, whose terms of reference are confined to the Hospital Health Service, receive complaints direct from the public and send their reports and two volumes a year of selected cases to the Secretary of State not to Parliament. When the Select Committee takes evidence on the annual report most of the witnesses are regional health authorities but one evidence session is usually reserved for Whitehall departments. The method of work of the Health Commissioners is similar to that of the Parliamentary Commissioner; Parliament, via its Select Committee, keeps a watch over his work, but is not directly linked with the case work.

On 3 April 1984 the committee had such an evidence session and invited the permanent secretary of the Department of Health to give his view of the role of the Health Commissioners and of the committee itself. He commented:

> I think it is most important to emphasise what we believe to be the immense impact on the Health Service of that steady flow of reports from the Commissioner about these cases. Why does the department think it has had such an impact? I can offer a number of reasons. First of all, what I would loosely describe as the status of the investigations that take place under this procedure: they are personal to the

Commissioner and made on his personal responsibility. Secondly, they are backed by this committee and ultimately by Parliament and I think you will not need me to elaborate the point. There have been those in the Health Service who have had to learn, perhaps the hard way, that this committee does require the Commissioner's examination of complaints to be taken very seriously. I think that has been done. Thirdly, I think the Commissioner's reports have established, if I may say so again, a very high standard of objectivity: they have been critical of authorities, of individuals, of the department, and they have also been critical of some of the complainants. I think this objectivity has been of great value. Finally, the investigations have taken place under the spotlight of public hearings. The authorities, members, officers and officials of the department who have been brought into these investigations have learned, many of them, that the ultimate destination of such an investigation is an appearance before this committee and cross-examination by its Members as to what all this is about. So taking those together, I think they add up to a very powerful force having a beneficial impact on the Health Service.[16]

The Commissioners described above are concerned with Great Britain. Northern Ireland has its own Northern Ireland Parliamentary Commissioner and also Commissioner of Complaints, both posts held by the same person. The Northern Ireland Parliamentary Commissioner for Administration has to make an annual report to Parliament and this is examined by the same Select Committee which then reports to the House of Commons. It takes evidence from the Commissioner and his staff. Most of the report consists of a summary of all (rather than a selection) of the cases investigated and these cases will have been referred to the Commissioner by a member of the Northern Ireland Assembly not a Westminster Member and be concerned with maladministration in one of the Northern Ireland departments. About 150 complaints are received a year and about 70 per cent are rejected. This is a rejection rate very close to the figure of the Parliamentary and Health Commissioners. Where a member of the public complains directly to the Commissioner then he writes to the complainant referring him to section 5 of the Parliamentary Commissioner (NI) Act (which says a complaint must be forwarded by a member of the Assembly), giving him the names of the Assembly members for his area and asking him to nominate one as sponsor of his complaint.

It is estimated by the Commissioner that about 10 per cent of his work is as Northern Ireland Parliamentary Commissioner and the rest as Commissioner for Complaints. The mechanics of obtaining information from departments is cogently set down in a recent reply by the Commissioner when asked about his working methods:

> We send a copy of the complaint by way of a statutory notice to the government department involved and we ask that they should let us have a reply within two weeks if possible. We realise that in planning cases, for example, it is not right to insist on a two-week time limit. In due course we get a reply from the department and we will study that reply very carefully; we may have to go to the department and ask for papers or go through their files, which we do, to take photostats of all the relevant documents. If it relates to interview panels we may ask for copies of all the applications and the marking sheets of the interview panel. We have an investigative department, an investigative section, and they will check out everything which the department sends.[17]

The Parliamentary Commissioner recently commented on his position in the following terms:

> The office of Parliamentary Commissioner stands curiously poised between the legislature and the executive, while discharging an almost judicial function in the citizen's dispute with his Government; and yet it forms no part of the judiciary. It is from the centre of that triangle that I have been able to appreciate the virtues of our unwritten and therefore flexible constitutional arrangements and still more the goodwill of those men and women, legislators and administrators, who govern us. For it is one thing to pass an act of Parliament and another to make it work. My office could not discharge its function of investigating the citizen's grievances half so well were it not for the willingness of officials in the civil service to make the Parliamentary Commissioner Act 1967 function as Parliament intended.[18]

This gives him a unique role as well as a new one, that of a parliamentary officer who on behalf of Parliament quarries out the information from departments which is then taken up by the traditional select committee system and tested, if necessary, against senior civil servant or minister alike. The evidence quoted in this chapter suggests that ministers may make statements of policy, administrators may explain departmental mistakes and report on methods of avoiding them, both in public, and that all this is based on the Parliamentary Commissioner looking over the shoulder of civil servants in a fashion that must have changed the traditional relationship of Whitehall and Westminster.

NOTES

1. Parliamentary Commissioner for Administration (Cmnd. 2767), para. 4
2. Parliamentary Commissioner for Administration, Third Report (1983/84), HC 190 p.85
3. *Ibid.* p.43
4. *Ibid.* p.44
5. Parliamentary Commissioner for Administration, First Report (1983/84), HC 44 p.23
6. *Ibid.* p.31
7. Parliamentary Commissioner for Administration, Fourth Report (1983/84), HC 191 p.3
8. *Ibid.* p.23
9. Third Report from the Select Committee on the Parliamentary Commissioner for Administration (1983/84), HC 423 p.3
10. *Ibid.* p.5
11. *Ibid.* p.6
12. *Ibid.* p.6
13. *Ibid.* pp.9–10
14. *Ibid.* p.4
15. Fifth Report from the Select Committee on the Parliamentary Commissioner for Administation (1983/84), HC 620 pp.43–44
16. *Ibid.* p.43
17. Second Report from the Select Committee on the Parliamentary Commissioner for Administration (1983/84), HC 422 p.7
18. Parliamentary Commissioner for Administration: Annual Report for 1983 (1983/84), HC 322 p.1

PART THREE: PAPERS

13. The Published Record: Bills, Reports, Accounts and Papers, Debates etc.

Words are sometimes seen as the weapons of Government — a smokescreen, some sceptics might say, to hide a lack of deeds. Whether you see any truth in this or not, it is certain that as its very name makes clear, the printed and the spoken word are the very lifeblood of Parliament. Parcelled words make documents and this chapter is concerned with documents of the written word, parliamentary papers and documents of the spoken word, the various forms of parliamentary debates.

A. Parliamentary Papers

Printed parliamentary papers as defined for this chapter consist of public bills (both Houses), House papers (both Houses) and command papers (only in the set of House of Commons papers). The Government is the originator of most public bills, many House papers and by definition all command papers, i.e. papers laid before Parliament by command of the Crown. All these documents are published by Her Majesty's Stationery Office (HMSO) and they are organised into four sets of papers.

It should be mentioned in passing that there are a large number of other papers which are laid before Parliament for information but which are subsequently not ordered to be printed by either House. These include a few command papers and a number of accounts, together with a large number of statutory instruments which are laid before both Houses but which have already been printed when they are laid. All papers whether ordered to be printed or not are listed in the daily Minutes of Proceedings of the House of Lords or Votes and Proceedings of the House of Commons and ultimately are to be found in the indexes of the journals of each House, in Part I of the index in the case of the House of Commons. The actual papers themselves are kept initially in the library of the House before which they were laid, just for current parliamentary use. Later the originals of those not ordered to be printed are transferred to the House of Lords Record Office in the Victoria Tower in the Palace of Westminster for preservation and archival use. This Record Office is open to the public, who may examine these original papers and other parliamentary records such as the original acts of Parliament or the evidence given to select committees which it is decided does not merit ordering to be printed. In the interest of economy and because of the growing work of the House of Commons departmental select committees, this latter is a growing quantity of information.

The four sets of printed papers consist of the following:

(1) House of Lords Public Bills and Papers, which are in one numerical sequence starting with the number (1) at the beginning of each parliamentary session. There are on average about 300 documents per session in this Public Bills and Papers Series. Bills are given a new number each time they have to be

printed during the legislative journey through the House and amendments to bills are given a letter after the number of the bill which they seek to amend e.g. (147a).

(2) House of Commons Public Bills, which are in one numerical sequence starting with (Bill 1) at the beginning of each parliamentary session. There are about 150–200 public bills in an average session. These bills also are given a new number each time they have to be printed passing through the House but amendments are published in a quite separate sequence of papers from the public bills, namely in the Supplement to the Votes and Proceedings.

(3) House of Commons Papers, which are in one numerical sequence starting with (1) at the beginning of each parliamentary session. There are about 400–650 papers in an average session and some of the papers are in several parts, e.g. evidence to select committees, in which case each part or evidence session when published is sub-numbered in roman figures: eg. (147–i).

(4) Command Papers, which with a lettered prefix (currently CMND) have a running number 1–9999. There are 350 or more such papers in an average session.

The first group of papers, House of Lords Public Bills and Papers, when collected together at the end of the session total about a dozen large volumes. This collection is given a first page "Titles and Tables of Contents for the Sessional Papers of the House of Lords" followed by the session. Although having one numerical sequence, the set of papers have, since 1979/80, been divided for binding into three groups. The first group is public bills, which are arranged alphabetically by title. These public bill volumes are not paginated. The title page gives the title of the bill, its number (100) and individual amendments, which are separately published and given letters (100a) (100b) etc. Amendments are marshalled before the bill is actually debated and this paper keeps the same bill number for that particular stage of proceedings and adds a roman number (100–I). Later stages of a bill, when it is reprinted as amended, have different numbers as already indicated, so that an actual bill's history in 1980/81 reads: Companies (No 2) Bill HL 72, 72 I–IV; 125, 125 I–II; 145, 145–I; 283, 283a.

The second group of House of Lords papers is reports from committees, i.e. select committees. The most regular select committees to work for the House include:

Consolidation Bills, Joint Committee with the House of Commons
European Communities Committee*
House of Lords Offices Committee
Procedure Committee
Science and Technology Committee*
Selection Committee
Statutory Instruments, Joint Committee with the House of Commons.

Committees marked with an asterisk above quite frequently take and publish evidence from government departments. The arrangement of these reports is by the alphabetically arranged name of the committee. The third and final group of House of Lords papers is called "miscellaneous" and normally fills only part of the final volume of the series of volumes for each session. It includes the Roll of the Lords published at the beginning of each session, and amendments to or new editions of Standing Orders. In groups two and three (select committee reports and miscellaneous), the title page refers to an overall pagination number which is of course useless unless the volumes are given manually the correct overall numeration. But these title pages are useful for checking a paper's correct title, number and length, if it is missing. The House of Lords papers contain no annual reports and no command papers, simply the bills passing through the House including amendments, papers of their committee work and a few domestic papers. There is no index to these papers.

The second of the four groups of papers consists of House of Commons Public Bills. Up until session 1968/69 these bills were arranged alphabetically by title in a few volumes at the beginning of each set of House of Commons sessional papers. Because it was arranged by title, amended versions of bills were bound in the volume next to earlier printings although their number was not sequential. The title page of the set of sessional papers reads "Parliamentary Papers (House of Commons and Command)" and makes no mention of the bills. During the decade 1969/70 to 1978-79, these volumes of public bills had added to them the Minutes of Proceedings of the Standing Committees which considered them, together with the reports and evidence of the Joint Committee on Consolidation Bills. These Minutes of Standing Committees are published as House of Commons Papers and the reports and evidence of the Joint Committee as House of Commons/House of Lords Papers, so during this decade the volumes of published public bills included all the bills and some House of Commons papers. From session 1979/80, however, this first group of House of Commons sessional papers has returned to being public bills only, and now they are arranged strictly by number. This means that the various printings of the same public bill during the different stages it passes through the House are separated, even scattered over a number of volumes, so that it is more difficult to follow through a detailed legislative history. But the numerical clarity of the arrangement goes some way to make up for this.

The third of the four groups of papers consists of House of Commons Papers — those papers laid before the House of Commons which are ordered to be printed. There are five main collections of papers to be found in this group. First, there are those papers which are connected with the House's select commitee work, namely minutes of proceedings, minutes of evidence, reports and appendices and finally special reports. Secondly, there are the papers connected with the House's standing committee work, namely their Minutes of Proceedings which, as already mentioned, during the decade 1969/70 to 1978/79 were bound up with the relevant bill. A third collection of papers is connected with the House's financial business. These include the Autumn Statement, and the Financial Statement and Budget Report concerning policy. There are also the vote on account and the estimates in all their different forms (see table 8) together with the volumes of appropriation accounts. The fourth collection are the annual Reports, the annual accounts and the annual returns which are laid and ordered to be printed (see Appendix 5). Finally, there are a number of papers of more domestic interest such as the Standing Orders and the Register of Members' Interests.

The last of the four groups are the command papers. These are "Presented to Parliament by [the Minister named] by Command of Her Majesty". These are therefore government papers laid before the House for the information of Parliament. They include individual statements of government policy or indeed more specific proposals. There are also some of the government replies to select committee reports where such a reply gives the Government an opportunity to make a statement of policy. There are also a number of annual or periodical reports and sometimes accounts especially by Commissions which will have been set up by the Government (see appendix 6). Finally, foreign affairs, as has been noted in chapter 10, is very much a matter of royal prerogative and therefore a government responsibility, so that all the various papers in the treaty series are command papers.

While the group of House of Lords papers has no published index, references to the three groups of House of Commons sessional papers are brought together in the published House of Commons Sessional Index, which is discussed in the next chapter. Copies of all these papers, which from session 1986/87 it is planned to publish in A4 format, are available from HMSO either singly or on a subscription basis. In addition, Chadwyck Healey Ltd has made available each month a micro-film of the three groups of House of Commons sessional papers. This is of course a much cheaper way of buying the information than by purchasing a set of the original papers.

Is all this documentation adequate for Parliament? As we have seen (at the conclusion of chapter 9), the House wants improvements to be made in the supply by the Government of financial information, and, there would appear to be other reasons for replying clearly in the negative to this question. Firstly, however, let us look at the more satisfactory side. Bills are printed as required and, while the printing and numbering of amendments to these bills are treated differently in each House and while the arrangement of the bills in the sessional volumes is different in each House, the system, though complicated, works. The papers created by the work of each House are also published satisfactorily either as House of Lords or House of Commons papers. One qualification is that the numbering of some select committee evidence and its relation to the final report could be simplified. There is also the problem that for sound reasons of economy a growing proportion of select comittee evidence is not ordered to be printed; although this is mentioned in the individual reports, the unprinted evidence is nowhere regularly listed. It is, however, when we move into the area which is the particular concern of this book, namely where Government informs Parliament and the papers needed for this purpose that the unsatisfactory nature of the present position becomes clear.

The papers which Parliament needs from Government are of two main kinds: regular reports covering administration and ad hoc reports covering policy etc. Appendices 5 and 6 list the regular reports appearing either as House of Commons papers or as command papers in 1984. But there is nothing reliable about these lists. For instance, the first annual report of the Equal Opportunities Commission was a House of Commons paper ordered to be printed; subsequent reports have not been published in the set of parliamentary papers. The first two annual reports of Parliament's own printer, Her Majesty's Stationery Office, covering 1978/79 and 1979/80 were House of Commons papers and contained a great deal of information. From 1980/81 HMSO has published a Trading Fund Account, required by Parliament as a House of Commons paper, but the annual report is just a glossy public relations brochure called "Review of the Year". For 1982/83 the latter contained a report on parliamentary printing (probably the most important raison d'être for the existence of HMSO) which I quote in full: "Efforts and resources were concentrated in providing a comprehensive service to HMSO's prime customer — Parliament. The Hansard Press continues to improve its service."

The list of such regular reports from departments which have been trivialised or are no longer published by HMSO or have dried up altogether is a long one. A different point is that many government departments which use huge funds voted by Parliament never report regularly on their activities. Even where a department has recognised and responded to such a need for an annual report, such as with the Department of the Environment for 1982/83, it is often not published as a parliamentary paper. Parliament itself has contributed to this situation as far as nationalised industries are concerned. On 22 February 1972 the House of Commons (Services) Committee resolved: "That the report and accounts of the nationalised industries should in future not necessarily be printed by the Stationery Office but should be produced independently in British Standard sizes and presented to Parliament as non-parliamentary publications."[1] This important information for Parliament is therefore no longer in the set of parliamentary papers. In addition, there is often less information in the reports which are published. It is possible that the general question of annual departmental reports may be reviewed. With the appointment of departmental select committees there is now a formal and sustained relationship between departments and Parliament. And with annual reports, prepared centrally but arranged by departments, on the progress of the "financial management initiative" programme, there is the embryo of a system of annual departmental reports to Parliament. The possibilities of these changes was picked up in a report of the Treasury and Civil Service Committee,[2] which, after arguing that the Public Expenditure White Paper should be arranged on a departmental basis, had this to say on the question of departmental annual reports:

At present very few departments make annual reports to Parliament, although they are compulsory for nationalised industries and are also presented in a wide variety of forms by most "associated public bodies". We welcome the initiative of the Department of the Environment in producing their own report in 1983, but regret that it has not been repeated. The Overseas Development Administration now produces an annual review. There are other variants, the best known being the traditional Statement on the Defence Estimates. Other useful practices have grown up, sometimes following requests from the departmentally-related select committees, as in the case of the Scottish Office and the Department of Transport.

If early progress were to be made in developing the Public Expenditure White Paper on a departmental basis, we believe this should lead to later developments in the direction of departmental reports. In due course we would like to see the Treasury and the Management and Personnel Office persuading departments to produce their own documents and encouraging a degree of uniformity in their format. Naturally a prime purpose of the reports would be to enable departments to explain their policies. But there would be other important information which could be included. For example, we have for some years drawn attention to the need for improved performance indicators in Volume II of the Public Expenditure White Paper and pointed to the inconsistency in the number and quality of those produced in the 18 sections. We continue to have a difference of opinion with the Treasury about the value of reintroducing information on a "volume" basis, without in any way undermining the new system of cash planning which we believe has been successful in many of its aims. All these kinds of information, together with the material linked to the Estimates and the Public Expenditure

White Paper, might well be most effectively presented in separate departmental reports, which each select committee could study in detail.

In this connection, we have a suggestion about the Annual White Paper on the Financial Management Initiative.[3] It has been right that the early reports to Parliament on this important new activity within Government should have been collated centrally. But we believe there is a danger that this paper will become regarded as little more than an annual chore for departments. We do not consider that even now it is presented at a time of year when the House and its committees can give it the scrutiny it merits. We therefore believe there is a case for bringing it forward to budget time and in due course incorporating the relevant information into one or more of the documents then produced. Departmental reports could well be the right place for such information.[4]

The government response to these proposals was published in March 1985.[5] What is notably absent is any requirement in the report that departmental annual reports should be published by HMSO and thus included in the regular set of parliamentary papers.

In the area of ad hoc reports etc. there is a similar situation, namely that important papers no longer necessarily appear in the set of parliamentary papers. Many of the most important policy reports of committees appointed by ministers and chaired by household names — Beeching on railways, Crowther "15 to 18" on eduction, Plowden on primary schools, Newsom/Donnison on public schools, Serpell on railway finances to name but a few, were not published as command papers. They were of course of great importance to Parliament, leading to many parliamentary questions and debates not to mention thousands of letters from constituents; but they were not included in the information papers set before Parliament and therefore not included in its collection of published papers.

The result of this is twofold. At a domestic level for the House of Commons and House of Lords the papers are not automatically available for Members through the normal Vote Office or Printed Paper Office method for supplying parliamentary papers. Of more general concern, if the department chooses not to publish using the Stationery Officer as its agent, then the bibliographical control of appearing in the Stationery Office daily list and their monthly and annual catalogue is missing. On top of this, the British National Bibliography is not comprehensive in this area of government reporting. With the growing independence of departments in publishing information, the resulting disintegration of documentary control has become serious and it is now causing concern.

There would appear to be no clear and coordinated government policy on this question. With publishing becoming more expensive, there is considerable temptation for departments to cut corners in the area of their publishing. It might have been thought that Parliament, with its long history of securing and publishing official information, would have tightened its grip. This has not happened. Instead private enterprise has stepped into the vacuum in the form of the publishing firm of Chadwyck Healey Ltd, which since 1980 has brought out the "Catalogue of British Official Publications Not Published by HMSO". This has greatly helped to establish bibliographical control over the growing library of papers published by departments but not through HMSO. The catalogue appears every two months and then as an annual volume. It covers "over 400 organisations financed or controlled completely or partially by the British

Government". In addition to this publication by Chadwyck Healey, a few departmental libraries such as that of the Department of Trade and Industry publish lists of non-HMSO publications put out by their departments.

To summarise, government-published information now appears in three groups. First there are the bills, reports, accounts, returns and command papers discussed in this chapter, which are all published by HMSO, which have their own published index discussed in the next chapter and which by definition appear in HMSO catalogues. Secondly, there are departmental publications brought out by HMSO which appear in the same HMSO catalogues. Finally, there is the growing number of departmental publications not published by HMSO which are sometimes listed by departments but for which the most comprehensive, reliable and systematic source are the Chadwyck Healey catalogues.

B. Debates

The report of each day's parliamentary debate is prepared by skilled reporters who sit in the gallery behind the clock above and behind Mr Speaker's chair and take down the proceedings in shorthand in 10-minute shifts (or less) at a time. They then retire from the Chamber to an office to prepare their copy for the printer. At this point the parliamentary clerk of the minister (if one has spoken at the despatch box) may, if it is appropriate to do so, check that the reporter got his minister's facts down correctly before the text is sent to the *Hansard* press for overnight computer typesetting and printing. The definition of what is printed is: "A report which, though not strictly verbatim, is substantially the verbatim report with repetitions and redundancies omitted and with obvious mistakes corrected, but which on the other hand leaves out nothing that adds to the meaning of the speech or illustrates the argument."[6]

If the debate continues after 10.30 p.m. the remaining text prepared up until the House rises will be added to that of the following day. Each day has its own issue and each issue is internally numbered by column not by page, a number which is continued in use until the individual issues add up to a volume. To the report of what is said in the House, which includes oral questions, there is added at the back of the issue with its own sequence of column numbers the written answers to questions. Sometimes there are so many written answers that a special supplement devoted just to them is printed, but it remains part of that particular day's issue. These daily parts are gathered together at the end of the week into bright green folders and sold as the *Weekly Hansard*. Many libraries take *Hansard* in this form, as it is considerably cheaper than subscribing for each daily issue.

It is important to remember that the text of *Hansard* at this stage, whether a daily issue or a weekly one, is uncorrected. Each daily issue prints instructions to Members telling them the day by which they may send corrections to the editor. He makes the corrections if in his view "they do not alter substantially the meaning of anything that was said in the House". Once all corrections have been incorporated, the Official Report is finally published in bound volume form, each volume normally covering a fortnight. The indexes to these Official Reports are discussed in the next chapter.

Ministers giving information to the House, especially when answering questions and occasionally when making statements, may with the permission of the House wish to present very detailed facts or tables of data. To a limited extent they may do this by including them in the main text of the Official Report — reading them as it were into the record. However, the text really is what was said. With written questions and answers the position is quite different and these regularly contain information from the Government, especially statistical information, where the tables compiled in answer to one question may take up many columns.

The reports of the House of Lords' debates are similar. There are of course only four oral questions a day, the House debates for a shorter period overall and the number of written questions and answers is far fewer than in the House of Commons. Unlike in the House of Commons *Hansard*, all this text is in one sequence of columns. If the debate continues after 9.30 p.m., which is not very often, then the rest of the report of the sitting appears in the following day's issue. The indexes to these Official Reports are discussed in the next chapter.

Reporting the debates of standing committees in the House of Commons is the responsibility of the same staff who report the debates in the Chamber. Standing committees normally sit for two and half hours in the morning — 10.30 a.m.–1 p.m. — and the report of each sitting is published as a separate issue. If the committee also sits later in the same day, then a separate issue is published. In view of the number of standing committees which may be sitting on the same morning (see appendix 1) considerable text may be prepared. Whether these standing committee debates are concerned with legislation or with matters, they do not receive any indexing, although quite detailed information on the contents of each issue is to be found on its title page. There is a delay of a few days before these debates are printed. Corrections to these standing committee debates are made in the same way as corrections to the debates in the Chamber. However, the end-of-session gathering together of these debates into volumes arranged by the letter of the committee (A, B, etc.) for legislation, or by the name of the committee for matters, is a very protracted matter, as they would seem to have a very low priority in the Stationery Office's publishing programme.

*   *   *   *   *

All these debates and possibly half of the papers described in this chapter emanate from Parliament. The other half of the papers described are nearly all presented to Parliament by the Govenment. Together they add up to several metres of publishing each session, about 50 to 60 volumes of papers and nearly as many volumes of debates. They are a very rich and important source of information on current national affairs and, especially where the United Kingdom is concerned, on international affairs. It would seem therefore appropriate that on behalf of Members their Library at the House of Commons should set up a system of analysing and indexing this archive of contemporary affairs created sometimes by and sometimes for Parliament. This indexing work is described in the next chapter, but the background to this development has been four major changes in the work, and hence in the needs of Parliament itself, and one major change in the method of meeting them.

The first change has been the enormous growth of parliamentary work. This has resulted in a great increase in its documentation, whether we are talking about the number of parliamentary questions, the work of select committees or the growth of legislation. The second change has been the growth in demand for information on Parliament's work by Members themselves and their increasing personal staff. Thirdly, there has been a comparable growth of interest in, and clearly need for, information about Parliament from the public, who range from sophisticated professionals such as those from the media, from business or lobbyists, to worried and sometimes confused constituents. Finally, with the growth of parliamentary activity and therefore of staff, especially in the Library Department, these have become more widely scattered through several buildings outside the Palace of Westminister.

The method of responding to these greater demands was to turn to the computer. In the next chapter we consider the way in which the many strands of Parliament's work — an example of which during one session is set out in appendix 1 — are drawn together into a pattern both by traditionally produced published indexes and most recently through a computer-created database, which is available not just for the use of Parliament, but also for all those who need or wish to know about the work being done at Westminster.

NOTES

1. Minutes of Proceedings of the Select Committee on House of Commons (Services) (1971/72), HC 72–ii, p.5
2. Second Report from the Treasury and Civil Service Committee: The Structure and Form of Financial Documents presented to Parliament (1984/85), HC 110
3. The objective of the Financial Management Initiative is: "to promote in each department an organisation and a system in which managers at all levels have (a) a clear view of their objectives, and means to assess, and whenever possible measure, outputs or performance in relation to these objectives; (b) well-defined responsibility for making the best use of their resources, including a critical scrutiny of output and value for money; and (c) the information (particularly about costs), the training and the access to expert advice which they need to exercise their responsibilities effectively." (*Progress in Financial Management in Government Departments*, (Cmnd. 9297, 1984, p. 1-2)
4. Second Report from the Treasury and Civil Service Committee: The Structure and Form of Financial Documents presented to Parliament (1984/85), HC 110, paras 24-26
5. See chapter 9, note 9
6. Select Committee on Parliamentary Debates (1907), HC 239

14. Finding Out: Indexes to the Proceedings and Papers of Parliament, POLIS and Other Sources

In this chapter we look at the published indexes to Parliament's proceedings and papers, the Parliamentary On-Line Information System (POLIS) and the Public Information Offices of the two Houses of Parliament.

Traditionally Parliament has been a rather private institution. It was only in 1680 that the House of Commons passed a resolution instructing its Speaker to publish its Votes and Proceedings (Minutes) each day and it was only in 1825 that the House of Lords started to print its daily Minutes of Proceedings. It was the 18th century before each House ordered its Journal to be printed — just for the convenience of the Members. Both Houses created great difficulties for those who wished to report their debates until the late 18th century and it was as late as the mid-1830s before the House of Commons had a reporters' gallery. Indeed it was not until 1909 that Parliament accepted responsibility for issuing a report of its own debates to its members and the public at large.

With regard to the publication of House of Commons papers etc., it was 1800 before the whole subject was reviewed by Speaker Abbot, who set down an arangement of sessional papers in volumes of bills, accounts and papers, reports of committees and reports of commissioners which was to last until session 1969/ 70. The House of Lords similarly set their papers in order in the early 19th century. A systematic method of selling much of this material to the public dates from the 1830s. But a healthy democracy implies an informed electorate and in this century, and especially since 1945, the information-broking role of Parliament and of its staff has become of considerable importance. Members in various ways are in a position to use parliamentary procedures to examine and publicise government activities. As we have seen, much of their work in this connection is published.

Each sitting day of Parliament there are produced two sets of working papers. One is for the House of Lords, called the Minutes of Proceedings, and the other for the House of Commons, called colloquially the "Vote Bundle" and made up of various sets of papers starting with the Votes and Proceedings.[1] These publications are quite distinct from those discussed in the previous chapter. These working papers, compiled by the clerks of each House and printed each night in Parliament's own press, record what has been done in Parliament, not what has been said, and list all the papers which the Government has laid before the respective Houses. These listed papers, like deposited papers mentioned on page 8, are information for Parliament and for the most part can only be laid by a minister. Although there are no published indexes to these two sets of working papers, at the end of the session much of the information in them is included in the Journal of each House. These are both subsequently published as separate sessional volumes and each of them is indexed. Every 10 years these indexes are published in large cumulated volumes which are the key to the official record of Parliament's work and the papers laid before it. It is possibly surprising that less than 200 copies of the

Journal of the House of Commons and its indexes are required to be printed and still fewer copies of the Journal of the House of Lords.

In the first part of the previous chapter the four sets of parliamentary papers were described. There is no published index to the set of House of Lords bills and papers. The three House of Commons sets, however, have a single sessional index which is itself a House of Commons paper. Since 1979/80[2], the index has been compiled in the House of Commons Library with the indexers using the list of subject headings (or "thesaurus") used for the Library's parliamentary on-line computer-based indexing system (POLIS), which is discussed later in this chapter. This sessional index covers House of Commons bills, including all their separate reprintings at different stages of their legislative journey, House of Commons papers which have been ordered to be printed, and printed command papers. In the past these indexes have been cumulated and three 50-year indexes cover the whole of the 19th century and the first half of the 20th century. There are further cumulations, mostly decennial, which carry the story up until session 1969/70. There are no plans to cumulate thereafter (for the period 1969/70 to 1978/79 the index was compiled in a different form by the library of the Board of Trade, later the Department of Trade and Industry), and because the arrangement of these different papers and hence their indexing will have changed at least three times during the second half of the 20th century, there is obviously doubt as to whether early in the next century it will be practical to compile a fourth 50-year index covering the second half of this one. Future researchers may well not bless these changes!

Since January 1984 the published indexes to the House of Commons *Hansard* have also been compiled in the House of Commons Library. As with the sessional index to papers, the subject indexing is based on the thesaurus used for POLIS. The first index to be published is the fortnightly index to the House of Commons debates. This is an index to the uncorrected daily parts and it later appears in a corrected version at the back of the *Hansard* bound volumes of corrected text. Finally the cumulated index for the session is published as a separate volume. Very long sessions, which sometimes occur after an election depending when in the year it takes place, may sometimes need a two-volume cumulated index. This was the case in 1983/84. There are, however, no published indexes to standing committee debates. When a bill is referred for its second reading to a standing committee — which after debate may recommend that the House should read it formally but can also recommend against a second reading — the report of this second-reading debate used to be published in the main text of *Hansard* covering debates in the Chamber. In recent years this has changed and the second-reading debates in standing committee have been published like other standing committee debates as separate "books". The result of this is that they are no longer indexed.

The published indexes to the House of Lords *Hansard* are compiled for the Stationery Office by outside contractors, as happened with the Commons *Hansard* until the end of 1983. They first appear as "Index to the House of Lords Parliamentary Debates" in respect of the relevant weekly *Hansard*. As with the Commons *Hansard* fortnightly index, this is an index to the unrevised text. Members of the House of Lords who wish to propose changes to the editor must do so within 14 days. The index to the unrevised text is cumulated volume by volume as a separate paper (a House of Lords volume of debates covering a longer period than a House of Commons volume depending on the actual number of sitting days). After the text has been finally revised, the corrected cumulations form the indexes to the bound volumes. The final bound volume of debates for a session therefore contains the revised index for that entire session.

So much for the traditionally published indexes of both Houses covering their Journals, their papers and their debates. But for several decades now the House of Commons has needed more detailed and elaborate indexes than those. In the mid-1950s the House of Commons Library decided that the indexes mentioned above — together with a number of copper-plate ledgers, some of which dated back to the 19th-century — were quite inadequate to deal with the growing number and sophistication of enquiries from hard-pressed Members. There were introduced therefore, over the decade 1955–65 and others still later, a series of visible strip indexes covering especially the proceedings and papers of Parliament discussed in this book. This system helped Library staff to respond not only to Members but also to the growing flow of enquiries from people outside the Palace of Westminster. These included government departments, the press and media, outside organisations with parliamentary connections, firms of solicitors, firms in the City, local authorities and, inevitably, individual citizens. This growth in the role of House of Commons staff giving information to those outside Parliament was finally recognised when a select committee looked into the whole question.[3] The implications of its report are discussed below.

Although these visible strip indexes worked well, their information was only in one sequence and for practical staffing reasons restricted to one copy. This limited their usefulness to Members and staff. There was also the fact that the number of people outside Parliament who appeared to need up-to-date information, not only about the institution generally but also about its current work in particular, was continuing to grow very quickly. The solution to the oft-repeated question "How does one find out?" seemed to be the computer.

The introduction of computer-based information retrieval in the House of Commons Library was a very protracted affair, the details of which need not detain us. The first detailed examination of the problem took place during 1970 and the scheme was introduced just 10 years later. In essence the task was to transfer the indexing for most of the visible strip indexes already mentioned to one computer-based source of information. What is important is that the comprehensive database finally created draws together a great number of the threads of government information referred to in this book and that in addition we are shown a fuller and more interrelated and intelligent picture of Parliament's work than had been achieved by traditional published indexes.

Each day there arrive on the top floor of a large building on the Embankment — the Norman Shaw (South) building — copies of all the papers of Parliament discussed in earlier chapters of this book. There they are examined and indexed by professionally qualified staff whose work demands a logical approach in analysis of the papers, accuracy, an ability to summarise, understanding of how Parliament works and to some extent how Whitehall works, clear comprehension of current affairs and flexibility enough to check their stride if need be and to respond to new concepts and information. This last ability is especially important because Parliament is concerned with such a wide and swiftly changing range of information and is sometimes involved in seeking to push back the frontiers of policy. The indexers prepare entries, pass them to secretaries who type them on to floppy disks and two or three times a day send them down one of three dedicated telephone lines to the computer used on a bureau basis at Scicon in Milton Keynes.[4] Because the retrieval service is required to be available at Westminster until 1 a.m. in the morning from Monday to Thursday, the database is up-dated overnight.

The papers regularly examined include the following (grouped by source):

Source	Paper
Government	Green Papers
	Command Papers
	Reports of Commissions etc.
	Deposited Papers
	Departmental Publications
House of Lords	Minutes of Proceedings
	Bills and Papers
	Hansard
House of Commons	Votes and Proceedings
	Bills and Papers
	Hansard including Standing Committees

References and sometimes brief summaries are prepared to these papers of Government and both Houses of Parliament. Below are listed the specific areas of parliamentary business covered by POLIS, most of which have been treated in this book.

(1)   All parliamentary questions both oral (including supplementary questions) and written
(2)   Private notice questions
(3)   Statements
(4)   Debates, legislative, non-legislative and public bill committee and standing committee debates
(5)   Bills (not individual or marshalled amendments)
(6)   Acts and laid statutory instruments
(7)   Early day motions
(8)   Select committee reports and special reports
(9)   Select committee oral and written evidence including named witnesses (except most civil servants) unless they represent an organisation, when then the latter is used
(10)   Annual reports, returns and accounts ordered to be printed
(11)   Miscellaneous reports
(12)   Treaty Series papers
(13)   Deposited papers from ministers or Mr Speaker
(14)   Departmental publications both HMSO and non-HMSO (selectively)
(15)   Unprinted papers

Also included in the POLIS database are the pamphlets, books etc. added to the House of Commons Library. The full database is set out in table 16 (see next page).

Something like 60,000 entries per year are added to the database. How does it work in practice? Material arriving in the Indexing Unit will vary from a three-line parliamentary question to a four-volume select committee report, but the basic indexing procedure remains the same. Before starting subject analysis, the indexer will deal with information about the document — type, (i.e. question, bill, debate etc.), date, issuing department, member or minister, title (if there is one), whether the document contains statistical information and so on. Virtually

Table 16
Official Published Material of Parliament and Government
etc. and House of Commons Library Collections in POLIS

Parliamentary Papers and Bills	Type code used in indexing and retrieval	Starting date
House of Commons papers	HC	May 1979
House of Commons public bills	Bill	May 1979
Command papers	Cmnd	May 1979
House of Lords papers and public bills	HL	4 Nov. 1981
Private bills	PB	3 Nov. 1982
Parliamentary Proceedings		
House of Commons oral questions	OPQ	27 Oct. 1980
House of Commons private notice questions	PNQ	27 Oct. 1980
House of Commons written questions	WPQ	27 Oct. 1980
House of Commons ministerial statements	CH	27 Oct. 1980
House of Commons general debates	CH	4 Nov. 1981
House of Commons legislative debates	CH	3 Nov. 1982
House of Commons special standing committees	SC	3 Nov. 1982
House of Commons standing committees		
Debates on legislation (including 2nd reading)	SC	3 Nov. 1982
Debates on statutory instruments etc.	SC	3 Nov. 1982
Debates on matters	SC	3 Nov. 1982
House of Lords starred questions	LPQ	4 Nov. 1981
House of Lords unstarred questions	LPQ	4 Nov. 1981
House of Lords written questions	LPQ	4 Nov. 1981
House of Lords statements	LH	4 Nov. 1981
House of Lords general debates	LH	4 Nov. 1981
House of Lords legislative debates	LH	3 Nov. 1982
Legislation		
Public and general acts	PGA	9 May 1979
Local and personal acts	LPA	3 Nov. 1982
Statutory instruments laid before Parliament	SI	3 Nov. 1982
Northern Ireland orders	SI	3 Nov. 1982
Official Publications		
United Kingdom HMSO & departmental papers (selectively)	OP	1 Jan. 1982
European Communities (EC)		
Draft legislation	EURL	1 Jan. 1983
Non-legislative documents	EUR	1 Jan. 1984
Other Information from Departments		
Unprinted papers	UP	1 June 1983
Unprinted command papers	UC	3 Nov. 1982

In addition POLIS contains
Library (House of Commons) Collections

Deposited papers	DEP	22 June 1983
Pamphlets	BK	1 Jan. 1983
Books	BK	1 Jan. 1985
Library produced papers etc.		
Reference sheets*	RS	1 Nov. 1982
Background papers*	BGD	1 Nov. 1982
Research notes*	RN	1 Nov. 1982
Factsheets	FS	1 Nov. 1982

* Material for House of Commons use only

---

all this information will be available later to users of POLIS to enable them to retrieve exactly what they want from the system. Additional help is given in the next stage, which is the creation of a "description" for the document; this is especially important for questions which have no title. Finally, subject analysis by the indexer leads to the addition of (i) terms from the House of Commons Library subject-indexing thesaurus (known as T1), which as already mentioned is used also for the published Sessional Index of House of Commons papers and the published index of House of Commons proceedings (*Hansard*), (ii) free indexing terms (known as T2 or "identifiers") and (iii) where necessary the names of official committees or titles of legislation.

A fairly straightforward example would be material received recently on the film industry. First came the White Paper:

Type:	CMND	(command paper)
Group:	PP	(parliamentary papers)
Date:	19.07.84	
Source:	CMND 9319	
Statistics:	S	(contains statistics)
Department:	Dept. of Trade & Industry	
Description:	Film policy. White Paper	
Subject Indexing:	1. Film industry	
	2. National Film Finance Corporation	
	3. Satellite broadcasting	
	4. British Film Institute	
	5. Finance	
Legislation:	Films Bill 1984/85	
Title:	Film Policy White Paper	
Identifiers:	1. CMND 9319	
	2. Eady Levy	
	3. National Film School	
	4. Childrens Film & Television Foundation	

This gives the POLIS user many ways of approaching the document. Every element of the record is searchable with the exception of the source (which is repeated anyway) and the description (which can be searched on individual words only). Then came the Bill:

Type:	BILL	
Group:	PP	(parliamentary papers)
Date:	08.11.84	
Source:	Bill 6 1984/85	
Member:	Tebbit, Norman	
Dept:	Dept. of Trade & Industry	
Description:	Films Bill	
Subject Indexing:	1. Film industry	
	2. Finance	
	3. National Film Finance Corporation	
	4. Cinematograph Films Council	
	5. British Film Fund Agency	
	6. Government grants	
Legislation:	Films Bill 1984/85	
Title:	Film Policy White Paper	
Identifiers:	1. Eady Levy	
	2. Film quotas	

This again gives the user many avenues of approaching the subject. Note how although the bill followed the White Paper, the system is flexible enough to allow the title of the bill to be subsequently added to the original record. The story so far is completed by the subsequent debate:

Type:	CH	(Commons *Hansard*)
Group:	P	(parliamentary proceedings)
Date:	19.11.84	
Source:	68 c29–110	(HC Deb., vol.68 cols.29–110)
Members:	Lamont, Norman	(opening and closing two speakers)
	Gould, Bryan	
	Buchan, Norman	
	Trippier, David	
Description:	Films Bill. Second reading debate. Agreed to on division & committed to a Standing Committee	
Subject Indexing:	1. Second reading, specific cases	
	2. Film industry	
	3. Finance	
	4. Cinemas	
	5. British Film Fund Agency	
	6. Video recordings	
	7. National Film Finance Corporation	
Legislation:	Films Bill 1984/85	
Identifiers:	1. Eady Levy	
	2. National Film School	
	3. Film quotas	

Note how many approaches from the bill and White Paper are also present in the indexing of the debate, thus making it much easier for the POLIS user to draw all the threads together. This would continue whatever the physical form or origin of the material: the example could easily have been expanded to cover select committee or European Parliament material, questions in the House of Commons or Lords, House of Commons early day motions or even books and pamphlets in the Library.

In the summer of 1984, because of its sheer size, it became necessary to transfer the part of POLIS made up of parliamentary questions sessions 1980/81 to 1982/83 inclusive to a reserve database. This remains on-line.

By the end of April 1985, POLIS had over 190 external organisations subscribing to its services. Table 17 gives a broad breakdown of users which shows that it is a service becoming available to bureaucrat, businessman, student and citizen. All applications to take out a subscription need to be approved by the Computer Sub-Committee of the House of Commons (Services) Committee.

Table 17
POLIS External Subscribers

Central Government	19
Government agencies	17
Local authorities	54
Education	34
Businesses	30
Media	6
Consultants	11
Overseas	8
Miscellaneous	11

Mention was made earlier in the chapter of the Select Committee on House of Commons (Services) report *Services for the Public*.[3] It was clear by the mid-1970s that Parliament needed to respond to the public's interest in its work and this took a number of forms such as increasing Members' allowances so that they could hire more personal staff and, towards the end of the decade, introducing the broadcasting of their proceedings. But the *Services for the Public* report also had a number of direct results. First there was established a Public Information Office to provide a telephone and letter answering service concerning the House of Commons as an institution and more importantly its current and recent work. Currently the Office answers about 70,000 enquiries a year. It covers not only what happens in the House of Commons within the Palace of Westminster, but also the whole range of Government—Parliament activities covered in this book. Secondly, the Office compiles the *Weekly Information Bulletin* which is published by HMSO. Available on Saturdays, it sets down first the House of Commons business of the week just completed and then the business of the forthcoming week. It lists the departments answering questions, the minister who made a statement, and the minister or Member who moved a motion in debate. It lists current bills by title, indicates what stage they have reached in both Lords and Commons and whether they are government bills, in which case the minister in charge is named. It notes the meetings of select committees and indicates witnesses who have appeared or will appear to give evidence. Ministers and permanent secretaries are mentioned by name, other civil servants by their department. When evidence is published, this is listed together with the witness whose evidence it was, e.g. HM Treasury. It sets down the European consultative documents and draft instruments that the Government sends to Parliament and also their White Papers. It also lists the Government's Green Papers or consultative documents and most usefully indicates how copies are obtainable, since departments have so many different methods of issuing these Green Papers. In many cases this information is being published for the first time.

The *Weekly Information Bulletin* has a great deal of other information but the sections mentioned above are specifically concerned with the theme of this book. Thirdly, the Public Information Office is contributing more concise information to the approximately 250 frames of PRESTEL devoted to information on the current proceedings etc. of Parliament. This is updated once a week.

The most recent service to be started by the House of Commons Library's Public Information Office is the first number of the *Sessional Information Digest*, which appeared in January 1985 and which covers the long session 1983/84. With reference to government information for Parliament it included subject indexes of the 222 consultative documents and of the 44 White Papers on Government policy that were set before Parliament, and lists of both the departmental and other select committee reports. The subjects debated during the 19 opposition days are noted as are the 16 private Members' motions. But certain information available in the *Weekly Information Bulletin* is not found in the *Sessional Information Digest*, such as the EC documentation that the Government regularly submits to Parliament.

The House of Lords also has a Public Information Office within its Journal Office (not its Library), which responds to telephone and letter enquiries, contributes information on the House of Lords to PRESTEL, but no longer publishes a weekly information bulletin.

All the tools of the trade described in this chapter are designed to help people elucidate and follow Parliament's work including the flow of information from Government and to satisfy what is clearly a growing interest, both by Members and their staff and by those outside Westminster, in its changing relationship with Whitehall. But this Whitehall—Westminster axis is part of a more extensive network of information to which we turn by way of conclusion.

NOTES

1. A description of these papers is to be found in Dermot Englefield's *Parliament and Information* (Library Association, 1981), pp.11–13.
2. The Sessional Index for session 1979/80 was published in May 1985 (1979/80, HC 849)
3. Eighth Report from the Select Committee on House of Commons (Services): *Services for the Public* (1976/77), HC 509.
4. POLIS was designed and implemented by SCICON (a subsidiary of BP) and is mounted on a SCICON Univac 1100/61 series computer at Milton Keynes, about 50 miles north of London. Three tariff T private lines operating at 9600 baud connect the computer to Westminster and equipment at each end enables all terminals to share any line.

    The retrieval terminals distributed through the Palace of Westminster are Cifer 2632 VDUs and are equipped with small, quiet thermal printers. Some Cifer 2884s are being introduced during 1985. The input terminals in the Computer and Technical Services Section of the House of Commons Library are Cifer 2684s and are equipped with magnetic diskettes for the immediate storing of input. They can also be used for retrieval. The Computer and Technical Services Section has a PDP–11/34 system with printers and disk storage for high-speed printing of references retrieved. Users can direct print-out on this system from all terminals.

There are two elements of software: (a) programmes developed by SCICON to handle data input at the Cifer terminals; (b) UNIDAS, a Univac information retrieval package, including a user dialogue which is an adaptation of Euronet standard common language. UNIDAS runs under OS1100 on the Univac 1100. The database is manipulated by DMS1100 with full CODASYL implementation.

The on-line system is available to the Palace of Westminster from 9 a.m.–1 a.m. on Mondays to Thursdays, 9 a.m.–6 p.m. on Fridays and 10 a.m.–1 p.m. on Saturdays. The thesaurus, which has about 8,500 preferred terms and 1,500 non-preferred terms, is an integral part of the database. It is also available as hard copy.

CONCLUSION

15. Conclusion

The previous chapters have treated the different ways in which members at Westminster individually, through their work in committees and in the two Chambers, or collectively as Parliament, are given, sometimes willingly and sometimes not so willingly, information by the Government. These procedures are mostly carried out in public and the results are normally published. There are also, however, a few less publicised ways whereby Members may secure information, which are carried out in private.

First, Members may be briefed by a government department. The most usual occasion is when Members of either side of either House are making a visit abroad when, if they wish, they may be briefed by the Foreign Office. As suggested in chapter 10, foreign affairs is a prerogative matter, many aspects of which are seen by most Governments as a rather private affair, so that it is not surprising that these briefings take place behind closed doors.

Secondly, Members can and quite often do write personal letters to ministers. Such letters are handled by the minister's private office and are treated with considerable respect. They receive priority treatment and replies are carefully drafted by a senior civil servant who notes any implications the question raised may pose for the future, as the letter may be a siting shot for the start of a campaign which will be taken up in Parliament. The replies are signed personally by the minister. Any government figures in the reply must be checked with special care, as the Member may be using alternative but still authoritative statistics and may later wish to challenge the minister in public. The last point is important because, although these are private letters, information once supplied to a Member is really in the public domain and he may frequently regard it as his duty to make public information which he has received from a government department. If a reply does not satisfy the Member, and as a matter of constitutional propriety he will expect a careful answer, and he does not wish to pursue the matter in the public forum of Parliament, then the proximity of life in the Palace of Westminster means that he can usually follow up a letter by having a word with a minister after a division, or during a chance meeting in a corridor.

Thirdly, and at the other extreme from the personal letter to a minister, Members of both Houses each have another service, namely their respective libraries. These are private libraries for Members and therefore when they seek information from the staff their enquiries are assured of confidential treatment. This is important to them as they may be checking on information being prepared for them by a department, or may be using the library services to prepare themselves for the start of a campaign of questioning the Government. The House of Commons Library has a research service for Members which has some 40 staff, including economists, lawyers, statisticians, foreign affairs specialists and others.

The libraries also play the more traditional role of holding or securing documentation and organising it for immediate use by their staffs or by Members themselves or their growing personal staff. One important group of material available in the Libraries of both Houses is that prepared by departments and reading it helps Members to understand the Government's proposals, decisions and the administration of their policies. These sources are public ones and they are very extensive. Included are (i) the hundreds of press releases sent out by press officers of all departments, often having appended very useful background notes for editors; and (ii) the huge library of departmental leaflets made available to explain acts of Parliament, encourage applications for grants, elucidate social security payments, remind the forgetful of necessary action and in general keep the citizen up to the mark. Finally, there are the departmental circulars, which are often the way in which central Government formally communicates its requirements to local authorities or other organisations with statutory responsibilities.

Access to these sources for Members is vital, because these documents all focus on and are prepared to instruct those beyond Whitehall and Westminster. Although not immediately the concern of this book, this wider world is the background to the work of civil servant, minister and Member. The press notices are aimed at journalists and editors fighting for space in tomorrow's papers or that evening's broadcast news. The leaflets are for public libraries, citizens advice bureaux and post offices so that citizens then learn how they should adjust their conduct as the law and its administration require. The circulars are for officials to read and then promulgate so that other officials further down the line can ensure that government policy, especially when based on legislation, is carried out. And finally, at the end of these spreading government messages is the citizen himself, who, because he has a vote, is of perennial interest to the Member. He needs to study these messages and learn whether government instructions are pinching the life of his constituents. These papers thus remind us how interlocking in modern society are Government, Parliament, the press, local government, lobbies and pressure groups, statutory bodies and finally, the electorate — all needing to inform, instruct and check each other.

This book then has been concerned with only one relationship of many. But if we spread the network still wider, we find that the press feeds on Parliament for copy while Members are great readers of the press.[1] Public relations officers bombard those who are thought to be interested in (and preferably influential concerning) their cause, and seek support. Select committees call for witnesses and government departments consult with lobbyists and experts. Pressure groups lobby Parliament while Parliament itself hires specialist advisers. Interviewers demand on-the-spot comment and even academics undertake instant often number-crunching research. And all this leads to institutions having their spokesmen, experts pronouncing, statisticians calculating, the computer informing until, in the middle of this aptly named information society producing a circulating cacophany, we seem to be close to T. S. Eliot's prophetic lines written half a century ago:

Where is the wisdom we have lost in knowledge?
Where is the knowledge we have lost in information?

(Choruses from *The Rock*)

But even if we are tempted to hold the poet's Olympian view of information, we have to accept that these new pressures have transformed the facts of political life. Technical developments of the last few decades have quite literally obliterated not only the importance but also the protection of space and time. Such a cultural shock has made it more difficult for thoughts, views and hence policies to mature. Public figures are asked only for their instant reactions, seldom their reflected knowledge, and there is no time to wait for wisdom. And Parliament is in the middle of this nexus of spinning viewpoints.

Finally, therefore, the question must be asked as to what purpose does Parliament put the information discussed in this book. The answer must depend on your view of the role of Parliament. Here are two definitions which assume that there will be a sustained flow of information from Government to Parliament:

> Parliament is the forum where the exercise of Government is publicly displayed and is open to scrutiny and criticism — Michael Ryle, *The Commons Today* (1977), p.13
>
> The main task of Parliament is still what it was when it was first summoned, not to legislate or govern, but to secure full discussion and ventilation of all matters. . . . — Leo Amery, *Thoughts on the Constitution* (1947), p.12

And if you push the questioning still further back, asking why you have a Parliament at all, then you must grapple with the great abstractions, freedom of this or that . . . and return to the great 17th–century debates which were mentioned on the first page of this volume.

NOTES

1. The importance of the press and now the media's relationship with Parliament was given its classic formulation long ago: "Without publicity there can be no public spirit, and without public spirit every nation must decay" — Disraeli.

APPENDICES

Appendix 1
Portrait of a Session (1980/81)

Appendix 2
Extract from Memorandum of Guidance for Government Officials appearing before Parliamentary Select Committees (May 1980)

Appendix 3
Letter from Sir Douglas Allen to Heads of Government Departments on the Disclosure of Official Information — Croham Directive (July 1977)

Appendix 4
The Duties and Responsibilities of Civil Servants in relation to Ministers, by Sir Robert Armstrong (February 1985)

Appendix 5
Annual and Periodical Reports and Accounts laid before Parliament and ordered to be printed as House of Commons Papers.

Appendix 6
Annual and Periodical Reports and Accounts laid before Parliament and printed as Command Papers.

Appendix 1

Portrait of a Session (1980/81)

Introduction

Appendix 1 sets out to give a chronological account of the work of Parliament during the session 1980/81. The session was chosen because with no General Election it was of normal length. The appendix gives the date of sitting, the departments answering oral parliamentary questions, the main type of proceedings of the day in the Chamber excluding those which were formal, the department involved in this work, the subjects of debate, standing committee work and, finally, select committee work. All this concerns the House of Commons. There then follows for the House of Lords the main type of proceedings of the day in the Chamber and the subject of debate, together with its select committee work. The whole appendix is designed to illustrate three things.

First, it shows how on a given sitting day Government may be informing Parliament through answering parliamentary questions, making statements, proposing or opposing motions or responding to subjects raised on adjournment motions and by other means in one or both Houses. They may also be steering legislation through standing committees of the House of Commons and be giving evidence to select committees of both Houses. The sheer range of information that Parliament requires in any one session is enormous and must run to a library of a hundred or so large volumes.

Secondly, the appendix shows the shape of work during the session as a whole. In the early days there are no oral parliamentary questions, but rather broad debates on the Queen's Speech. This is followed by the introduction of major bills with their second readings normally in the Chambers, followed by their transfer in the House of Commons to standing committees. Standing committee work between Christmas and Easter is especially heavy. Fridays early in the session are usually devoted to private Members' motions with private Members' bills starting to be introduced on Fridays some time after the Christmas recess. Select committee work early in the session is usually spent taking evidence. In the Spring there are several days spent debating the Budget. By the summer many of the select committees are deliberating in private and considering draft reports, while the House of Commons is considering House of Lords amendments to bills. And later still, in the Autumn, the House of Lords is busy dealing with legislation first introduced in the House of Commons and which the Government needs to have passed before the prorogation at the end of October.

Finally, the appendix reminds us that superimposed on this broad pattern of parliamentary work, most of it introduced by the Government, there are the irregular private notice questions, statements, the critical motions moved by the Opposition and above all the torrent of parliamentary questions which press the Government in a sustained manner to inform Parliament about the more immediate events and problems of the day. Appendix 1, if studied in detail, whether over the period of a sitting week or month, clearly shows that

151

Parliament is an institution as exacting on itself as it is on others — but above all on the Government and its civil servants. The distribution of the work connected with Parliament as between departments is suggested in table 18.

Key to Appendix 1 Arrangement and Abbreviations

1. Columns in Appendix 1

Date — Gives the date of sitting or proceeding across the columns.

Commons Chamber

PQs Dept — Shows the department answering oral questions (see section 2 below for key).

Proc — Identifies the type of proceeding (see section 3 below for key).

Dept — Shows the department responding to the proceeding (see section 2 below for key).

Major Debates etc. — Identifies the subject of the proceeding (see section 3 below for key to legislation abbreviations).

Commons Committees — Standing

Com — Identifies standing committee (see section 4 below for key).

Bills, Orders etc. — Shows subject under consideration.

Commons Committees — Select

Com — Identifies select committee (see section 4 below for key)

Subjects — Shows subject under consideration.

Lords Chamber

Proc — Identifies type of proceeding (see section 3 below for key).

Major Debates etc. — Identifies the subject of the proceeding (see section 3 below for key to legislation abbreviations)

Lords Select Committees

Com — Identifies select committee (see section 4 below for key).

Subjects — Shows subject under consideration.

NB. General abbreviations used throughout the tabulation are listed in section 5 below.

2. Government Departments

The key to identifying the government departments whose ministers were answering oral parliamentary questions, making statements or conducting other business in the House of Commons (as indicated in the second and fourth columns of appendix 1 under the heading **Dept** is set out below. (The numbering is not applied to the House of Lords, since responsibility there is governmental rather than departmental.)

1 = Agriculture, Fisheries and Food	13 = Scottish Office
2 = Defence	14 = Welsh Office
3 = Education and Science	15 = Leader of the House of Commons
4 = Employment	16 = Law Officers' Department
5 = Energy	17 = Lord Advocate's Department
6 = Environment	18 = Lord Chancellor
7 = Foreign and Commonwealth Office	19 = Lord Privy Seal
8 = Health & Social Security	20 = Northern Ireland Office
9 = Home Office	21 = Paymaster General
10 = Industry/Trade	22 = Privy Council Office
11 = Transport	23 = Prime Minister
12 = Treasury/Civil Service	

Table 18

House of Commons: Type of Business and its Distribution between Departments, Session 1980/81

Government Department	Oral Questions Sessions	Statements and PNQs[1]	Motion (Legislation)	Motion (Subjects)[2]	Motion (Delegated legislation)	Motion (Adjournment)	Select Committees Evidence Sessions	Standing Committees Legislation Sessions[3]	Standing Committees SI and other Sessions[4]
Agriculture, Fisheries & Food	8	11	6	5	—	6	7	14	3
Defence	9	4	2	7	—	5	10	—	—
Education & Science	15	1	3	5	—	16	13	10	1
Employment	8	1	4	5	4	18	17	9	3
Energy	8	5	5	4	5	7	9	7	1
Environment	8	10	14	10	8	37	8	32	3
Foreign & Commonwealth Office	15	5	7	9	1	8	19	4	3
Health & Social Security	8	3	9	8	4	19	15	12	2
Home Office	6	8	24	11	4	24	8	60	2
Trade & Industry	17	17	20	19	4	23	12	55	15
Transport	7	2	5	3	4	15	3	35	1
Treasury & Civil Service	15	8	10	17	2	7	15	26	4
Scottish Office	8	6	12	4	11	8	16	46	13
Welsh Office	8	2	2	2	—	3	10	—	7
Leader of the House	10	—	2	8	—	1	—	10	2
Law Officers	9	—	10	—	—	1	—	—	—
Lord Advocate	8	—	—	—	—	—	—	—	—
Northern Ireland Office	8	4	—	2	23	3	2	—	3
Paymaster General	9	—	—	—	—	—	—	—	—
Prime Minister	63	7	—	1	—	—	—	—	—

1. PNQ = private notice question (excluding business questions to the Leader of the House).
2. Including European Community Documents
3. Includes Standing Committees A–G, Scottish Standing Committees, Special Standing Committees and Second Reading Committees.
4. Includes European Documents, Northern Ireland, Scottish Grand, Six Statutory Instruments and Welsh Grand Standing Committees.

3. Proceedings in the Chambers

The type of proceedings for a particular item of parliamentary business is identified in the third (Commons) and 10th (Lords) columns — under the heading **Proc** — according to the following abbreviations:

A = Motion to adjourn These motions are normally followed by one or more short debates. They include the half-hour adjournment debate held at the end of business each day. The subject is shown in the next column of appendix 1. (For general abbreviations, see section 5 below.)

L = Legislation The titles of bills being debated are given in the next column of appendix 1, where the following abbreviations are used:

AM = Amendment in the title of a bill
AsA = As amended
B = Bill
Comp = Completed
HCA = House of Commons amendment
HLA = House of Lords amendment
(Misc Prov) = (Miscellaneous Provisions)
Money Res = Money Resolution
Rep = Report Stage
RS = Remaining Stages
2R = Second Reading
3R = Third Reading

M = Motion The subjects of such motions are given in the next column of appendix 1. (For general abbreviations, see section 5 below.)

Q = Unstarred question In the House of Lords only, in cases where such questions led to short debates. The four unstarred questions allowed in the Lords eash day are not indicated in the table, nor are written questions and answers in either House, since they are not proceedings of Parliament.

S = Statement Normally made by the Government in both Chambers at the same time.

4. Proceedings in Committees

The various parliamentary committees referred to under the heading **Com** in columns 6, 8 and 12 of the tabulation are, respectively, the standing committees of the House of Commons, the select committees of the Commons and the select committees of the House of Lords. The key to the abbreviations used is given below (the Commons committees being identified by number and those of the Lords by letter).

In the House of Commons the department handling the bill in standing committee is of course the same as the department noted during the earlier proceedings in the Chamber. If select committees have taken evidence from a government department, this is noted with an asterisk in the **Subjects** columns 9 and 13.

The work of the Joint Committee on Statutory Instruments and the Joint Committee on Consolidation Bills is to be found in the column of select committee work of the House of Lords. With regard to committee work, only public meetings are listed. This means that in the select committee columns there is no mention for instance of the work of the Services Committee (HC) or the Offices Committee (HL) nor other domestic committees, nor of the many deliberative meetings committees held to plan their work and prepare their reports. (For general abbreviations see section 5 below.)

House of Commons Select Committees (excluding Domestic matters committees)

1 = Agriculture	13 = Scottish Affairs
2 = Defence	14 = Welsh Affairs
3 = Education, Science and Arts	15 = Consolidation Bills (Joint Committee)
4 = Employment	16 = European Legislation
5 = Energy	17 = Parliamentary Commissioner for Administration
6 = Environment	
7 = Foreign Affairs	18 = Public Accounts
8 = Social Services	19 = Statutory Instruments (Joint Committee
9 = Home Affairs	20 = Statutory Instruments
10 = Industry & Trade*	21 = Procedure
11 = Transport	22 = Armed Forces Bill
12 = Treasury and Civil Service	

* This was renamed Trade & Industry in session 1983/84.

House of Commons Standing Committees

23 = A	32 = Northern Ireland
24 = B	33 = Regional Affairs
25 = C	34 = Scottish Grand
26 = D	35 = Second Reading
27 = E	36 = Welsh Grand
28 = F	37 = Statutory Instruments
29 = G	38 = European Documents
30 = First Scottish	39 = Special Standing
31 = Second Scottish	

House of Lords Select Committees (excluding Domestic matters committees)

Eccl C.	= Ecclesiastical Committee
EC	= European Communities Committee
	= European Communities Sub-Committees (A to G):
A	= (Finance, Economics and Regional Policy)
B	= (External Relations, Trade and Industry)
C	= (Education, Employment and Social Affairs)
D	= (Agriculture and Consumer Affairs)
E	= (Law)
F	= (Energy, Transport, Technology and Research)
G	= (Environment)
Un	= Unemployment
S&T I	= Science & Technology Sub-Committee I
S&T II	= Science & Technology Sub-Committee II
LD	= Development Corporation (Area and Constitution) O
BR	= British Railways (Victoria) B
PB	= Preston Borough Council B
CA	= County of Avon B
CU	= Cumbria B
DE	= Derbyshire B
JCS	= Joint Committee on Statutory Instruments
JCC	= Joint Committee on Consolidation Bills

5. General Abbreviations

Add	= Address	O	= Order
Comm	= Committee	R	= Regulation
D	= Document	Rep	= Report
Deb	= Debate	(S)	= Scotland
(E)	= England	(S Day)	= Supply Day
(EC)	= European Communities	(W)	= Wales
(NI)	= Northern Ireland		

Parliamentary Proceedings, November 1980—October 1981
(see pages 152–55 for keys)

				Commons Chamber		**Commons**
Date	**PQs Dept**	**Proc**	**Dept**	**Major Debates & Statements Bills, Orders etc. & Subjects**	**Com**	**Standing Committes Bills, Orders etc. & Subjects**
20 Nov. 1980		M A	9	Debate on the Address (Day 1) Prisons Education Service		
21 Nov. 1980		M S A	8 4 14	Social Services (Deb on Add, Day 2) Employment measures Unemployment (South Wales)		
24 Nov. 1980	10 16	S M A	12 7 5	Economic policy (Deb on Add, Day 3) Foreign affairs & defence Coal (liquefaction)		
25 Nov. 1980	3 23	M A	6 4	Housing (Deb on Add, Day 4) Manpower Services Commission (new area office)		
26 Nov. 1980	13 17	M M A	4 1 10	Unemployment (Deb on Add, Day 5) Fisheries policy (EC) Marriage bureaux		
27 Nov. 1980	20 23	M M A	12 9 10	Industry and the economy (Deb on Add, Day 6) Imprisonment (Temp. Prov.) O Bolton (assisted area)		
28 Nov. 1980		M A	12 6	Draft Budget (EC) Mr J.A. Maudsley		
1 Dec. 1980	10	L A	10 4	Industry B 2R Byssinosis compensation scheme		
2 Dec. 1980	2 23	S S L M A	2 7 10 8 10	Service women and arms Falkland Islands British Telecom B 2R NHS (drugs & appliances charges) R Small businesses (Liverpool)		
3 Dec. 1980	7	S L M M A	23 9 10 12 8	European Council meeting (EC) European Assembly Elections B 2R Shipbuilding (EC) D Excise duties (EC) D Legal aid	37	Draft Veterinary Surgeons (EC
4 Dec. 1980	1 23	M A	10 2	Engineering industry (S Day 1) Hydrographic Service		

Parliamentary Proceedings, November 1980—October 1981
(see pages 152–55 for keys)

	Committees		Lords Chamber		Lords Select Committees	
	Select Committees Subjects	**Proc**	**Major Debates & Statements Unstarred Questions Bills, Orders etc. & Subjects**	**Com**		**Subjects**
9	Racial disadvantage	M	Debate on the Address			
8	Role of Comptroller & Auditor General*					
3	Dispersal of civil servants to (S)*	M	Home affairs (Deb on Add, Day 2)	G		Environmental impact assessment
7	Hotel devel., Turks & Caicos*			A		Regional policy
4	Broadcasting in Welsh	M	Foreign affairs & defence (Deb on Add, Day 3)	B		Aid enquiry*
8	Role of Comptroller & Auditor-General*			C		Labour marketing policy (EC)*
0	Import-export trade*					
8	Medical education*					
2	Role of CSD*					
	Animal welfare — poultry, pig & veal	M	Economic affairs (Deb on Add, Day 4)	Un		Micro-technology
		M	Imprisonment (Temp. Prov.) O			
	Admin. of Prison Dept. Govt. economic policy* Role of Comptroller & Auditor-General*					
		L	Anguilla B 2R	A		Regional policy
		S	Falkland Islands			
		M	Housing (NI) O			
		M	Building socs. & tax (NI) O			
		M	Leasehold (NI) O			
		M	Education (NI) O			
		M	Wisley Airport			
	Foreign affairs*	S	European Council meeting (EC)	B		Aid enquiry*
	UK Parl. and British North America Acts	M	Defence	Un		Micro-technology*
	Broadcasting in Welsh Import/export trade* Dept. of Employment Group* Role of Comp./Aud-General* Medical education*			D		Fruit & vegetable policy (EC)*
	Animal welfare	L	Judicial Pensions B 2R			
	Racial disadvantage	M	Vet Qualifications (EC) O			
		M	Apple etc. Dev. Council O			
		L	Bill of Rights B 2R			
		Q	East Timor (Annexation)			

Parliamentary Proceedings, November 1980—October 1981

(see pages 152–55 for keys)

| | | | | Commons Chamber | | Commons |
Date	PQs Dept	Proc	Dept	Major Debates & Statements Bills, Orders etc. & Subjects	Com	Standing Committes Bills, Orders etc. & Subject
5 Dec. 1980		M A	8 3	Perinatal and Neonatal mortality Rep. Open University		
8 Dec. 1980	5 15 21	L M M A	8 6 4 7	Social Security (Contributions) B 2R Whale products (EC) D Employment protection O World Information Order		
9 Dec. 1980	4 23	S L M A	8 13 20 8	Social Security (payments) Local Govt. (Misc. Prov. (S)) B 2R Education (NI) O N. Ayrshire District Gen. Hosp.	23 24 37 34	Industry B British Telecom B Statutory Instruments Colleges of education (S)
10 Dec. 1980	11 12	S M M M A	13 20 20 20 7	Forestry policy (S) Appropriation (NI) O Financial Provisions (NI) O Emergency Provisions (NI) O Gibraltar	37 36	Statutory Instruments Housing (W)
11 Dec. 1980	12 21	L A	8 8	Social Security (Contributions) B 3R Supplementary benefit (school leavers)	23 24	Industry B British Telecom B
12 Dec. 1980		M A	7 4	Brandt Report Propane gas (storage)		
15 Dec. 1980	14 15	S S S M L M A	9 6 10 13 7 9 8	Immigrants (medical exam.) Housing US synthetic textiles (imports) Scotland (govt. policies) Anguilla B 2R & 3R Prisons Blood transfusion service		
16 Dec. 1980	8 23	S S M M M A	6 14 10 10 5 11	Rate support grant (E) Rate support grant (W) Steel industry (S Day 2) Newsprint quota (EC) Coal ind. (concessionary coal) O Railway services (London)	23 24 30 37 37 37 37	Industry B British Telecom B Local Govt. (Misc. Prov.) (S) Elections (Welsh Farms) No 2 Customs Duties etc. O Draft Hill Livestock etc. O Draft Building Socs. etc. O
17 Dec. 1980	6	S M L A A A A A A	13 15 2 10 6 11 13 9	Rate support grant (S) Adjournment (various subjects) Consolidated Fund B 2R — Royal ordnance factories — Paper and board industry — Great London Govt. assistance — Road safety — Colleges of education (S) Alan Chard (Parkhurst Jail)	37	Draft Housing (Improvement Grants) (S) O

Parliamentary Proceedings, November 1980—October 1981
(see pages 152–55 for keys)

	Committees		Lords Chamber	Lords Select Committees	
om	Select Committees Subjects	Proc	Major Debates & Statements / Unstarred Questions / Bills, Orders etc. & Subjects	Com	Subjects
9	Admin of Prison Dept.	L	Anguilla B Comp.		
		L	Constitutional Referendum B 2R		
4	Broadcasting in Welsh	M	Companies (fees) R		
7	Reports of Health Service Comm.*	M	Building Socs. (Special Advances) O		
		S	Social Security (payments)		
		L	Contempt of Court B 2R		
		Q	Insurance contracts (EC) Rep.		
7	UK Parl. and British North America Acts*	M	Training in industry	D	Fruit & vegetable policy (EC)
8	Medical education*	S	Forestry policy	C	Proprietary medicinal products*
				C&E	Rights of residence
				Un	Micro-technology
				JCC	Judicial Pensions B*
5	Industry energy pricing	L	Energy Conservation B 2R	S&T	Hazardous waste disposal*
	Animal welfare	M	Appropriation (NI) O	II	
	Racial disadvantage	M	Emergency Powers (NI) O		
		M	Financial Prov. (NI) O		
		M	Harbours, Piers, etc. (S) O		
		M	Fishing Vessels (Grants) O		
		L	Parl. Comm. (Consider Complaints) B 2R		
		L	International Orgs. B 2R		
		L	Road traffic (seat belts) 2R		
		S	Housing		
		S	US synthetic textiles		
		L	Disused Burial Grounds (AM) B 2R		
	Hotel devel., Turks & Caicos*	L	Wildlife & Countryside B 2R		
		S	Rate support grant (E)		
		S	Rate support grant (W)		
	DES expenditure plans*	M	Reorg. of Local Govt. (S)	D	Fruit & vegetable policy (EC)
	Broadcasting in Welsh	S	Rate support grant (S)	B	Aid enquiry
	Medical education	M	UN: Britain's role		
		L	Criminal Justice (AM) B 2R		
		M	Biotechnology (EC)		

Parliamentary Proceedings, November 1980—October 1981
(see pages 152–55 for keys)

				Commons Chamber		Commons
Date	PQs Dept	Proc	Dept	Major Debates & Statements Bills, Orders etc. & Subjects	Com	Standing Committes Bills, Orders etc. & Subject
18 Dec. 1980	9 23	S M A	13 20 7	Fisheries meeting (EC) European Community (S Day 3) Falkland Islands		
19 Dec. 1980		S A A A A A A A A A	20 5 11 7 9 6 9 3 10 6	Prisons (NI) North Sea gas Commuter rail services (London) Anglo-Canadian relations BBC (licence fee) Water supply (Sowerby) Privacy Adult education Imported goods (labelling) British motor racing industry		
12 Jan. 1981	10 16	S L A	10 1 6	Nat. Union of Seamen (dispute) Fisheries B 2R Rates (Lambeth)		
13 Jan. 1981	3 23	L M M A	11 11 11 13	Transport B 2R Motor vehicles (licences) R Heavy goods vehicles (licences) R Corsbie Hall School (S)	24 30	British Telecom B Local Govt. (Misc. Prov.) (S) F
14 Jan. 1981	13 17	M M A	6 14 7	Rate support grant (E) Rep. Rate support grant (W) Rep. Iran (British detainees)	37	Sheep (Variable Premium) (Protection of Payments) (No 2
15 Jan. 1981	20 23	M M A	12 10 13	Economic policies (S Day 4) Steel industry (EC) D Housing assoc. (Glasgow)	23 24 30	Industry B British Telecom B Local Govt. (Misc. Prov.) (S) I
16 Jan. 1981		M A	15 11	Select committees (powers) Barnstaple (roads)		
19 Jan. 1981	10 7	L L M M A	9 6 13 13 4	Criminal Attempts B 2R Greater Manchester B 2R Local Auth. Grants (S) O Highlands & Islands shipping Benzidine-based dyes		
20 Jan. 1981	2 23	S L L A	2 7 6 7	Defence Estimates 1980–81 European Assembly Elections B 3R Comp Water B 2R Visas (USA)	24 26 30	British Telecom B Fisheries B Local Govt. (Misc. Prov.) (S)

Committees		Lords Chamber		Lords Select Committees	
Com	**Select Committees Subjects**	**Proc**	**Major Debates & Statements Unstarred Questions Bills, Orders etc. & Subjects**	**Com**	**Subjects**
9	Immigration topics*	L	Cons. Fund B (all stages)	S&T II	Hazardous waste disposal
		L	Supreme Court B 2R		
		L	Merchant Shipping B 2R		
		M	Imprisonment (Temp. Prov.) O		
		M	Hill Livestock (Compensatory Allowances) R		
		M	Employment Protection (Limits) O		
		L	Laboratory Animals Protection B 2R		
7	Hotel devel. in Turks & Caicos*	L	Social Security (Contributions) B 2R		
		M	Firearms (NI) O		
		M	Clean Air (NI) O		
		M	Road Traffic (NI) Os		
8 4	Medical education Manpower Services Commission plan 1981–85*	M	International Year of the Disabled	C	Employee participation in asset forming*
		L	Bill of Rights B Comm.		
		Q	Aid to UNRWA		
		L	Contempt of Court B Comm. (Day 1)		
		M	Sheep Variable Premium (Protection of Payments) O		
3	Funding the arts*	L	International Organisations B 3R		
		L	Deep-sea Mining (Temp. Prov.) B 2R		
		L	Energy Conservation B Comm.		
		M	Control of pollution (special waste) R		
7	Non-departmental public bodies*	M	Judgement Enforcements (NI) Os		
		M	Elections (Welsh Farms) (No 2) Regs.		
		S	Defence expenditure		
		L	Contempt of Court B Comm. (Day 2)		

Parliamentary Proceedings, November 1980—October 1981
(see pages 152–55 for keys)

				Commons Chamber		Commons	
Date	PQs Dept	Proc	Dept	Major Debates & Statements Bills, Orders etc. & Subjects	Com	Standing Committes Bills, Orders etc. & Subjects	
21 Jan. 1981	7	M M M A	5 13 13 9	Energy policy (S Day 5) Rate support grant (S) O Housing support grant (S) O Criminal procedure (Royal Commission)	32	Enterprise zone in Belfast	
22 Jan. 1981	1 23	M M A	14 18 11	Welsh affairs Firearms, Clean Air, Road Traffic, Leaseholds, Housing, Building Socs. (all NI) Os Railway preservation	24 26 27 30	British Telecom B Fisheries B Transport B Local Govt. (Misc. Prov.) (S) B	
23 Jan. 1981		S M A	10 12 8	*Times* newspapers Financial institutions Rep. Univ. College Hospital			
26 Jan. 1981	5 15 21	S L M A	10 13 13 8	BL (corporate plan) Forestry B 2R Rents (S) O Electro-convulsive therapy (Broadmoor)			
27 Jan. 1981	4 23	M A M A	10 11 9 8	*Times* newspapers Lorries & environment Rep. Imprisonment (Temp. Prov.) O Hospital services (Bolton)	23 24 27 30	Water B British Telecom B Transport B Local Govt. (Misc. Prov.) (S) B	
28 Jan. 1981	11 12	L M A	9 20 3	British Nationality B 2R Judgements Enforcement (NI) O Village schools	37	Motor vehicles (speed limits) (No 2) R	
29 Jan. 1981	12 23	S M A A	10 12 3 3	Motor industry Public Accounts Comm. Reps. (S Day 6) Education (Cambridgeshire) Education Act 1980	23 24 26 27 30	Water B British Telecom B Fisheries B Transport B Local Govt. (Misc. Prov.) (S) B	
30 Jan. 1981		L L L L A	9 8 10 6 6	Indecent Displays (Control) B 2R Industrial Diseases (Notification) B 2R Aircraft & Shipbuilding industry (AM) B 2R Local Govt. & Planning (AM) B 2R Housing etc. premises (demolition)			
2 Feb. 1981	14 15 3	S L L A	9 3 10 20	Brixton Prison (Security) Education B 2R Insurance Companies B 2R Parole (NI)			

Parliamentary Proceedings, November 1980—October 1981
(see pages 152–55 for keys)

	Committees		Lords Chamber		Lords Select Committees	
om	Select Committees Subjects	Proc	Major Debates & Statements Unstarred Questions Bills, Orders etc. & Subjects	Com	Subjects	
3 14 8	Secondary school curriculum & exams Broadcasting in Welsh Medical education	M L	Transport policy Criminal Justice (AM) B Comm.	Un B	Micro-technology Aid enquiry	
1 9	Animal welfare Racial disadvantage	L M L L	T & C Planning (Minerals) B 2R Social Fund (EC) Animal Health B 2R English Ind. Estates Corporation B 2R	F S&T I	New information technologies* Hazardous waste	
9	Admin. of Prison Dept.	L S M L	Social Security (Contributions) B Comm. BL (corporate plan) Local Authority Grants (Termination) (S) O Forgery and Counterfeiting B 2R			
1 7	Supply procedure British aid to Zimbabwe*	L M L	Wildlife & Countryside B Comm. (Day 1) Imprisonment (Temp. Prov.) Act 1980 (Continuance No 3) O Bill of Rights B Rep.			
3 ↓) 7 ↓ ↓	First scrutiny by Committee* Housing capital allocation* Broadcasting in Welsh Cost of Concorde Afghanistan* Medical education Energy pricing policy*	M M L	Gibraltar English-simplification Licensing (AM) (off-licences) B 2R	B C Un	Aid enquiry Employee participation in asset forming Micro-technology*	
	Animal welfare	L S L L L Q	Social Security (Contributions) B 3R Nissan Company in UK Representation of the People B 2R Trees (Replanting etc.) B 2R Pet Animals Act 1951 (AM) B 2R Sugar from Commonwealth			
	Admin. of Prison Dept. Control of army load- carrying vehicles: defence cash limits and excess votes*	L S M	Wildlife & Countryside B Comm. (Day 2) Brixton Prison escape Education (EC) Rep.			

Parliamentary Proceedings, November 1980—October 1981
(see pages 152–55 for keys)

				Commons Chamber		Commons	
Date	PQs Dept	Proc	Dept	Major Debates & Statements Bills, Orders etc. & Subjects	Com	Standing Committes Bills, Orders etc. & Subject	

Date	PQs Dept	Proc	Dept	Major Debates & Statements / Bills, Orders etc. & Subjects	Com	Standing Committes / Bills, Orders etc. & Subject
3 Feb. 1981	8 / 23	M / M / M / M / A	8 / 20 / 20 / 5 / 10	Poverty (S Day 7) / Election Expenses (NI) O / Fisheries AM (NI) O / Gas Levy Money Res B / Tankers (hazardous cargoes)	23 / 24 / 26 / 27 / 30 / 39	Water B / British Telecom B / Fisheries B / Transport B / Local Govt. (Misc. Prov.) (S) B / Criminal Attempts B — Evidence*
4 Feb. 1981	6	S / S / L / A	6 / 3 / 10 / 11	New Towns / ILEA's future / Industry B 3R / Roadline depot (Kirkdale)	37 / 38	Draft representation of the people (variation . . .) O / Hormones in domestic animals (EC)
5 Feb. 1981	9 / 23	M / A	10 / 8	Economic and industrial policy / Cottage hospital (Faversham)	23 / 24 / 26 / 27 / 30 / 39	Water B / British Telecom B / Fisheries B / Transport B / Local Govt. (Misc. Prov.) (S) B / Criminal Attempts B — Eviden
6 Feb. 1981		L / A	12 / 9	Freedom of Information B 2R / Community radio broadcasting		
9 Feb. 1981	10 / 16	S / L / M / A	6 / 4 / 6 / 9	Inner cities policy / Employment and Training B 2R / Toxic waste disposal R / Citizens Band radio		
10 Feb. 1981	3 / 23	L / L / M / A	5 / 2 / 11 / 3	Atomic Energy (Misc. Prov.) B 2R / Armed Forces B 2R / BR Board (increase of compensation limit) O / School meals (Lancashire)	23 / 24 / 27 / 28 / 30 / 39	Water B / British Telecom B / Transport B / British Nationality B / Local Govt. (Misc. Prov.) (S) B / Criminal Attempts B — Eviden
11 Feb. 1981	13 / 17	S / S / M / M / M / A	13 / 10 / 6 / 20 / 20 / 6	Talbot (Linwood) / Brit. Steel Corp. (finance) / Housing & building industry (S Day 8) / Legal Aid (NI) O / Weights & Measures (NI) O / All-night parties	25	Indecent Displays (Control) B
12 Feb. 1981	20 / 23	S / L / A	1 / 13 / 4	Fisheries ministers' meeting (EC) / Education (S) (No 2) B 2R / School leavers (training)	23 / 24 / 26 / 27 / 28 / 30	Forestry B / British Telecom B / Fisheries B / Transport B / British Nationality B / Local Govt. (Misc. Prov.) (S)
13 Feb. 1981		L / A	/ 8	Gaelic (Misc. Prov.) B 2R / Health Services (Kent)		
16 Feb. 1981	10 / 7	S / M / L / A	10 / 3 / 5 / 1	*Times* newspapers / Adult education / Gas Levy B 2R / Fish imports		

Parliamentary Proceedings, November 1980—October 1981
(see pages 152–55 for keys)

Committees		Lords Chamber		Lords Select Committees	
Com	**Select Committees Subjects**	**Proc**	**Major Debates & Statements / Unstarred Questions / Bills, Orders etc. & Subjects**	**Com**	**Subjects**
21	Supply procedure	L L M M	Wildlife & Countryside B Comm. (Day 3) Bill of Rights B 3R Fisheries (AM) (NI) O Election Expenses (Candidates) (NI) O	G Un JCC	Asbestos risks* Micro-technology Statutory Instruments*
3 14 10 8 4	Funding the arts* Broadcasting in Welsh Cost of Concorde* Medical education Training, mobility & unemployment	L M S L	Wildlife & Countryside B 3R Industry: public sector ILEA's future Criminal Justice (AM) B 3R	B JCC	Aid enquiry* Various bills*
		L L L	Energy Conservation B Rep. Deep-sea Mining (Temp. Prov.) B Comm. T & C Planning (Minerals) B Comm. (Day 1)	F S&T I	New information technologies Hazardous wastes
3 9	Secondary school curriculum & exams Admin. of Prison Dept.	L	Wildlife & Countryside B Comm. (Day 4)		
21	Supply procedure	M L L L	Procedure Rep. Statute Law (Repeals) B 2R Energy Conservation B 3R Contempt of Court B Rep.	LD A	Devel. Corp. (Area & Constitution) O Motor liability insurance
14 4 16 8 3 18	Broadcasting in Welsh Winter Supplementary Estimates* EC reflections on CAP* Medical education Future of Times Supplements Purchases of defence imports*	M S S Q	Economic recovery Talbot (Linwood) Brit. Steel Corp. (finance) Concorde support	D B C	Fruit & vegetable policy (EC)* Aid enquiry Employee-participation in asset forming
9	British overseas (citizenship)*	L L	Wildlife & Countryside B Comm. (Day 5) European Assembly Elections B 2R		
		L	Wildlife & Countryside B Comm. (Day 6)		
8 4	Medical education Broadcasting in Welsh	L M	T & C Planning (Minerals) B Comm. (Day 2) Motor vehicles (speed limits) (No 2) R	LD	Development Corp. (Area & Constitution) O

Parliamentary Proceedings, November 1980—October 1981
(see pages 152–55 for keys)

				Commons Chamber		Commons	
Date	PQs Dept	Proc	Dept	Major Debates & Statements Bills, Orders etc. & Subjects	Com		Standing Committes Bills, Orders etc. & Subjects
17 Feb. 1981	2 23	S M M A	5 10 1 7	Coal industry Talbot (Linwood) (S Day 9) Sugar (EC) (S Day 9) Commonwealth Dev. Corp.	23 24 26 27 28 30 39 39		Forestry B British Telecom B Fisheries B Transport B British Nationality B Local Govt. (Misc. Prov.) (S) B Criminal Attempts B Draft shipbuilding Os
18 Feb. 1981	7	L L M M A	4 10 20 20 8	Redundancy Fund B 2R & 3R Iron & Steel (Borrowing Powers) B 2R & 3R Agricultural Trust (NI) O Museums (NI) O Social Security claimants (information)	25 35 35 35 38		Indecent Displays (Control) B International Orgs. B Merchant Shipping B Parl. Comm. for Admin. (Consular Complaints) B Income tax (EC) D
19 Feb. 1981	1 23	S L L M A	5 6 15 15 9	Coal industry Water B 3R HC Members' Fund and Parl. Pensions B All stages Members' pensionable pay Police (Kent)	23 24 26 27 28 30 39 39		Forestry B British Telecom B Fisheries B Transport B British Nationality B Local Govt. (Misc. Prov.) (S) B Education B Evidence* Criminal Attempts B
20 Feb. 1981		L A	9 10	Shops B 2R Corby			
23 Feb. 1981	5 15 21	S L A A	2 5 11 6	Dockyard (Rosyth) Energy conservation B 2R A12 road (Martlesham) Police houses (Gateshead)			
24 Feb. 1981	4 23	S L M A	10 8 8 11	Steel industry Social Security B 2R Medical, dental, etc. professions (EC) Roads (North-West E.)	23 24 26 27 28 30 39 39		Forestry B British Telecom B Insurance Companies B Transport B British Nationality B Local Govt. (Misc. Prov.) (S) B Criminal Attempts B Education B Evidence
25 Feb. 1981	11 12	S L L A	1 5 6 6	Agriculture Ministers' meeting (EC) Gas Levy B 3R GLC (Gen. Powers No 2) B Rep. Dev. Corp. (Redditch)	25		Indecent Displays (Control) B

Parliamentary Proceedings, November 1980—October 1981
(see pages 152–55 for keys)

Committees		Lords Chamber		Lords Select Committees	
Com	**Select Committees** **Subjects**	Proc	**Major Debates & Statements** **Unstarred Questions** **Bills, Orders etc. & Subjects**	Com	**Subjects**
8 14 5	Medical education Broadcasting in Welsh Energy pricing policy	L S L L	Industry B 2R Coal industry Contempt of Court B 3R Wildlife & Countryside B Comm. (Day 7)	JCS	Statutory Instruments*

3
10
7
11
4
8
	Funding of the arts
	Financing of BL*
	Gibraltar*
	Transport in London
	Dept. of Employment
	  Group*
	Medical education
		M
		Q
		L
			Civil aviation industry
			Middle East (EC)
			Trees (Replanting and
			  Replacement) B Comm.
				D
				
				JCC
					Agricultural policy
					  (EC)*
					Various bills*

9	British overseas
	  (citizenship)
		L
		
		S
		L
			Wildlife & Countryside
			  B Comm. (Day 8)
			Coal industry
			Deep-sea Mining (Temp.
			  Prov.) B Rep.
				F
				
				S&T
				II
					New information
					  techniques
					Hazardous waste disposal

9
18
	Admin. of Prison Dept.*
	Advances to Comm. Dev.
	  Corp.*
		M	Forestry	LD	Development Corp.
					  (Area & Constitution)
					  O

4
21
11
	Homeworking*
	Supply procedure*
	Transport in London
		S
		L
		
		L
		
		M
		M
		
		L
		
		Q
			BSC corporate plan
			Iron & Steel (Borrowing
			  Powers) B 2R
			Matrimonial Homes (Family
			  Protection) (S) B 2R
			Museums (NI) O
			Agricultural Trust (Abolition)
			  (NI) O
			Pet Animals Act 1951 (AM)
			  B Comm.
			Hong Kong
				A
				JCS
					Motor liability insurance
					Statutory Instruments*

3
 	
4
1
 	
8
 	
1
4
	Secondary school
	  curriculum
	  and exams*
	Broadcasting in Welsh
	Lorries, people &
	  environment
	Effectiveness of bilateral
	  aid*
	Transport in London
	Work of Dept. of
	  Employment Group*
		M
		M
		L
			Air defence
			Trident system
			Marriage Enabling B 2R
				D
				C
				
				S&T
				I
					Agricultural policy (EC)
					Employee participation in
					  asset-forming
					Science & Government*

Parliamentary Proceedings, November 1980—October 1981
(see pages 152–55 for keys)

| | | | | Commons Chamber | | Commons |
Date	PQs Dept	Proc	Dept	Major Debates & Statements Bills, Orders etc. & Subjects	Com	Standing Committes Bills, Orders etc. & Subjects
26 Feb. 1981	12 23	M A A	10 4 8	Textile, clothing & footware industries (S Day 10) Employment & the economy (South E.) (S Day 10) Baby milk products and developing countries (WHO)	23 24 26 27 28 30 39	Forestry B British Telecom B Insurance Companies B Transport B British Nationality B Local Govt. (Misc. Prov.) (S) B Education B Evidence
27 Feb. 1981		L L A L	9 13 6	Horserace Betting Levy B 2R Development of Tourism (S) B 2R Cost of living (London) Disused Burial Grounds (AM) B 2R		
2 Mar. 1981	14 22	S L A	23 16 8	Prime Minister (US visit) Contempt of Court B 2R Mr Penney (Benefit)		
3 Mar. 1981	8 23	S M M A	20 2 6 6	Prisons (NI) Nuclear deterrent T & C Planning (Fees) R Crinan Moss, Argyll	23 24 26 27 28 29 30	Forestry B British Telecom B Insurance Companies B Transport B British Nationality B Social Security B Education (S) (No 2) B
4 Mar. 1981	6	L M A	1 7 9	Fisheries B Rep. & 3R International Devel. Assoc. O Electoral arrangements (Humberside)	25 31 37 37 37	Indecent Displays (Control) B Countryside (S) B Draft. Judges O Draft. Export O Abortion (AM) R
5 Mar. 1981	9 23	S M A	12 3 3	Civil Service pay Education Service (S Day 11) Dyslexia	27 28 29 30 39	Transport B British Nationality B Social Security B Education (S) (No 2) B Education B
6 Mar. 1981		L L L L A	6 9 10 6	Zoo Licensing (No 2) B 2R Licensing (Alcohol Education etc.) B 2R Small Firms Expansion (Enquiry) B 2R Local Govt. Planning (AM) B 2R Mr M. O'Hara		
9 Mar. 1981	10 16	S M M A	10 15 20 2	Cable and Wireless Transport B (Allocation of Time) Appropriation (NI) O Min. of Defence (dispersal)		

Parliamentary Proceedings, November 1980—October 1981
(see pages 152–55 for keys)

Committees		Lords Chamber		Lords Select Committees	
Select Committees **Subjects**	**Proc**	**Major Debates & Statements** **Unstarred Questions** **Bills, Orders etc. & Subjects**	**Com**	**Subjects**	
Racial disadvantage*	L	Iron & Steel (Borrowing) B 3R			
	L	Redundancy Fund B 2R			
	L	Companies (No 2) B 2R			
	L	Deep-sea Mining (Temp. Prov.) B 3R			
Medical education Admin. of Prison Service	L S M	Supreme Court B Comm. PM's visit to USA Environment policy (EC) Rep.			
Medical education Supply procedure* Transport in London British aid to Zimbabwe	M L S L Q	Number of Judges O Water B 2R Prisons (NI) Industry B Comm. Local Auth. & privatisation			

Funding the arts
Arms sales: foreign
  policy*
Closure of colleges*
Broadcasting in Welsh*
Regional incentives*
Finance for BL
Work of Dept. of Employ.
  Group
Reflections on CAP*
Medical education
	M	Unemployment			

Animal welfare in poultry,
  pigs, etc.
Brandt Report*
	S
	L
	M
	L
		Civil Service pay
		European Assembly Elections
		  B Comm.
		Medical (Linguistic
		  Knowledge) (EC) O
		T & C Planning (Minerals)
		  B Rep.
			F	New information
				  technologies	

Funding of the arts
Regional incentives*
	L
	L
	
	S
	L
	M
	L
	
	L
	Q
		Gas Levy B 2R
		HC Members' Fund & Parl.
		  Pensions B 2R
		Cable and Wireless
		Industry B Rep.
		T & C Planning (Fees) R
		Matrimonial Homes &
		  Property B 2R
		Interpretation of Legis. B 2R
		Right of Residence (EC) D			

Parliamentary Proceedings, November 1980—October 1981
(see pages 152–55 for keys)

| | | | | Commons Chamber | | Commons |
Date	PQs Dept	Proc	Dept	Major Debates & Statements / Bills, Orders etc. & Subjects	Com	Standing Committes / Bills, Orders etc. & Subje
10 Mar. 1981	3 23	M L M A	12 11 20 16	Budget and economic situation / British Railways (No 2) B 2R / Local Govt. Planning & Land (NI) O / Magistrates' Advisory Comm.	26 27 28 29 30 39	International Orgs. B / Transport B / British Nationality B / Social Security B / Education (S) (No 2) B / Education B
11 Mar. 1981	13 17	S S M A	1 8 12 4	Fisheries Ministers' meetings (EC) / Social Security benefits / Budget (Day 2) / Wages Councils	25 31 37	Indecent Displays (Control) B / Countryside (S) B / Draft Carriage by Air Acts O
12 Mar. 1981	20 23	M A	12 10	Budget (Day 3) / Industrial building (Manchester)	23 24 27 28 29 30 39	Energy Conservation B / Merchant Shipping B / Transport B / British Nationality B / Social Security B / Education (S) (No 2) B / Education B
13 Mar. 1981		M A	6 4	London (govt. policies) / Mr C. Banton (TU procedure)		
16 Mar. 1981	10 7	M M A	12 6 10	Budget (Day 4) / T & C Planning Os / Performing Rights Society		
17 Mar. 1981	2 23	S L A A A	7 7 8 8 13	Belize / Consolidated Fund (No 2) B / London hospital medical schools / Preventive medicine / Colleges of education (S)	23 24 26 27 28 29 30 39	Energy Conservation B / Parl. Comm. (Complaints) B / Employment & Training B / Transport B / British Nationality B / Social Security B / Education (S) (No 2) B / Education B
18 Mar. 1981	7	M M M M M A	20 9 5 5 9 3	Economic situation (NI) (S Day 12) / Prevention of terrorism / Coal Ind. (Redundancy Payments etc.) O / Mineworkers Pension Scheme (Contributions) O / Prevention of Terrorism (Temp. Prov.) O / Comprehensive education (Bolton)	25 37 37	Ind. diseases (Notification) B / Draft Suppl. Benefit R / Draft Mortgaging Aircraft O
19 Mar. 1981	1 23	S S L M A	10 10 10 6 6	Fishing vessel Celerity / ICL / Iron and Steel B 2R / Merseyside Dev. Corp. O / Vale of White Horse District Council	23 26 27 28 29 30 39	Energy Conservation B / Employment & Training B / Transport B / British Nationality B / Social Security B / Education (S) (No 2) B / Education B

Parliamentary Proceedings, November 1980—October 1981
(see pages 152–55 for keys)

Committees		Lords Chamber		Lords Select Committees	
Com	**Select Committees Subjects**	**Proc**	**Major Debates & Statements Unstarred Questions Bills, Orders etc. & Subjects**	**Com**	**Subjects**
		L	Wildlife & Countryside B Rep. (Day 1)	A	Motor liability insurance
		M	Carriage by Air Acts (Application of Provisions) (Third AM) O	S&T I	Science & Government
7	Foreign affairs*	L	Companies (No 2) B 2R	C	Employee participation in asset-forming
3	Secondary school curriculum & exams	S	Social Security benefits		
10	Effects of BSC Corp. plan	M	Industry: efficiency	JCC	Various bills*
18	Accounting (magistrates' courts)*	M	Appropriation (NI) O		
4	Work of Dept. of Employment Group*	M	Local Govt. etc. (NI) O		
16	CAP price proposals 1981–82* (EC)	L	Licensing (AM) B 2R		
8	Medical education				
1	Animal welfare in poultry, pigs, etc.	L	Wildlife & Countryside B Rep. (Day 2)	D	CAP prices etc. 1981–82
		L	T & C Planning (Minerals) B 3R		
		L	Trees (Replanting and Replacement) B 3R		
9	Racial disadvantage				
13	Youth unemployment (S)*	L	Wildlife & Countryside B Rep. (Day 3)		
9	Admin. of Prison Dept.*				
18	Staff/student ratios*	S	Belize	LD	Devel. Corp. (Area & Constitution) O
8	Science Research Council*	L	Companies (No 2) B Comm. (Day 1)		
4	Homeworking*			G	Oil pollution (EC)
21	Supply procedure				
7	Brandt Report*				
7	Parl. Comm. for Admin.*				
10	Effects of BSC corp. plan	S	Leader of the House visit to Zimbabwe	D	CAP prices etc. 1981–82* (EC)
7	Gibraltar				
4	Broadcasting in Welsh*	M	Education exp. cuts		
8	BM, V & A; Science Museum*				
2	Budget & govt. plans*				
4	Work of Dept. of Employment Group*				
8	Medical education				
1	Animal welfare in poultry, pigs, etc.	L	Companies (No 2) B Comm. (Day 2)	F	New information technologies
		S	ICL		
		L	Water B Comm. (Day 1)		

Parliamentary Proceedings, November 1980—October 1981
(see pages 152–55 for keys)

				Commons Chamber		Commons	
Date	PQs Dept	Proc	Dept	Major Debates & Statements Bills, Orders etc. & Subjects	Com	Standing Committes Bills, Orders etc. & Subjects	
20 Mar. 1981		M A	9 9	Criminal justice Police (detained persons) (injuries)			
23 Mar. 1981	5 15 21	S S L M A	12 1 13 13 2	Civil Service (dispute) Foot and mouth disease Local Govt. (Misc. Prov.) (S) B Rep. 3R NHS (Functions of Health Boards) (S) O NATO (weapons)			
24 Mar. 1981	4 23	S M L L L A	6 7 10 10 7 4	Canvey Island (planning) Overseas aid (S Day 13) Lloyd's B 2R Merchant Shipping B 3R International Orgs. B 3R Young persons (military service)	23 26 27 28 29 30 39	Energy Conservation B Employment & Training B Transport B British Nationality B Social Security B Education (S) (No 2) B Education B	
25 Mar. 1981	11 12	S L L M A	23 13 11 6 14	European Council (Maastricht) (EC) Local Govt. (Misc. Prov.) (S) B Rep. & 3R Ports (financial assistance) B 2R BR Board (Payments) O BRD factory (new town)	25 37 37 36	Horserace Betting Levy B Rating of Ind. (S) O Draft British Nuclear Fuels O Budget and Wales	
26 Mar. 1981	12 23	S M M M M A	23 1 20 20 20 12	Security CAP (EC) Enterprise zones (NI) O Planning Blight Compensation (NI) O Public Order (NI) O Civil servants (pol. activities)	26 27 28 29 30 39	Employment & Training B Transport B British Nationality B Social Security B Education (S) (No 2) B Education B	
27 Mar. 1981		M A	5 1	Industrial fuel costs Poultry industry			
30 Mar. 1981	14 3	S S A L A	12 1 4 7 6	Civil Service (dispute) Fisheries Ministers' meeting (EC) Unemployment (Midlands) (S Day 14) Parl. Comm. (Consular Complaints) B 3R Palace of Westminster			
31 Mar. 1981	8 23	S L L M A	6 1 9 8 6	GLC (housing transfer) Forestry B 3R Criminal Attempts B 3R NHS (charges) Rs Rate support grant (Rugby)	23 26 27 28 29 30 39	Atomic Energy (Misc. Prov.) B Employment & Training B Transport B British Nationality B Social Security B Education (S) (No 2) B Education B	
1 Apr. 1981	6	L A	10 10	British Telecom B 3R Calderdale (assisted area status)	25 37	Horserace Betting Levy B Trade Descriptions O	

Parliamentary Proceedings, November 1980—October 1981
(see pages 152–55 for keys)

Committees		Lords Chamber		Lords Select Committees	
Select Committees Subjects	**Proc**	**Major Debates & Statements Unstarred Questions Bills, Orders etc. & Subjects**		**Com**	**Subjects**
Admin. of Prison Dept.* Fraud in Area Office* Housing subsidy claims* Funding of the arts	L S M	Companies (No 2) B Comm. (Day 3) Foot and mouth disease Prevention of Terrorism (Temp. Prov.) etc. O		LD	Devel. Corp. (Area & Constitution) O
Broadcasting in Welsh Supply procedure	M L L L Q	Merseyside Devel. Corp. (Area etc.) O Matrimonial Homes etc. (S) B Comm. Water B Comm. (Day 2) Forgery & Counterfeiting B Comm. Petrol tax increase		A E JCS	Motor liability insurance Bankruptcy Convention (EC) Statutory Instruments*
Armed Forces B* Gibraltar* Science policy* Youth unemployment (S)* Effects of BSC corp. plan* NHS (finance)* Medical education Budget & govt. plans*	M S M L Q	Agriculture European Council (Maastricht) (EC) Local Govt. (closed shop) Marriage (Enabling) B Comm. SE Africa		D C	CAP prices etc. 1981–82 Employee participation in asset-forming
Animal welfare in poultry, pigs, etc.	S L L M M	Security Supreme Court B Rep. Interpretation of Legis. B Comm. Human Rights (EC) Rep. Supplementary Benefits (Requirements) (AM) R			
Comm. for Racial Equality Funding of the arts Budget & govt. plans NHS (finance)*	L S	Wildlife & Countryside B 3R Fisheries Ministers' meeting (EC)		LD BR	Devel. Corp. (Area & Constitution) O British Railways (Victoria) B
Brandt Comm. (Mexico Summit)*	L S Q	Fisheries B 2R GLC (housing transfer) Mental after-care		EC	British business & EC legislation
Funding of the arts Youth unemployment (S) NHS (finance)* Effects of BSC corp. plan* Transport in London* Medical education Armed Forces B*	M Q	Trade union immunities London's third airport (Stanstead)		S&T I	Science & Government

Parliamentary Proceedings, November 1980—October 1981
(see pages 152–55 for keys)

		Commons Chamber				Commons	
Date	PQs Dept	Proc	Dept	Major Debates & Statements Bills, Orders etc. & Subjects	Com	Standing Committees Bills, Orders etc. & Subje
2 Apr. 1981				NO SITTING	23 24 28 29 30 39	Atomic Energy (Misc. Prov.) Iron & Steel B British Nationality B Social Security B Education (S) (No 2) B Education (B)
3 Apr. 1981		M S M A	3 1 6 1	Industry & school curriculum Agriculture Ministers' meeting (EC) Water authorities Meat hygiene		
6 Apr. 1981	10 16	M L M M A	15 10 10 10 8	Adjournment (Easter & May Day) Insurance Companies B 3R ICL (government aid) Biomolecular Engineering (EC) D Infectious diseases (transportation)		
7 Apr. 1981	3 23	M L L M M A	4 11 9 20 11	Youth unemployment (S Day 15) Greater Manchester B As A. Rep. Transport (No 2) B MEPs' (salaries) Queen's Univ. (Belfast) O Transport policy (EC)	23 24 26 28 30	Atomic Energy (Misc. Prov.) Iron & Steel B Employment & Training B British Nationality B Education (S) (No 2) B
8 Apr. 1981	13 17	S M L L A	20 7 6 5 10	Air services (NI) Developments (EC) (S Day 16) Water B (Lord's AM) Energy Cons. B 3R Gatwick (noise insulation)	25	Ind. Diseases (Notification) B
9 Apr. 1981	20 23	M A	12 8	Public expenditure, 1981–82/1983–84 Northampton Health Auth.	24 26 28 30	Iron & Steel B Employment & Training B British Nationality B Education (S) (No 2) B
10 Apr. 1981		M A	9 6	British constitution Plumbing (UK standards)		
13 Apr. 1981	10 7	S L A	9 12 14	Brixton riots Finance B 2R Unemployment (mid-Glamorgan)		
14 Apr. 1981	2 23	L A	11 8	Transport B AsA 3R Dr Dossetor (pension)	24 26 28 30	Iron & Steel B Employment & Training B British Nationality B Education (S) (No 2) B

Parliamentary Proceedings, November 1980—October 1981
(see pages 152–55 for keys)

Committees		Lords Chamber		Lords Select Committees	
Com	**Select Committees Subjects**	**Proc**	**Major Debates & Statements Unstarred Questions Bills, Orders etc. & Subjects**	**Com**	**Subjects**
		M	Queen's Univ. Belfast (NI) O	F	New information
		M	Enterprise Zones (NI) O		technologies
		L	Supreme Court B 3R	S&T	Hazardous waste disposal
		L	Water B 3R	II	
		L	Forgery & Counterfeiting B Rep.		
		L	Laboratory Animals etc. B. Comm.		
8	Medical Education	L	Companies (No 2) B Rep. (Day 1)	E	Trade Marks (EC) Draft Rs
9	Vagrancy offences			LD	Devel. Corp. (Area & Constitution) O
8	Govt. Depts. (Audit)*			PB	Preston Borough Council B
4	Homeworking	L	Companies (No 2) B Rep. (Day 2)		
1	Supply Procedure				
2	Armed Forces Bill*	L	Matrimonial Homes and Property B 3R		
7	Reports of Parliamentary Commissioner*				
3	Medical Education				
3	Medical Education	M	Expenditure, cuts and public services	C	Consultation with employees*
3	Secondary School Curriculum & exams	L	Prayer Book Protection B 2R		
3	Youth Unemployment (S)				
0	Effects of BSC Corp. Plan				
3	Govt. Depts. (Audit)*				
	Transportation in London				
4	Trade Unions (Immunities)*				
3	Medical Education	L	Matrimonial Homes (Family Protection) (S) B Rep.	S&T	Hazardous waste disposal*
	Animal Welfare in Poultry, Pig*	M	CAP (EC) Rep.	II	
	Secondary School Curriculum & exams*	L	Criminal Attempts B 2R	LD	Devel. Corp. (Area & Constitution) O
		S	Brixton riots		
	Vagrancy offences	M	Regional policy (EC) Rep.		
	Various subjects (NI)*	Q	Police Act 1964		
	Armed Forces Bill*	L	Matrimonial Homes (Family Protection) (S) B 3R		
	Homeworking				
	UK aid for Zimbabwe*	L	Local Govt. (Misc. Prov.) (S) B 2R		
	Supply Procedure*	L	Harbours (Transport of Farm Animals) B 2R		
		Q	El Salvador policy		

Parliamentary Proceedings, November 1980—October 1981
(see pages 152–55 for keys)

Date	PQs Dept	Proc	Dept	Major Debates & Statements Bills, Orders etc. & Subjects	Com	Standing Committes Bills, Orders etc. & Subj
				Commons Chamber		**Commons**
15 Apr. 1981	7	S	10	Telecommunications	25	Disused Burial Grounds B
		S	12	Civil Service (dispute)	36	Reorganisation of NHS (W)
		S	6	Council house sales	38	Divisions of Public Ltd
		M	10	Northern region (S Day 17)		Companies (Scissions) (E
		A	4	Sandbanks (employment)		
16 Apr. 1981	1	A	4	Unemployment (Leeds)	28	British Nationality B
	23	A	8	Health & social services (Fife)		
		A	9	Charity commissioners		
		A	5	Petrol & oil charges		
		A	10	Space programme		
		A	9	Rastafarians		
		A	7	Int. Cultural Centre Grant		
		A	10	Walsall industry		
		A	9	Prison transfer treaties		
27 Apr. 1981	5	L	6	Wildlife & Countryside B 2R		
	15	M	4	Health & Safety (Diving) R		
	21	A	20	Criminal injuries comp. (NI)		
28 Apr. 1981	4	M	6	Greater London (S Day 18)	23	Contempt of Court B
	23	A	9	Police (complaints proc.)	24	Iron & Steel B
					28	British Nationality B
29 Apr. 1981	11	M	15	British Nationality B (time allocation)	25	Zoo Licensing (No 2) B
	12	L	10	Deep-sea Mining (Temp. Prov.) B 2R		
		A	1	Turkeys (French exports)		
30 Apr. 1981	12	L	12	Finance B Comm. (Day 1)	23	Contempt of Court B
	23	A	5	Power plant industry	24	Iron & Steel B
					28	British Nationality B
					29	Ports (Fin. Prov.) B
1 May 1981		L	9	Indecent Displays (Control) B 3R		
		L	8	Disabled Persons (No 2) B 3R		
		A	3	National Youth Orchestra		
5 May 1981	8	L	12	Finance B Comm. (Day 2)	23	Contempt of Court B
	23	M	13	Education (S) R	28	British Nationality B
		A	3	Schools (marriage guidance)		
6 May 1981	6	L	12	Finance B Comm. (Day 3)	25	Zoo Licensing (No 2) B
		L	16	Judicial Pensions B 3R	28	British Nationality B
		L	16	Statute Law (Repeals) B All stages	35	T & C Planning (Minerals) B
		A	8	Health visitors	37	New To s (Borrowing) O

PORTRAIT OF A SESSION
Parliamentary Proceedings, November 1980—October 1981
(see pages 152–55 for keys)

Committees		Lords Chamber		Lords Select Committees	
Com	**Select Committees Subjects**	**Proc**	**Major Debates & Statements / Unstarred Questions / Bills, Orders etc. & Subjects**	**Com**	**Subjects**
3	Secondary school curriculum & exams	S	Civil Service (dispute)	C	Consultation with employees
10	Effects of BSC corp. plan	S	Telecommunications	S&T	Science and
11	Transport (expenditure)*	L	Forestry B 2R	I	Government
4	Work of Dept. of Employment Group*				
18	Various subjects (NI)*				
8	Medical education				
				F	Machine translation system*
		L	British Telecom B 2R	LD	Devel. Corp. (Area and Constitution) O
		Q	Children needs: ministerial responsibility		
2	Defence White Paper*	L	Insurance Companies B 2R	A	Restructuring Budget (EC)
4	Homeworking	L	Fisheries B Comm.		
21	Supply procedure	L	Energy Conservation B		
17	Health Service Comm. Rep.*		HCA		
14	Welsh Office*	M	Equality in society	C	Consultation with employees
4	Dept. of Employment Group*	M	Newspaper industry		
13	Youth unemployment (S)	L	Marriage (Enabling) B Rep.		
8	Medical education*				
2	Defence White Paper*	L	Animal Health B 3R	S&T	Hazardous waste disposal
1	Animal welfare in poultry, pigs, etc.	L	Companies (No 2) B 3R	II	
		M	Environment (EC) Rep.		
7	UK aid to Zimbabwe	M	HL procedure Rep.	LD	Devel. Corp. (Area & Constitution) O
21	Supply procedure*	L	Local Govt. (Misc. Prov.) (S) B Comm.	JCS	Statutory Instruments*
17	Reports of Parliamentary Commissioner*				
	Secondary schools curriculum & exams	M	New and smaller businesses	D	Cereal substitutes*
	Gibraltar*	Q	Naval hydrographers	S&T	Science and Government
7	Youth unemployment (S)			I	
3	Animal welfare in poultry, pigs, etc.				
1	Various tax subjects*				
8	Broadcasting in Welsh				
4	N. Sea oil depletion policy*				
5	Transportation in London				
1	Medical education*				
8	Trade unions (immunities)				
4					

Parliamentary Proceedings, November 1980—October 1981
(see pages 152–55 for keys)

				Commons Chamber		Commons	
Date	PQs Dept	Proc	Dept	Major Debates & Statements Bills, Orders etc. & Subjects	Com	Standing Committes Bills, Orders etc. & Subjects	
7 May 1981	9 23	M A	7 8	Foreign affairs Oxfordshire Health Auth.	23 28	Contempt of Court B British Nationality B	
8 May 1981		L L L A	9 9 16 12	Horserace Betting Levy B 3R Licensing (Alcohol, Ed. & Research) B 3R Bill of Rights 2R Civil Service (dispute)			
11 May 1981	14 22 3	S L M L A	6 12 12 6 6	Lead pollution Finance B Comm. (Day 4) Local Loans O T & C Planning (Minerals) B Money Res. Nuclear shelters (planning)			
12 May 1981	3 23	S L A	8 12 9	Social Security benefits Finance B Comm. (Final Day) Marches (London)	23 26 28 34	Contempt of Court B Wildlife & Countryside B British Nationality B Matrimonial Homes (S) B	
13 May 1981	13 17	L A	8 12	Social Security B Rep. (Day 1) People's bank	25 28 3	Zoo Licensing (No 2) B British Nationality B Draft Employ. Protection O	
14 May 1981	20 23	L L L A	8 10 4 3	Social Security B Rep. (Day 2) & 3R Iron and Steel B AsA Rep. Ports (Fin. Assistance) B 3R Old Vic Theatre	23 26 27 28	Contempt of Court B Wildlife & Countryside B Finance B British Nationality B	
15 May 1981		L L L L A	13 11 6 7 8	Countryside (S) B AsA RS Transport Act 1962 (AM) B RS Local Govt. & Planning (AM) B 3R British North America Act 1867 (AM) B 2R Orthopaedic Surgery			
18 May 1981	10 16	M L M M A	13 10 1 8 6	Housing policy (S) Iron and Steel B 3R Fisheries policy (EC) NHS (GP Loans) O Rate support grant (E & W)			
19 May 1981	2 23	M L M	2 2 20	Defence (Day 1) Armed Forces B 3R Employment (NI) O	23 26 27 29 37 37 39	Contempt of Court B Wildlife & Countryside B Finance B T & C Planning (Minerals) B Zimbabwe (EC) O Sheriff Courts (S) O Deep-sea Diving (Temp. Prov.) B Evidence*	

Parliamentary Proceedings, November 1980—October 1981
(see pages 152–55 for keys)

Committees	Lords Chamber			Lords Select Committees	
Select Committees **Subjects**	**Proc**	**Major Debates & Statements** **Unstarred Questions** **Bills, Orders etc. & Subjects**		**Com**	**Subjects**
	L M Q	Transport B 2R Proprietory medical products (EC) Rep. Economy (NI)		F	Safe containers*
Comm. for Racial Equality* Secondary school curriculum & exams* Taxation (casual workers)*	L S	Forestry B Comm. Lead pollution		LD	Devel. Corp. (Area & Constitution) O
Supply procedure* Govt. Exp. on social services*	L S	British Telecom B Comm. (Day 1) Social security benefits		E JCS	Competition policy (EC) Statutory Instruments*
Funding of the arts Welsh Office* Effects of BSC corp. plan Namibia* Transportation in London North Sea oil* Housing assoc. grants* Form of estimates	M Q	Housing MV *Derbyshire* Loss		C	Consultation with employees
Animal Welfare in Poultry, pigs, etc.	L L L M	Fisheries B Rep. Insurance Companies B Comm. Marriage (Enabling) B 3R Asbestos (EC) Rep.		S&T II	Hazardous waste disposal*
	L L	Food and Drugs (AM) B 2R Indecent Displays (Control) B 2R			
Comm. for Racial Equality* Secondary school curriculum & exams*	L	British Telecom B Comm. (Day 2)			
Homeworking	L M L	British Telecom B Comm. (Day 3) Accession of Zimbabwe to Lomé convention O Licensing (AM) B Comm.		G S&T II	Titanium dioxide industry waste* Hazardous waste disposal

Parliamentary Proceedings, November 1980—October 1981
(see pages 152–55 for keys)

				Commons Chamber		Commons
Date	PQs Dept	Proc	Dept	Major Debates & Statements Bills, Orders etc. & Subjects	Com	Standing Committes Bills, Orders etc. & Subjects
20 May 1981	7	M	2	Defence (Day 2)		
		L	5	Atomic Energy (Misc. Prov.) B 3R		
		A	1	Lobster fishermen		
21 May 1981	1	M	15	Adjournment (Spring)	26	Wildlife & Countryside B
	23	M	9	Broadcasting	29	T & C Planning (Minerals) B
		M	10	Shipping standards & oil pollution (EC)		
		A	11	Hatch Beauchamp, Somerset		
22 May 1981		A	5	Coal liquefaction		
		A	11	British Transport Police		
		A	1	Swine vasicular disease		
		A	4	People's march for jobs		
		A	11	Airliners safety		
		A	9	Mr Mariner (trial)		
		A	7	Torture		
1 June 1981	10	L	10	Companies (No 2) B 2R		
	7	M	3	Education (school information) R		
		A	6	Domestic rates		
2 June 1981	4	S	6	Local Govt. expenditure (E)	26	Wildlife & Countryside B
	23	S	14	Local Govt. expenditure (W)	27	Finance B
		L	9	British Nationality B AsA Rep. (Day 1)		
		L	1	Animal Health B All stages		
		A	17	Warrant sales		
3 June 1981	11	L	9	British Nationality B AsA Rep. (Day 2)	24	Supreme Court B
	12	M	10	Insurance contracts (EC)		
		A	6	Sporting links (South Africa)		
4 June 1981	12	S	13	Local Govt. expenditure (S)	39	Deep-sea Diving (Temp. Prov B Evidence*
	23	L	9	British Nationality B AsA Rep. (Day 3) 3R	26	Wildlife & Countryside B
		A	4	Unemployment (Leigh)	27	Finance B
5 June 1981		M	15	Members & ministers (salaries)		
		A	10	BL (Wellingborough Foundry)		
8 June 1981	5	S	12	Civil Service (dispute)		
	15	L	13	Education (S) B AsA Rep.		
	21	M	4	Health & Safety (Exams) R		
		A	9	Immigration (work permits)		
9 June 1981	8	L	4	Employment and Training B 3R	23	Companies (No 2) B
	23	L	13	Education (S) B 3R	26	Wildlife & Countryside B
		A	10	Multi-fibre arrangement	27	Finance B
					30	Matrimonial Homes (S) B
					39	Environmental assessment (E

PORTRAIT OF A SESSION
Parliamentary Proceedings, November 1980—October 1981
(see pages 152–55 for keys)

	Committees		Lords Chamber		Lords Select Committees
m	**Select Committees Subjects**	**Proc**	**Major Debates & Statements Unstarred Questions Bills, Orders etc. & Subjects**	**Com**	**Subjects**
	Secondary school curriculum & exams* Youth unemployment (S) NHS local autonomy* Transportation in London Homeworking* Form of estimates*	M M	Trading hours (shops) East/West trade (Madrid conference)	D S&T I	Fresh poultrymeat/ health* Science and Government
	Animal welfare in poultry, pigs, etc.	L L	Ports (Fin. Asst.) B 2R Criminal Attempts B Comm.	F LD	Safe containers Devel. Corp. (Area & Constitution) O
	Comm. for Racial Equality	L L L	Social Security B 2R Iron and Steel B 2R Local Govt. Planning (AM) B 2R		
	Govt. Exp. on Social Services*	L S L L	Local Govt. (Misc. Prov.) (S) B Rep. Local Govt. expenditure (E & W) Insurance Comp. B Rep. Food & Drugs (AM) B Comm.	G E EC JCS	Titanium dioxide industry — waste Competition policy (EC) Presidency of EC* Statutory Instruments*
	Welsh Office* Testing HGVs & PSVs Transportation in London Trade union (immunities) Youth unemployment (S) Supply Estimates Class II 1981–82*	M M L Q	Employment (Misc. Prov.) (NI) O Development aid (EC) Rep. Countryside (S) B 2R Leasehold tenure	D	Fresh poultrymeat/health (EC)
	North Sea oil*	L L S L	Licensing (A) B 3R Transport B Comm. (Day 1) Local Govt. exp. (S) Fisheries B 3R	F	Safe containers
		L L L	Industrial Diseases (Notification) B 2R Horserace Betting Levy B 2R Disabled Persons (No 2) B 2R		
	Nat. Ind. private finance* Nat. Ind. finance Energy conservation*	S L M	Civil Service (dispute) Transport B Comm. (Day 2) Employment Protection (Aided Schools) O		
	Testing HGVs & PSVs	M M L L	Lord's expenses Ministerial etc. Salaries O Local Govt. (Misc. Prov.) (S) B 3R Forestry B Rep.		

Parliamentary Proceedings, November 1980—October 1981
(see pages 152–55 for keys)

				Commons Chamber		Commons	
Date	PQs Dept	Proc	Dept	Major Debates & Statements Bills, Orders etc. & Subjects	Com	Standing Committes Bills, Orders etc. & Subje
10 June 1981	6	L	3	Education B AsA 3R	24	Supreme Court B
		L	13	Local Govt. (Misc. Prov.) (S) B	25	Forgery & Counterfeiting B
				HLA	26	Wildlife & Countryside B
		A	3	Greenside, spec. sch. Wombwell	37	Job Release Act O
					37	Customs Duties (Quota) O
					32	Housing Grants (NI) O
11 June 1981	9 23	S	20	Prison escape (NI)	23	Companies (No 2) B
		M	8	Women's rights (S Day 19)	26	Wildlife & Countryside B
		A	20	DeLorean Motor Co.	27	Finance B
					30	Matrimonial Homes (S) B
					39	Deep-sea Diving (Temp. Prov
12 June 1981		L	6	Zoo Licensing (No 2) B 3R		
		A	10	Book manufacturing industry		
15 June 1981	14 3	S	9	Trooping the Colour (incident)		
		M	4	North-west region (S Day 20)		
		M	7	Food aid management (EC)		
		A	10	Japanese imports		
16 June 1981	3 23	S	1	Agricultural Ministers' meeting (EC)	23	Companies (No 2) B
		S	5	NCB (finance)	26	Wildlife & Countryside B
		L	16	Contempt of Court B AsA 3R	27	Finance B
		M	15	Government (S) Rep.	30	Matrimonial Homes (S) B
		A	9	Animals (experiments)		
17 June 1981	13 17	S	13	Local Govt. (S) Stodart Rep.	24	Supreme Court B
		M	9	Domestic gas appliances (S Day 21)	26	Wildlife & Countryside B
		M	11	Lorries & Environment (S Day 21)		
		L	6	T & C Planning (Minerals) B 3R		
		A	4	Miss Woods (voluntary work)		
18 June 1981	20 23	S	11	National Freight Co. Ltd	23	Companies (No 2) B
		M	10	Multi-fibre Arrangement	26	Wildlife & Countryside B
		A	4	Unemployment (W. Midlands)	27	Finance B
					39	Deep-sea Diving (Temp. Prov
					34	Scottish Estimates
19 June 1981		L	8	Foods & Drugs (AM) B HLA		
		L	9	Forgery & Counterfeiting B RS		
		L	9	Criminal Justice (A) B RS		
		L	9	Imprisonment of Prostitutes (Abolition) B 2R		
		A	10	Cheap pianos (imports)		
22 June 1981	10 16	S	11	Railways (electrification)		
		L	9	Representation of the People B 2R		
		A	10	Mr G. Sheward (Receiver's conduct)		
23 June 1981	2 23	M	2	Royal Air Force (S Day 22)	23	Companies (No 2) B
		A	6	Sex shops (planning)	26	Wildlife & Countryside B
					27	Finance B
					39	Deep-sea Diving (Temp. Prov.
					37	Gypsy encampments O
					37	Draft Shipbuilding Redundancie
					34	Scottish Estimates

Parliamentary Proceedings, November 1980—October 1981
(see pages 152–55 for keys)

Committees		Lords Chamber		Lords Select Committees
Select Committees Subjects	**Proc**	**Major Debates & Statements Unstarred Questions Bills, Orders etc. & Subjects**	**Com**	**Subjects**
Supply Estimates Class II 1981–82* Youth unemployment (S) Transportation in London European air fares*	M L	Race & sex discrimination Indecent Displays (Control) B Comm.	D	Fresh poultrymeat/ health*
Supply Estimates Class III 1981–82* Civil Service, efficiency*	L S	Transport B Comm. (Day 3) Prison escape (NI)		
Public expenditure (S)* Energy conservation* Civil service, manpower* Nat. Ind. Finance*	L S M M	British Telecom B Rep. (Day 1) Trooping the Colour (incident) Sheep Variable Premium (AM) O Industrial Diseases (Notification) B		
	L L L	Social Security B Comm. Disabled Persons (No 2) B Comm. Licensing (Alcohol Ed. and Research) B 2R	JCS	Statutory Instruments*
European air fares HGVs & PSVs testing HMSO accounts* Transportation in London Civil Service, efficiency	M S L	UK membership of EC — advantages Local Govt. (S) Stodart Rep. Countryside (S) B Comm.	S&T I JCC	Science & Government* Various bills*
	L S L L	British Telecom B Rep. (Day 2) National Freight Co. Ltd Iron & Steel B Comm. Transport Act 1962 (AM) B 2R	F B	Safe containers Agricultural trade policy*
	L L	Horserace Betting Levy B Comm. Local Govt. & Planning (AM) B Comm.		
Youth unemployment (S) Comm. for Racial Equality Secondary school curriculum & exams Nat. ind. finance Carry-over of funds*	L L S	Trustee Savings Bank B 2R British Nationality B 2R Railways (electrification)		
Housing policies & expenditure plans*	L L M	Atomic Energy (Misc. Prov.) B 2R Education B 2R Fruit & Veg. (Policy) (EC) Rep.	B JCS	Agricultural trade policy Statutory Instruments

Parliamentary Proceedings, November 1980—October 1981
(see pages 152–55 for keys)

				Commons Chamber		Commons
Date	PQs Dept	Proc	Dept	Major Debates & Statements Bills, Orders etc. & Subjects	Com	Standing Committees Bills, Orders etc. & Subjec
24 June 1981	7	M M A	4 20 13	Unemployment Car-sharing (NI) O Burrough Machines (Cumbernauld)	26 37 37 37 32 36	Wildlife & Countrylife B Draft Yugoslavia (EC) O Draft Fin. Assist. O Employ. Subsidies O Housing Grants (NI) O Rural affairs (W)
25 June 1981	1 23	S L L A	2 1 9 10	Defence programme Fisheries B HLA Representation of the People B 3R ICL Ltd	23 26 27 34	Companies (No 2) B Wildlife & Countryside B Finance B Scottish Estimates
26 June 1981		M A	9 12	Obscenity & film censorship Rep. Civil Service (equal opportunities)		
29 June 1981	10 7	S M L M A	12 6 10 8 6	Civil Service (pay enquiry) Yorkshire and Humberside (S Day 23) Insurance Companies B HLA Proprietary medicines (EC) Gipsy camp (Streatham)	26	Wildlife & Countryside B
30 June 1981	4 23	M L L M A	6 13 7 8 13	Sec. of State (Environment) and GLC dwellings (S Day 24) Matrimonial Homes (Family Protection) (S) B AsA 3R Belize B All stages Supplementary Benefit (Requirements etc) R Hosp. broadcasting services (S)	23 27 34	Companies (No 2) B Finance B Scottish Estimates
1 July 1981	11 12	S M M A	23 10 6 6	European Council (Lux.) (EC) Motor Vehicle Industry (S Day 25) London Docklands Dev. Corp. O Agricultural land		
2 July 1981	12 23	S M A	12 20 8	Petroleum duty (Derv) Emergency Prov. (NI) O Office of population etc. (social survey div.)	23 34	Companies (No 2) B Scottish Estimates
3 July 1981		M A	8 2	Disabled persons (S Day 24 Part II) Equipment accounting centres (Liverpool & Reading)		
6 July 1981	5 15 21	S M M M M M A	9 10 12 12 12 12 3	Southall & Toxteth riots Flags of convenience Tobacco products General betting duty Bingo duty Gaming machine licence duty Rampton Report (West Indies)		

Parliamentary Proceedings, November 1980—October 1981
(see pages 152–55 for keys)

Committees		Lords Chamber	Lords Select Committees	
Select Committees Subjects	**Proc**	**Major Debates & Statements Unstarred Questions Bills, Orders etc. & Subjects**	**Com**	**Subjects**
Secondary school curriculum & exams European air fares HGV's & PSV's Testing* Transportation in London	L M	Transport B Rep. Higher etc. education	C	Consultation with employees
Civil Service efficiency*	L S L L M L Q	British Telecom B 3R Defence programme Education (S) B 2R New Towns B 2R Shipbuilding (Redundancy) Os Countryside (S) B Rep. Edinburgh outer by-pass	B	Agricultural trade policy
	L L L	Licensing (Alcohol Educ. & Research) B 3R Indecent Displays (Control) B Rep. Horserace Betting Levy B 3R		
Comm. for Racial Equality Funding of the arts Energy conservation Nat. indust. finance	S L L Q	Civil Service (pay enquiry) Armed Forces B 2R Zoo Licensing (No 2) B 2R Discounted air tickets		
	L L L L Q	Social Security B Rep. Iron & Steel B Rep. Employ. & Training B 2R Repres. of the People B 2R Falkland Islands (sovereignty)	A B	Prospectuses for unlisted securities* Outward processing*
Funding of the arts Youth unemployment (S) Dockyards Various subjects* Trade unions (immunities) etc.	S M L L L	European Council (Lux.) (EC) London Docks Devel. Corp. Os Contempt of Court B HCA Forestry B 3R Criminal Attempts B Rep.	S&T I CA JCC	Science & Government County of Avon B Various bills*
	L L L L	Repres. of the People B RS Transport Act 1962 (AM) B 3R Indecent Displays (Control) B 3R Countryside (S) B 3R	B	Agricultural trade policy*
	L L L	Disabled Persons (No 2) B RS T & C Planning (Minerals) B HCA Zoo Licensing (No 2) B Comm.		
Youth unemployment (S) Second Scrutiny, 1981* Energy conservation Nat. indust. finance Civil Service, manpower*	L L S M	Betting & Gaming Duties B 3R Education B Comm. (Day 1) Southall & Toxteth riots Definition of EC Treaties (Yugoslavia) O		

Parliamentary Proceedings, November 1980—October 1981
(see pages 152–55 for keys)

				Commons Chamber		Commons	
Date	PQs Dept	Proc	Dept	Major Debates & Statements Bills, Orders etc. & Subjects	Com		Standing Committes Bills, Orders etc. & Subje
7 July 1981	8 23	S M L A	7 2 10 5	Foreign Secretary's visit (Moscow) Defence programme British Telecomm. B HLA Fishing industry (fuel costs)	23 37 34		Companies (No 2) B Draft Meat & Livestock Levy Scottish Estimates
8 July 1981	6	S M M L M M A	10 10 3 1 7 10 5	Gas appliances (Rep.) Regional policy (S Day 26) Higher education (S Day 26) Forestry B HLA Antigua (Termination of Association) O Furniture Development Council O Wytch Farm oilfield	37		Draft Aviation Security Fund
9 July 1981	9 23	S M L M A	10 2 16 6 11	*The Observer* newspaper The Army (S Day 27) Supreme Court B 3R Merseyside (Urban Devel.) Os Mr J. Flint (pension)	23		Companies (No 2) B
10 July 1981		L L L L L L A	6 9 8 6 9 6 4	Local Govt. & Planning (AM) B HLA Indecent Displays (Control) B HLA Disabled Persons (No 2) B HLA Countryside (S) B HLA Licensing (AM) B 3R T & C Planning Act 1971 (AM) B 2R Community Service			
13 July 1981	14 3	L L A	10 6 6	Deep-sea Mining (Temp. Prov.) B 3R Wildlife & Countryside B Rep. (Day 1) River Torridge (sewage)			
14 July 1981	3 23	S M L M L A	7 23 12 9 12 6	Foreign Affairs Council (EC) HRH Prince of Wales & Lady Diana Spencer Finance B Rep. AsA (Day 1) Pool Competitions Act 1971 O Friendly Societies B All stages Tennis (Sports Council) Rep.	37 34		Draft County Court Jurisdicti Recommendations concerning colleges of education (S) (Stodart Committee)
15 July 1981	13 17	S L L L A	9 12 10 9 12	Police (equipment) Finance B Rep. AsA (Day 2) Iron & Steel B HLA Criminal Attempts B HLA Duty-free goods (airports)	37 37 36		Draft Comm. for Conservatio of Antarctic Marine Reso etc. O Draft European Centre for Medium-range Weather Forecasts O Development Agency (W)
16 July 1981	20 23	M A	9 10	Civil disturbances Tenerife air disaster			

Parliamentary Proceedings, November 1980—October 1981
(see pages 152–55 for keys)

	Committees		Lords Chamber		Lords Select Committees	
Com	Select Committees Subjects	Proc	Major Debates & Statements Unstarred Questions Bills, Orders etc. & Subjects	Com		Subjects
4	Trade unions (immunities) etc.	S	Foreign Secretary's visit (Moscow)	B		Outward processing
6	Housing policies & expenditure plans*	L	British Nationality B Comm. (Day 1)	A		Prospectuses for unlisted securities
		M	Car-sharing (NI) O	U		Micro-technology
		M	Supple. Benefit (Requirement etc.) (AM) R	E		Trade marks
2	Dockyards*	L	Transport B Rep. (Day 1)	CU		Cumbria B
3	Secondary school curriculum & exams	S	Gas appliances	B		Agricultural trade policy
4	Trade unions (immunities)	L	Armed Forces B Comm.	JCC		Various bills
5	North Sea oil	L	Zoo Licensing (No 2) B 3R			
2	Civil Service, efficiency*	L	British Railways B 3R			
		M	NI Act 1974 (Extension) O	Eccl		Pastoral (AM) Measure
		S	*The Observer* newspaper	C		
		L	Atomic Energy (Misc. Prov.) B Comm.			
		M	Aviation Security Fund (AM) R			
		L	Belize B 2R			
		M	Merseyside Devel. Corp. Os			
		M	New Information Technologies (EC) Rep.			
	Comm. for Racial Equality*	L	British Nationality B Comm. (Day 2)	CU		Cumbria B
	Secondary school curriculum & exams*	M	Meat & Livestock etc. O			
	Nat. indust. finance	M	Pool Competitions Act 1971 (Continuance) O			
	Overseas students fees	L	Education (S) B Comm. (Day 1)			
		M	Antigua (Termination of Association) O			
		M	European Centre for Medium-range Weather Forecasts O			
		M	Comm. for Conservation of Antarctic Marine Resources etc. O			
	Dockyards*	L	Transport B 3R	DE		Derbyshire B
	Funding of the arts*	S	Police (equipment)	JCC		Broadcasting B*
	Youth unemployment (S)*	L	Employment & Training B Comm.			
	Civil Service, efficiency					
	North Sea oil					
		L	British Nationality B Comm. (Day 3)			
		L	Armed Forces B Rep.			
		M	County Courts Jurisdiction O			
		L	Forgery & Counterfeiting B HCA			
		L	Trustee Savings Bank B 3R			

Parliamentary Proceedings, November 1980—October 1981
(see pages 152–55 for keys)

				Commons Chamber		Commons
Date	PQs Dept	Proc	Dept	Major Debates & Statements Bills, Orders etc. & Subjects	Com	Standing Committes Bills, Orders etc. & Subjects
17 July 1981		M	20	Industrial Investment (AM) (NI) O		
		M	20	Diseases of Animals (NI) O		
		M	20	Appropriation (No 2) (NI) O		
		A	6	Local auth. (functions)		
20 July 1981	10 16	S	10	Tenerife air disaster		
		M	12	Budget (EC)		
		L	12	Finance B 3R		
		M	1	Poultry Slaughterhouse (Hygiene) (EC) D		
		A	8	Non-contrib. invalidity pen.		
21 July 1981	2 23	M	13	Rate support grant (S)	37	Draft Build. Soc. R
		M	13	Western Ferries (Argyll) Ltd O	37	Draft Double Taxation RS
		A	10	Design skills		
22 July 1981	7	M	2	Royal Navy		
		L	16	Contempt of Court B HLA		
		M	10	Co-op Devel. Agency (Grants) O		
		M	13	Highlands & Islands Shipping etc. O		
		M	13	Hydro-Elect. Board (North (S)) O		
		A	6	Severn-Trent Water Auth.		
23 July 1981	1 23	S	23	Summit Meeting (Ottawa)	37	Draft Export Guarantees Os
		M	15	Adjournment (royal wedding and summer)		
		L		Consolidated Fund (Approp.) B 2R		
		A	3	— Aston University		
		A	7	— BBC External Services		
		A	3	— Manchester Univ. Ed.		
		A	12	— Economy		
		A	9	— Prisoners (Parole)		
		A	4	— Employment opportunities		
		A	9	— Immigration appeals		
		A	3	— Universities (govt. exp.)		
		A	12	— borrowing requirement		
		A	6	— Local Authority expenditure		
		A	6	Rates		
24 July 1981		M	7	Brandt Report		
		A	9	Mr P. Singh		
27 July 1981	10 7	M	12	Govt.'s economic & social policies		
		L	2	Armed Forces B HLA		
		M	5	Brit. Gas Corp. (Wytch oilfield)		
		M	5	Coal Industry (Finance) Os		
		A	8	Mentally handicapped (Surrey)		
28 July 1981	4 23	S	1	Fisheries Ministers (EC)	37	Draft Int. Dev. Assoc. O
		S	6	Local Govt. audit	37	Films (Quotas) O
		M	11	Transport B (allocation of time)	37	Teachers Colleges of Ed. (S) R
		L	11	Transport B HLA	37	Ed. (School Premises) R
		M	10	Steel Industry (EC) D	37	Ed. (School Gov. Bodies) R
		A	11	Midland Link motorways	38	Interregional Air Services (EC)

Parliamentary Proceedings, November 1980—October 1981
(see pages 152–55 for keys)

Committees		Lords Chamber		Lords Select Committees	
Select Committees Subjects	**Proc**	**Major Debates & Statements Unstarred Questions Bills, Orders etc. & Subjects**		**Com**	**Subjects**
	L	Education B Comm. (Day 1)			
Secondary school curriculum & exams Energy conservation	M	Defence			
Energy Estimates 1981–82* Overseas students fees*	L L	Education (S) B Comm. (Day 2) British Nationality B Comm. (Day 4)		B	Agricultural trade policy
Secondary school curriculum & exams Youth unemployment (S)* Govt. reply to Comm. Rep.* Relationship of Comptroller & PAC* North Sea oil	L L	British Nationality B Comm. (Day 5) Atomic Energy (Misc. Prov.) B 3R		D S&T I	CAP improvements (EC) Science & Government
	L S M M	British Nationality B Comm. (Day 6) Summit Meeting (Ottawa) Diseases of animals (NI) O Appropriation (No 2) (NI) O		D S&T I Eccl C	CAP improvements (EC) Science & Government Pastoral (AM) measures
	L L Q	Friendly Societies B RS Finance B RS Guyana-Venezuela dispute			
Energy conservation*	L L L M Q	Belize B RS Employment & Training B 3R Deep-sea Mining (Temp. Prov.) B HCA Furn. Dev. Council (Dissolution) O Namibian independence			
	L S M M Q	British Nationality B Comm. (Day 7) Local Govt. audit (E & W) Building Soc. (Authorisation) R Indust. Investment (NI) O Tenerife air disaster		S&T I	Science & Government

Parliamentary Proceedings, November 1980—October 1981
(see pages 152–55 for keys)

				Commons Chamber		Commons	
Date	PQs Dept	Proc	Dept	Major Debates & Statements Bills, Orders etc. & Subjects	Com	Standing Committes Bills, Orders etc. & Subject	
30 July 1981	12	S	10	British Telecommunications			
	23	L	14	Wildlife & Countryside B HLA Rep. (Day 2) & 3R			
		L	4	Employment & Training B HLA			
		M	6	London Docklands Dev. Corp.			
		A	6	Housing (Walsall)			
31 July 1981		M	8	Social Security Benefits Uprating Rs			
		A	6	Local Auth. houses (heating charges)			
		A	9	Special Constabulary			
		A	2	Amble (Naval Dock)			
		A	3	Social studies in schools			
		A	6	National housing survey			
		A	6	Opencast mining (Forest of Dean)			
		A	8	Inequalities in health rep. rates (London)			
		A	6	Local Govt. finance (Hackney)			
		A	6	Rate support grant scheme			
		A	6	Gleneagles Agreement			
6 Oct. 1981							
7 Oct. 1981							
8 Oct. 1981							
13 Oct. 1981							
14 Oct. 1981							
15 Oct. 1981							
19 Oct. 1981	5	S	5	Gas & oil indust. (disposal of assets)			
	15	L	10	Companies (No 2) B AsA (Day 1)			
	21	A	6	Properties services agencies			
20 Oct. 1981	8	S	1	Agriculture Ministers' meeting (EC)			
	23	L	10	Companies (No 2) B 3R (Day 2)			
		M	13	Grant-aided Colleges (S) R			
21 Oct. 1981	11	L	13	Matrimonial Homes (Family Protection) (S) B HLA			
	12	L	13	Education (S) B HLA			
		M	11	Road Traffic (Hereford etc.) O			
		M	13	Education (Lothian) O			
		A	4	Youth Opportunities Scheme			

Parliamentary Proceedings, November 1980—October 1981
(see pages 152–55 for keys)

Committees		Lords Chamber		Lords Select Committees	
Select Committees Subjects	**Proc**	**Major Debates & Statements Unstarred Questions Bills, Orders etc. & Subjects**	**Com**	**Subjects**	
	L	Education B Rep. (Day 1)			
	M	BBC (External Services)			
	M	HL Procedure Reps.			
	L	Education B Rep. (Day 2)			
	M	Social Security Benefits etc. Uprating Os and Rs			
	M	Films Quota O			
	M	London Docklands Southwark O			
	M	London Docklands Newham O			
	L	British Nationality B Rep. (Day 8)			
	S	Assassination of Pres. Sadat	C	Summer time	
	L	British Nationality B Rep. (Day 9)			
	L	Broadcasting B Comm.	F	Combined transport	
	L	Education (S) B Rep. (Day 3)	S&T I	Science & Government*	
	L	British Nationality B Rep. (Day 10)	A	Banks etc. annual accounts	
	L	Matrimonial Homes (S) B HCA	D	State aid to agriculture (EC)*	
	L	Education (S) B 3R			
	Q	Beverley Minster			
	L	Wildlife & Countryside B HCA (Day 1)	F	Combined transport	
	M	Building Societies (Authorisation) R			
	L	Education B 3R			
	L	Wildlife & Countryside B HCA (Day 2)			
	L	British Nationality B 3R	F	Combined transport	
			A	Banks etc. annual accounts	
	M	Employee Consultation (EC) D			
	M	Cereal Substitutes (EC) D			

Parliamentary Proceedings, November 1980—October 1981
(see pages 152–55 for keys)

| | | | | Commons Chamber | | Commons | |
| | | | | | | | |
Date	PQs Dept	Proc	Dept	Major Debates & Statements Bills, Orders etc. & Subjects	Com	Standing Committees Bills, Orders etc. & Subje
22 Oct. 1981	9 23	S L M A A	6 3 4 9 13	Rate support grant (judgement) Education B HLA Asbestos (EC) D Citizen's Band radio Drug abuse (Glasgow)		
23 Oct. 1981		M A	10 8	Information Technology (EC) D Royal Northern Hospital		
26 Oct. 1981	14 3	S M M M M A	23 7 11 9 6 11	Mexico Summit BBC (External Services) British Rail (investment) British Nationality B (allocation of time) Shorthold Tenancies Rent O Market Harborough (bypass)		
27 Oct. 1981	3 23	S L M M A	9 9 9 4 13	Bomb incidents (London) British Nationality B HLA Imprisonment (Temp. Prov.) Act 1980 O National Dock Labour Board O Unemployment (Kilmarnock)		
28 Oct. 1981	6	M A	12 10	Economic policies of Govt. Textile industry		
29 Oct. 1981	20 23	S S L L L L M M A	9 1 14 16 16 16 16 19 10	Police searches (Brixton) Fisheries Ministers' Meetings (EC) Wildlife & Countryside B HLA 3R Betting & Gaming Duties B 3R Acquisition of Land B 3R New Towns B 3R Magistrates' Courts (NI) O European Community (Mandate) Rep. British Leyland		
30 Oct. 1981						

Parliamentary Proceedings, November 1980—October 1981
(see pages 152–55 for keys)

	Committees		Lords Chamber		Lords Select Committees	
Com	Select Committees Subjects	Proc	Major Debates & Statements Unstarred Questions Bills, Orders etc. & Subjects	Com	Subjects	
		L	Laboratory Animals Protection B 3R	Eccl	Pastoral (AM)	
		S	Rate support grant (judgement)	C	measures	
		Q	Bankruptcy Convention (EC) D	B	Agricultural trade policy	
		Q	Extremist literature			
3	Funding of the arts					
5	Energy conservation in buildings					
		L	Companies (No 2) B HCA			
		S	Bomb incidents (London)			
12	Civil Service (efficiency)*	M	Imprisonment (Temp. Prov.) Act 1980 O			
		Q	Salmon fishing industry (S)			
		L	British Nationality B HCA			
		S	Police searches (Brixton)			
		M	Protected Shorthold Tenancies (Rent Registration) O			
		L	Betting & Gaming Duties B HCA			
		L	Acquisition of Land B HCA			
		L	New Towns B HCA			
			Queen's Speech			

Extract from Memorandum of Guidance for Government Officials appearing before Parliamentary Select Committees (May 1980)*

Provision of Evidence

General. (1) The general principle to be followed is that it is the duty of officials to be as helpful as possible to committees, and that any withholding of information should be limited to reservations that are necessary in the interests of good government or to safeguard national security. Departments should, therefore, be as forthcoming as they can (within the limits set out in this note) when requested to provide information whether in writing or orally. This will also help to secure that the reports of committees are as soundly based on fact as possible. Oral evidence is recorded verbatim. When oral evidence is to be given, it is advisable for departments to send at least two witnesses so that they can divide between themselves the responsibility for answering questions. Because officials appear on behalf of their ministers, departments might want to clear written evidence and briefing with ministers. It may only be necessary for ministers to be consulted should there be any doubt among officials on the policy to be explained to the committee. However, ministers are ultimately responsible for deciding what information is to be given and for defending their decisions as necessary, and ministers' views should always be sought if any question arises of withholding information which committees are known to be seeking.

Accuracy of evidence. (2) Officials appearing before select committees are responsible for ensuring that the evidence they give is accurate. They are reminded to take particular care to see that they are fully and correctly briefed on the main facts of the matters on which they expect to be examined. Should it nevertheless be discovered subsequently that the evidence unwittingly contained errors, these should be made known to the committee at the earliest possible moment.

Informal discussions. (3) Some committees may occasionally conduct informal discussions in addition to taking formal evidence. When that occurs, officials should apply the same considerations as apply to formal evidence, because the supply of information informally can affect a committee's report as much as formal evidence.

Status of information supplied. (4) Once information has been supplied to a committee, it becomes "evidence" and, subject only to the conventions governing classified information (see paragraphs 31, 32), it is entirely within the competence of the committee to report and publish it or to refrain from doing so. Letters addressed to the clerk to the committee, however informal, are strictly speaking "evidence" and liable to be published.

Inter-departmental liaison. (5) Generally speaking the subjects of enquiry by select committees will fall clearly within the responsibilities of particular departments. Occasionally, however, committees may enquire into subjects which span the work of more than one department, or where departmental responsibility is not self-evident. The aim must be to ensure that committees direct their questions on each aspect of such

* The CPRS was disbanded at the end of July 1983.

subjects to the department chiefly concerned with that aspect, and do not question departments whose role is that of co-ordination about matters which go outside that role. This indicates that where in such cases the committee needs a memorandum covering the interests of several departments, it may be better for this to be submitted by the department with the predominant role in the field concerned (rather than by a co-ordinating office such as the Cabinet Office). If the committee then asks that department questions (whether in writing or orally) proper to some other department, they can be re-directed.

(6) In these cases it is clearly desirable for all the departments concerned, in accordance with normal procedure, to keep in touch in the preparation of their evidence — e.g. by exchanging drafts. Where there is no co-ordinating machinery already available for this purpose, it may be best for the department with the predominant role to act as a central point. Since there is no separate select committee for Northern Ireland, a department with this role should particularly ensure that Northern Ireland interests are taken into account as necessary. It is important that departments should clear with any other department which may have an interest both memoranda and the line to be taken in oral evidence, even if the time for this is short.

(7) Greater difficulties may arise when the subject under enquiry is one in which no department can be said to have a predominant interest. In such cases the committee needs a memorandum covering the interests of several departments — e.g. setting out the range of government activities in the field concerned — and it may well be necessary for the body which co-ordinates government action in that field to submit it. It seems desirable, however, so to organise such memoranda as to indicate, for each aspect covered, which department is primarily responsible and at least by implication the limitations of the co-ordinating responsibility. This should assist the committee in summoning the witnesses appropriate to the aspects it wishes to investigate at each session; and if the questions asked are misdirected, no doubt the witnesses will say so.

(8) Normally the Cabinet Office and other similar co-ordinating offices will not be required to give evidence to a committee, but the Central Policy Review Staff* may give evidence about their published work. Requests for CPRS evidence on other matters, and requests for other evidence from co-ordinating offices such as the Cabinet Office and "non-departmental" units or officials, should be referred to ministers. A committee might seek evidence from a particular official (for example, the head of the Government Statistical Service) who is not directly answerable to a departmental minister but who in his professional capacity has a special knowledge of the subject of an enquiry. In these cases too, ministers should be consulted.

Limitations on the Provision of Information

General. (9) Committees' requests for information should not be met regardless of cost or of diversion of effort from other important matters. It might prove necessary to decline requests which appeared to involve excessive costs. It may be necessary for a department to consult their minister if a particular request seems to involve an unreasonable amount of extra work.

(10) The Procedure Committee recognised that there may be occasions when ministers may wish to resist requests for information on grounds of national security. Appendix C of the committee's report (the memorandum by the Clerk of the House) reproduces the text of a letter of 9 May 1967 to the chairmen of certain select committees from the then Lord President of the Council and Leader of the House, which refers (among other limitations on the provision of information) to "information affecting national security,

* Drafted and circulated by the Head of the Civil Service in May 1980.

which would normally be withheld from the House in the national interest". Guidance to departments on the release of classified information to committees is given in the manual *Security in Government Departments*. This manual is the overriding authority; what follows must be read subject to its guidance. Officials must not disclose information which the manual says must be withheld; they should consult their departmental security officers if in doubt.

(11) Officials should not give evidence about or discuss the following topics:

(i) In order to preserve the collective responsibility of ministers, the advice given to ministers by their departments should not be disclosed, nor should information about inter-departmental exchanges on policy issues, about the level at which decisions were taken or the manner in which a minister has consulted his colleagues. Information should not be given about cabinet committees or their discussions (see paragraphs 12–14).

(ii) Advice given by a Law Officer (see paragraph 17).

(iii) The private affairs of individuals or institutions on which any information held by ministers or their officials has been supplied in confidence (including such information about individuals which is available to the Government by virtue of their being engaged in or considered for public employment).

Officials should also, where possible, avoid giving written evidence about or discussing the following matters (where appropriate further guidance is provided in the succeeding paragraphs):

(iv) Questions in the field of political controversy (see paragraphs 15–16).

(v) Sensitive information of a commercial or economic nature, e.g. knowledge which could affect the financial markets, without prior consultation with the Chancellor of the Exchequer; sensitive information relating to the commercial operations of nationalised industries, or to contracts; commercial or economic information which has been given to the Government in confidence, unless the advance consent of the persons concerned has been obtained (but see paragraph 48 on the kind of contract information which may, in certain circumstances, be provided).

(vi) Matters which are, or may become, the subject of sensitive negotiations with Governments or other bodies, including the European Community, without prior consultation with the Foreign and Commonwealth Secretary, or in relation to domestic matters the ministers concerned (see paragraph 18).

(vii) Specific cases where the minister has or may have a quasi-judicial or appellate function, e.g. in relation to planning applications and appeals, or where the subject-matter is being considered by the courts, or the Parliamentary Commissioner (see paragraphs 19–20).

Where, exceptionally, matters such as iv–vii have to be discussed, application may be made for "side-lining" (see paragraph 32). There is no objection to saying in general terms why information cannot be given and it is very unusual for a committee to press an official who indicates that he is in difficulty on such grounds in answering a question. If however, this happens, it may be best to ask for time to consider the request and to promise to report back.

Collective responsibility. (12) Departmental witnesses, whether in closed or open session, should preserve the collective responsibility of ministers and also the basis of confidence between ministers and their advisers. Except in a case involving an accounting officer's responsibility the advice given to ministers, which is given in confidence, should not therefore be disclosed, though departments may of course need to draw on information submitted to ministers. It is necessary also to refuse access to documents relating to inter-departmental exchanges on policy issues. Equally, the methods by which a current study is being undertaken, e.g. by the Central Policy Review Staff, should not normally be disclosed without the authority of ministers, unless they have already been made public. Nor should departments reveal the level at which decisions were taken. It should be borne in mind that decisions taken by ministers collectively are normally announced and defended by the minister responsible as his own decisions, and it is important that no indication should be given of the manner in which a minister has consulted his colleagues (see also paragraph 17 on the special position of the Law Officers).

(13) In no circumstances should any committee be given a cabinet paper or extract from it, or be told of discussions in a cabinet committee. Nor should information be given about the existence, composition or terms of reference of cabinet committees, or the identity of their chairmen, beyond that information disclosed by the Prime Minister in answer to a parliamentary question on 24 May 1979, and, if witnesses are questioned on such matters they must decline to give specific answers. There is, however, no objection to pointing out in general terms that consultation between departments runs through the whole fabric of Government and occurs at all levels both official and ministerial.

(14) Departmental files will tend to concern the matters referred to in paragraph 11 above, and departments should consult their ministers, and should also advise the Civil Service Department when dealing with any request by a committee to see or have quoted verbatim any inter-departmental correspondence or internal minutes. The Public Accounts Committee is in a special position in view of the Comptroller and Auditor General's access to departmental papers, and in considering any request from it for access to departmental papers the Treasury should be consulted in addition to the Civil Service Department. In the special case of the Select Committee on the Parliamentary Commissioner, it may be necessary to quote from departmental documents in connection with Parliamentary and Health Service Commissioner cases. But it is not the practice of the committee to require evidence which would amount to the "re-trial" of a Parliamentary or Health Service Commissioner case.

Policy. (15) Official witnesses, whether administrative, professional or Services, should as far as possible confine their evidence to questions of fact relating to existing government policies and actions. Officials should be ready to explain what the existing policies are and the objectives and justification, as the Government sees them, for those policies, and to explain how administrative factors may have affected both the choice of policy measures and the manner of their implementation. It is open to officials to make comments which are not politically contentious but they should as far as possible avoid being drawn, without prior ministerial authority, into the discussion of alternative policy. If official witnesses are pressed by the committee to go beyond these limits, they should suggest that the questioning be addressed, or referred, to ministers. If there is a likelihood of a material issue of policy being raised by a committee in its questioning of official witnesses, departments will wish to consult ministers beforehand.

(16) A select committee may invite specialist (as opposed to administrative) civil servants to discuss the professional or technical issues underlying controversial policies. This may raise particular problems in the case of, for example, economists, if committees discuss issues of economic reasoning which bear upon controversial policy questions and which are also matters of technical and professional controversy among economists. When this is so, and where economic advisers to the Government appear as official witnesses, they may find themselves in the difficulty that their own judgement on the professional issues has, or might easily appear to have, implications critical of the Government's policies. It is not open to them to explain the advice which they have given to the Government on such a matter, or would give if asked by the Government. They cannot, therefore, go beyond explaining the economic reasoning which, in the government's view, justifies their policy. This will only be possible where the underlying theory has indeed been explicitly formulated; and the status of what was being presented would have to be made clear. If there is no quotable public evidence of a government

view and the witness is asked for his own professional judgement on the issue, or his judgement of the view that the Government would be likely to take, he should refer to the political nature of the issue and suggest that the questioning be addressed or referred to ministers. Similar considerations apply in the case of other specialist civil servants.

Advice given by a Law Officer. (17) There should not be disclosed to a committee any advice that may have been given by the Law Officers. There is a well-established convention that the advice which Law Officers give to ministers is confidential. It is only when Law Officers expressly authorise the disclosure of that advice, or themselves report to or advise Parliament or a committee, that such advice is revealed.

International relations. (18) Negotiations with other governments are normally conducted in strict confidence. Officials should take care in discussing or giving written evidence on matters which may affect relations with other governments or bodies, including the European Community, or relations between British officials and those of other governments. Texts of communications between governments, unless already made public, should be regarded as confidential and should not be submitted as evidence without prior approval of the minister concerned.

Matters sub-judice. (19) Committees are subject to the rules by which the House regulates its own conduct and that of its Members. It is normally possible to work on the assumption that if a matter already before the courts seemed likely to come up for discussion before a committee, the staff of the House would have drawn the attention of the chairman to the relevant rules of the House relating to discussion of sub-judice questions. But the chairman has an overriding discretion to determine what is appropriate in the hearing of evidence.

(20) Officials should take care in discussing or giving written evidence on matters which may become the subject of litigation but which as yet do not strictly come under the rules which preclude discussion on sub-judice questions. Such caution should be exercised whether or not the Crown is likely to be a party to the litigation. If such matters seem likely to be raised when a committee takes evidence, officials should first consult with their own departmental solicitor or the Treasury Solicitor for advice on how to handle the questions which might arise.

Reports commissioned by departments. (21) On a number of occasions committees have made requests to see copies of reports commissioned by departments. These requests can often cause particular difficulty. Such reports may come from a variety of sources, ranging from the purely internal working group to the major outside committee, but where publication was not intended. The fact that a report is known to have been prepared does not of itself oblige a department to reveal its contents. In deciding whether to accede to requests for particular reports the primary consideration must always be the contents of the document concerned, i.e. whether it contains classified information or information of the kinds discussed elsewhere in this memorandum which should not normally be disclosed.

(22) In addition the following considerations may be relevant:
  (i) While select committees should not press for internal advice to ministers to be revealed, they are less likely to accept without argument a refusal to reveal a report from a departmental committee containing outside members, and even less likely to accept a refusal in the case of a wholly external committee. In particular, they will be understandably reluctant to accept a refusal where the establishment of the committee in question has been announced, together with its membership and terms of reference, and where its report is known to exist. These implications need to be taken into account in deciding how much publicity should be given to the establishment of committees of this kind.

(ii) In particular cases departments may consider that, while a report cannot be published, it would be helpful to provide it to a committee, provided it was treated in onfidence (see paragraph 29).

(iii) In certain cases, where a select committee might reasonably expect to receive a ertain amount of detailed information, departments may be able to provide a written memorandum in place of the report itself. If departments can assist committees in this way, it is generally desirable to do so.

(iv) Departments should always seek the views of ministers before refusing a request rom a select committee for a particular report, since the minister might be called on to defend the decision to the committee personally.

Documents Relating to the internal administration of Government. (23) The Procedure Committee recommended that: "Select committees should regard any refusal by government departments to provide information relating to departmental or inter-departmental organisation — unless fully explained and justified to their satisfaction — as a matter of serious concern which should be brought to the attention of the House."

A considerable amount of information about the internal distribution of business is already available in published form (e.g. in *The Civil Service Year Book*) and the normal presumption should be that more detailed information about departments' organisational structure, such as directories and organisation charts, should be provided to committees f it is requested. Where a description of duties of a sensitive nature necessitates the revelation of classified information, the considerations relating to classified documents see paragraphs 29–32) should apply.

(24) Requests for documents which go beyond a description of the existing organisation of a department and deal with methods of operation (e.g. arrangements for formal and informal co-ordination or for delegation of authority) or with reviews of existing departmental organisation or methods may raise more difficult questions, since these will frequently be internal working papers. Even here, however, the presumption should be that information on these matters should be provided, in an appropriate form, unless it would conflict with the guidance in paragraph 11 above. Ministers should be consulted about any requests for information of this kind. Except where particular arrangements have been made public, information about inter-departmental organisation may present more difficulty (see paragraphs 12–13).

Documents of a previous administration. (25) There are well-established conventions which govern the withholding of policy papers of a previous administration from an administration of a different political complexion. Since officials appear before select committees as representatives of their ministers and since select committees are themselves composed on a bipartisan basis, it follows that officials should not provide a select committee with papers of a previous administration which they are not in a position to how to present ministers. If such papers are sought, ministers should be consulted about the request. The general rule is that documents of a former administration which have not been released or published during the period of that administration should not be released or published by a subsequent government. Where ministers propose to make an exception, it would be necessary to consult a representative of the previous administration before showing the papers either to present ministers or, with ministers' agreement, releasing them to a select committee.

Treatment of Evidence

Open sessions. (26) Unclassified memoranda prepared by departments for a committee may be published by the committee before its full report is presented to the House, and may be available to the press and public at the time of the related session.

Open sessions of committees often attract publicity since evidence before them may be reported forthwith by the press. Departments are in these circumstances free to comment immediately to the press on matters raised in their evidence. If a select committee takes evidence in public from a minister or senior official, therefore, it may be considered desirable for a press officer also to attend, so as to be able to answer press queries. Such press briefing should not, however, extend to comment on matters of policy, since such comment might be regarded as impeding the committee in its task and hence as contempt. Care should be taken not to go beyond the evidence given by the minister or official in commenting on any suggestion made by another witness, e.g. the chairman of a nationalised industry, at the same hearing, or to disclose information not yet given publicly.

(27) Written memoranda of evidence on which departmental witnesses are examined in public and which are included in the printed copy of the proceedings reported that day to the House, inasmuch as they may have been available to the public attending the session, may at the department's discretion be issued to other interested parties thereafter. Copies of oral evidence given in public, however, should not be disclosed by departments until the final published version is available, as the first copies are confidential proofs subject both to correction and to explanation by footnotes. Amendments to the proofs of evidence sent to witnesses by the clerk cannot normally go beyond minor corrections of grammar and transcription, although the chairman may be willing to consider suggestions about "side-lining" (see paragraph 32).

(28) Evidence critical of a department may be given in open session by persons outside the department on occasions where departmental witnesses are not also present. In these circumstances departments should not seek publicly to respond to such criticism outside the ambit of the committee. Instead, the chairman of the committee concerned may be asked to consider inviting the department to express their view also to the committee as soon as possible.

Disclosure of confidential information in general. (29) The general aim of departments should be to assist committees by disclosing to them whatever official information they may require for the carrying out of their parliamentary functions, provided that there are not overriding reasons of security or other grounds for withholding such information. It may be, however, that particular information requested by a committee, or other information, which a department consider might have a relevant bearing on a committee's enquiries, should only be made available on the basis that it will not be published and will be treated in confidence. Where this is so, the department should inform the clerk to the committee that the information can be made available only on this basis, explaining the reasons in general terms. Such information should not be made available until the committee has agreed to treat it accordingly; or, in the case of information with no security classification, at least until the department are satisfied that the committee is prepared to agree to a reasonable degree of side-lining (see paragraph 32b). The interpretation of "evidence" at paragraph 4 should be noted in this context. In considering the submission of confidential evidence to a committee, departments should bear in mind that the final authority as to whether or not evidence shall be published rests with the committee. Arrangements have occasionally been made whereby certain classified evidence is given only to a sub-committee of a main Commons select committee. Formally, however, departments should proceed on the basis that main committees and sub-committees represent a single entity. No evidence given to committees in closed sessions (i.e. when the public and the press are not admitted) should be disclosed by departments before the evidence has been published by the committee.

Disclosure of confidential information in oral evidence. (30) It would clearly be inappropriate for any evidence which a department wished to be treated as confidential to be given at a session of the committee to which the public and press are admitted.

cordingly, if it appears likely that topics to be discussed at a forthcoming public
sion of a committee are such that the departmental witnesses would only be able to
e substantive answers if they could be treated in confidence, the department should
te to the chairman or the clerk to the committee explaining why this is so: in most
es it is likely that it would be appropriate for the departmental minister to write to the
irman. If, despite such an approach, a committee questions an official witness in
blic session on what he considers confidential matters, or if such matters are raised
expectedly, he should inform the committee that he cannot answer the question on
unds of confidentiality: he should not himself suggest that the committee should go
o closed session. In certain technical fields (e.g. defence research) it may be useful for
epartment to hold off-the-record "presentations" for committee members.

Procedures for avoiding publication of confidential evidence. (31) Where con-
ential written evidence is submitted to a committee on the understanding that it will
: be published, this understanding should be made clear in the covering letter to the
rk to the committee accompanying the evidence.

32) In the case of confidential evidence given orally to a committee in closed session,
following procedures should be followed in order to ensure that such evidence is not
de public:

a) *Information with a security classification* — TOP SECRET, SECRET, CONFIDENTIAL,
STRICTED. In cases where information with a security classification is revealed to a
mmittee, the following procedure should be followed in order to prevent publication.
1e disclosure of TOP SECRET information may only be made on the personal authority
the minister concerned.)
  (i) The witness, before leaving the committee room, should let the clerk to the
mmittee know what portions of his evidence contain matters with a security
ssification.
  (ii) The clerk will then instruct the shorthand writer not to send for printing the
nscript of those portions, but instead to send three copies to the clerk (five copies in
case of the Public Accounts Committee).
  (iii) The clerk will send two copies to the witness: one is for his retention; on the
er he should side-line any passage containing information which, in his opinion, it
uld be undesirable on grounds of security to print.

Since this procedure involves delay in the printing of evidence, it should only be used
ere strictly necessary.

b) *Other confidential information.* If a department propose to reveal confidential (but
classified) information which, in the view of the department, it would not be
irable on grounds other than security to include in the published evidence, they
uld first ask the committee to agree that it should not be published or at least be
tain that the committee is prepared to agree to a reasonable degree of side-lining.
cedures on the lines of a above will then be followed, and the attention of the clerk to
committee should be drawn to passages marked in accordance with the procedure at a
: which do not have a security classification (see also paragraph 11). Alternatively it
y be sufficient to settle the details of side-lining at a later stage when the proof of
dence is available from the clerk. It should be noted that select committees may
netimes challenge a request for side-lining, and officials must always be sure that they
justify such a request if they make one. Challenges are more likely to arise, and side-
ng is likely to be more difficult to defend, in the case of b above than where the
ormation has a standard security classification.

Appendix 3

Letter dated 6 July 1977 from Sir Douglas Allen* on the Disclosure of Official Information (the Croham Directive)

Dear Head of Department

During the Debate on the Address on 24 November [1976] the Prime Minister announced that it would be the Government's policy in future to publish as much as possible of the factual and analytical material used as the background to major policy studies:

> When the Government make major policy studies, it will be our policy in future to publish as much as possible of the factual and analytical material which is used as the background to these studies. This will include material used in the programme analysis reviews, unless — and I must make the condition — there is some good reason, of which I fear we must be the judge, to the contrary.
> I am trying to help. I assure the House that we shall not endeavour to pull back the information. We shall look at every case to see whether we can make it available. The cost to public funds is a factor here, and we should like to keep that cost to a minimum. Therefore, arrangements will not be of a luxurious nature, but we shall make available what information we can to provide a basis for better informed public debate and analysis of ministerial policy conclusions. (HC Deb. vol. 921, c. 27).

I am writing in terms which the Prime Minister has specifically approved to let you know how his statement affects present practice and to ask you to ensure that your department gives effect to it. You may wish to let your minister see this guidance, drawing particular attention to paragraph 10.

(2) The change may seem simply to be one of degree and of timing. But it is intended to mark a real change of policy, even if the initial step is modest. In the past it has normally been assumed that background material relating to policy studies and reports would *not* be published unless the responsible minister or ministers decided otherwise. Henceforth the working assumption should be that such material *will* be published unless they decide that it should *not* be. There is, of course, no intention to publish material which correctly bears a current security classification or privacy marking; at the same time, care should be taken to ensure that the publication of unclassified material is not frustrated by including it in documents that also contain classified material.

(3) In effect, what is proposed is an increase in the already considerable amount of material put out by departments. The additional material will mainly consist of deliberate presentations in the later stages of discussion and development of new policy. Some of these will probably, as now, take the form of Green Papers. Some may have kindred form, like the recent Orange Paper on Transport. While most material will be released on the intiative of the department, probably through HMSO, some of lesser importance, or of interest to a limited audience, may well be put out through other means such as publication in magazines or in response to specific requests in the same way that a good deal of unpublished material is already made available to bona fide researchers. In some cases it may be preferable simply to publicise the existence of certain material which would be made available to anyone who asked. Consideration should also be given to the issue of bibliographies or digests so that interested parties are advised what material is available.

(4) In adopting the working assumption described in paragraph 2 above for policy studies, including PARs [i.e. programme analysis reviews], the normal aim will be to

---

* then Head of the Home Civil Service

blicise as much as possible of the background material subject to ministerial decision ce they have seen the study and reached their conclusions on it. When ministers decide hat announcement they wish to make, therefore, they will also wish to consider whether d in what form the factual and analytical material may be published, since there may, as e Prime Minister made clear in his statement, be circumstances in which ministers will t wish to disclose such material.

(5) It is not the intention to depart from the present practice of not disclosing PARs nor entifying them publicly; any question of releasing PAR material in circumstances not vered by a ministerial decision should be referred to the Treasury.

(6) In his November statement the Prime Minister said that it was the Government's sh to keep to a minimum the cost to public funds of the new initiative on disclosure. One hibition to the publication of background material in the past has been that it has often en incorporated in submissions to ministers which could not be published in their tirety. Re-writing material specially for publication is wasteful and expensive in staff ne. Therefore when policy studies are being undertaken in future, the background aterial should as far as possible be written in a form which would permit it to be published parately, with the minimum of alteration, once a ministerial decision to do so has been ken. It will generally assist ministers to reach their decisions on publications if they can e an identifiable separate part of the report, appropriately written for this purpose.

(7) The form and way in which material is released will have to be considered on each casion. The cost of any extra printing, or publishing, falls under present arrangements the HMSO Vote, and HMSO is of course affected by the current restrictions on public penditure in the same way as other departments. HMSO is also responsible for deciding hat prices should be charged for published material. You should ensure that discussions th HMSO are initiated at the earliest possible opportunity on any proposal which will d to expenditure. The following particular considerations should also be borne in mind:
Great care should be taken to keep costs to a minimum. If copies are to be run off in vance of demand, the quantity should be carefully and prudently assessed, to avoid aste rather than to offer instant response. (But, of course, there is a countervailing need to m where appropriate for the economics of longer reproduction runs. The right balance re may be difficult and decisions should not be left to too low a level.)
) In general, double printing should be avoided, e.g. the published form of the material ould be the same as that used internally (and the same print).
i) There should be a charge for all material, at a price set by HMSO for each item, to clude all aspects of reproduction and handling, but not of course any of the costs of the imary study itself.
v) As regards Crown Copyright, attention is drawn to CSD [Civil Service Department] eneral Notice GEN 75/76 dated 12 August 1975 (and corrigendum of 8 October 1976).

(8) The Government's decision on this question is in a form which should not involve bstantial additional work but which could all too easily be lost to view. There are many ho would have wanted the Government to go much further (on the lines of the formidably rdensome Freedom of Information Act in the USA). Our prospects of being able to oid such an expensive development here could well depend on whether we can show that e Prime Minister's statement had reality and results. So I ask all of you to keep this estion of publicising material well on your check-list of action in any significant areas of licy formulation, even at divisional level; and to encourage your ministers to take an terest in the question.

(9) Since the Prime Minister may well be asked what effect his announcement has had on e amount of information made available, I should be grateful if you could arrange to have me kind of record kept of the relevant items made available by your department. Where

the material is of an unusual kind, or of a variety not usually made available in the past, it would be useful if a copy could be sent to CSD. In cases where it has been decided not to publish material which might be expected to be of considerable public interest, I suggest that the reasons should be briefly recorded.

(10) The greater publicising of material can hardly fail to add to one cost — that of responding to the additional direct correspondence to which it may well give rise. In a Service operating under tight resource constraints, it may not always be possible to afford to give to such additional correspondence the kind of full and studied replies to which we have long been accustomed within the sort of timescale that has hitherto been customary. Nevertheless, departments must do their best in these matters, and should inform a correspondent if the timescale for a reply is likely to be longer than normal.

Yours sincerely
Douglas Allen

The Duties and Responsibilities of Civil Servants in relation to Ministers, by Sir Robert Armstrong, Head of the Home Civil Service (February 1985)*

During the last few months a number of my colleagues have suggested to me that it would be timely to restate the general duties and responsibilities of civil servants in relation to ministers. Recent events, and the public discussion to which they have given rise, have led me to conclude that the time has come when it would be right for me, as head of the Home Civil Service, to respond to these suggestions. I am accordingly setting out the guidance in this note. It is issued after consultation with permanent secretaries in charge of departments, and with their agreement.

(2) Civil servants are servants of the Crown. For all practical purposes the Crown in this context means and is represented by the Government of the day. There are special cases in which certain functions are conferred by law upon particular members or groups of members of the public service; but in general the executive powers of the Crown are exercised by and on the advice of Her Majesty's ministers, who are in turn answerable to Parliament. The civil service as such has no constitutional personality or responsibility separate from the duly elected Government of the day. It is there to provide the Government of the day with advice on the formulation of the policies of the Government, to assist in carrying out the decisions of the Government, and to manage and deliver the services for which the Government is responsible. Some civil servants are also involved, as a proper part of their duties, in the processes of presentation of government policies and decisions.

(3) The civil service serves the Government of the day as a whole, that is to say Her Majesty's ministers collectively, and the Prime Minister is the Minister for the Civil Service. The duty of the individual civil servant is first and foremost to the minister of the Crown who is in charge of the department in which he or she is serving. It is the minister who is responsible, and answerable in Parliament, for the conduct of the department's affairs and the management of its business. It is the duty of civil servants to serve their ministers with integrity and to the best of their ability.

(4) The British civil service is a non-political and disciplined career service. Civil servants are required to serve the duly elected Government of the day, of whatever political complexion. It is of the first importance that civil servants should conduct themselves in such a way as to deserve and retain the confidence of ministers, and as to be able to establish the same relationship with those whom they may be required to serve in the future administration. That confidence is the indispensable foundation of a good relationship between ministers and civil servants. The conduct of civil servants should at all times be such that ministers and potential future ministers can be sure that that confidence can be freely given, and that the civil service will at all times conscientiously fulfil its duties and obligations to, and impartially assist, advise and carry out the policies of the duly elected Government of the day.

(5) The determination of policy is the responsibility of the minister (within the convention of collective responsibility of the whole Government for the decisions and actions of every member of it). In the determination of policy the civil servant has no

HC Deb. vol. 74, c. 130–132W (26.2.85).

constitutional responsibility or role, distinct from that of the minister. Subject to the conventions limiting the access of ministers to papers of previous administrations, it is the duty of the civil servant to make available to the minister all the information and experience at his or her disposal which may have a bearing on the policy decisions to which the minister is committed or which he is preparing to make, and to give to the minister honest and impartial advice, without fear or favour, and whether the advice accords with the minister's view or not. Civil servants are in breach of their duty, and damage their integrity as servants of the Crown, if they deliberately withhold relevant information from their minister, or if they give their minister other advice than the best they believe they can give, or if they seek to obstruct or delay a decision simply because they do not agree with it. When, having been given all the relevant information and advice, the minister has taken a decision, it is the duty of civil servants loyally to carry out that decision with precisely the same energy and good will, whether they agree with it or not.

(6) Civil servants are under an obligation to keep the confidences to which they become privy in the course of their official duties; not only the maintenance of trust between ministers and civil servants but also the efficiency of Government depend on their doing so. There is and must be a general duty upon every civil servant, serving or retired, not to disclose, in breach of that obligation, any document or information or detail about the course of business, which has come his or her way in the course of duty as a civil servant. Whether such disclosure is done from political or personal motives, or for pecuniary gain, and quite apart from liability to prosecution under the Official Secrets Acts, the civil servant concerned forfeits the trust that is put in him or her as a servant of the Crown, and may well forfeit the right to continue in the Service. He or she also undermines the confidence that ought to subsist between ministers and civil servants and thus damages colleagues and the Service as well as him or herself.

(7) The previous paragraphs have set out the basic principles which govern civil servants' relations with ministers. The rest of this note deals with particular aspects of conduct which derive from them, where it may be felt that more detailed guidance would be helpful.

(8) A civil servant should not be required to do anything unlawful. In the very unlikely event of a civil servant being asked to do something which he or she believes would put him or her in clear breach of the law, the matter should be reported to a superior officer or to the principal establishment officer, who should if necessary seek the advice of the legal adviser to the department. If legal advice confirms that the action would be likely to be held to be unlawful, the matter should be reported in writing to the permanent head of the department.

(9) Civil servants often find themselves in situations where they are required or expected to give information to a parliamentary select committee, to the media, or to individuals. In doing so they should be guided by the general policy of the Government on evidence to select committees and on the disclosure of information, by any specifically departmental policies in relation to departmental information, and by the requirements of security and confidentiality. In this respect, however, as in other respects, the civil servant's first duty is to his or her minister. Ultimately the responsibility lies with ministers, and not with civil servants, to decide what information should be made available, and how and when it should be released, whether it is to Parliament, to select committees, to the media or to individuals. It is not acceptable for a serving or former civil servant to seek to frustrate policies or decisions of ministers by the disclosure outside the Government, in breach of confidence, of information to which he or she has had access as a civil servant.

(10) It is ministers and not civil servants who bear political responsibility. Civil
vants should not decline to take, or abstain from taking, an action merely because to
so would conflict with their personal opinions on matters of political choice or
gement between alternative or competing objectives and benefits; they should con-
er the possibility of declining only if taking or abstaining from the action in question is
t to be directly contrary to deeply held personal conviction on a fundamental issue of
science.

(11) A civil servant who feels that to act or to abstain from acting in a particular way, or
acquiesce in a particular decision or course of action, would raise for him or her a
damental issue of conscience, or is so profoundly opposed to a policy as to feel unable
nscientiously to administer it in accordance with the standards described in this note,
uld consult a superior officer, who can and should if necessary consult the Head of the
me Civil Service. If that does not enable the matter to be resolved on a basis which the
il servant concerned is able to accept, he or she must either carry out his or her
tructions or resign from the public service — though even after resignation he or she
l still be bound to keep the confidences to which he or she has become privy as a civil
vant.

Robert Armstrong

Annual and Periodical Reports and Accounts laid before Parliament and ordered to be printed as House of Commons Papers

Reports

Ancient Monuments Board for England
Ancient Monuments Board for Scotland
Broadcasting Complaints Commission
Charity Commission
Chief Electoral Officer (Northern Ireland)
Chief Inspector of Constabulary
Cinematograph Films Council
Commission for the New Towns
Comptroller and Auditor General (Reports on Matters)
Continental Shelf Act 1964
Council on Tribunals
Development Commission and COSIRA
Ecclesiastical Committee (reports on measures)
Equal Opportunities Commission (Northern Ireland)
European Communities Act 1972 and Customs and Excise Duties (General Reliefs) Act 1979
Export Guarantees and Overseas Investment Act 1978
Gaming Board
General Practice Finance Corporation
Health Service Commissioner (all reports)
Historic Buildings Council for England
Historic Buildings Council for Scotland
Historic Buildings Council for Wales
House of Commons Commission
Housing Support Grant (Scotland) (orders, reports)
Human Rights (Northern Ireland) Standing Advisory Committee
Industrial Development Act 1982 (report on exercise of powers)
Law Commission (Scotland) (periodical reports)
Legal Aid (Northern Ireland) Incorporated Law Society and Advisory Committee Reports
Limits on Guarantee Payments
National Heritage Memorial Fund
Parliamentary Commissioner for Administration (all reports)
Parliamentary Commissioner for Administration (Northern Ireland)
Parole Board
Parole Board for Scotland
Patents, Designs and Trade Marks
Police Complaints Board
Police Complaints Board (Northern Ireland)
Prisons (England and Wales) (report of Chief Inspector)
Public Accounts Commission
Public Record Office
Scottish Hospital Endowments Research Trust
Scottish Hospital Trust

Social Services for Children (triennial reports)
Solicitors' Lay Observer
Solicitors' Lay Observer (Scotland)

N.B. It should be noted that the reports of some bodies appear at one time in the House of Commons, and at another in the Command Paper Series.

Reports and Accounts

British Film Fund Agency
Fair Employment Agency (Northern Ireland)
Forestry Commission
National Film Finance Corporation

Accounts

ACAS, Certification Officer and Central Arbitration Committee
Aviation Security Fund
British Tourist Authority
Civil Aviation Authority
Co-operative Development Agency
Commission for Local Authority Accounts (Scotland)
Commission for Racial Equality
Community Land Surpluses (Wales and Scotland)
Contingencies Fund
Countryside Commission (England & Wales and Scotland)
Crown Agents Holding and Realisation Board
Crown Estates Commissioners
Czechoslovak Compensation Fund
Development Board for Rural Wales
Development Fund
Duchy of Cornwall
Egyptian Nationalised Property Compensation Fund
Election Expenses Return
Equal Opportunities Commission
Erskine Bridge Tolls Act 1968
Funds in Court
Gas Levy
General Lighthouse Fund
Greenwich Hospital and Travers Foundation
Health Authorities
Health Boards and Common Services Agency
HMSO Trading Fund
Highland and Islands Development Board
Home Grown Sugar Beet (Research and Education) Fund
House of Commons Members' Fund
House of Commons Refreshment Department
Independent Broadcasting Authority Programme Contractors' Additional
        Payments
Industrial Organisation and Development Act 1947
Insolvency Services (Accounting and Investment)
Intervention Board for Agricultural Produce
Irish Land Purchase Fund
Ironstone Restoration Fund
Land Authority for Wales

Land Purchase (Northern Ireland)
Legal Aid Fund (England, Scotland and Northern Ireland)
Local Employment Act 1972
Manpower Services Commission
Marshall Aid Commemoration Commission
Maternity Pay Fund
Mineral Exploration and Investment Grants Act 1972
National Biological Standards Board
National Boards for Nursing and Midwifery and Health Visiting (and
    predecessors)
National Insurance Fund
National Oil Account
National Radiological Protection Board
National Research Development Corporation
National Savings Banks (Deposits and Fund)
Nature Conservancy Council
Northern Ireland Trading Funds
Parliamentary Contributory Pension Fund
Police Authority (Northern Ireland)
Police Complaints Board
Public Health Laboratory Service Board
Redundancy Fund
Royal Hospital Chelsea
Royal Mint Trading Fund
Royal Ordnance Factories Trading Fund
Savings Banks Fund
Scottish Development Agency
Severn Bridge Tolls Act 1965
Supreme Court (Northern Ireland) Land Purchase Fund
Tithe Act 1936
Tourist Boards
United Kingdom Atomic Energy Authority
Welsh Development Agency

Appendix 6

Annual and Periodical Reports and Accounts laid before Parliament and printed as Command Papers

Reports

ACARD and ABRC (chairman's joint periodic reports)
Agriculture (Scotland)
Ancient and Historical Monuments of England Standing Royal Commission
Armed Forces Pay Review Body
Boundary Commissions
Customs and Excise
Doctors and Dentists Pay Review Body
Education & Library Boards (Northern Ireland) (statements and summary accounts only)
Environmental Pollution Standing Royal Commission
Fire Services (Chief Inspector)
Fire Services (Scotland)
Foreign Compensation Commission
Government Actuary (reports on bills and statutory instruments)
Industrial Injuries Advisory Council ("matters" reports)
Inland Revenue
Intervention Board for Agricultural Produce
Law Commission ("matters" reports)
Law Commission (Scotland) ("matters" reports)
Law Reform Committee
Library and Information Matters (report by minister)
Marshall Aid Commemoration Commission
Memorandum on the Estimates
Metropolitan Police Commissioner
Monopolies and Mergers Commission (substantive reports)
Occupational Pensions Board (reports on statutory instruments)
Police (Scotland) (Chief Inspector of Constabulary)
Prison Department
Prisons (England and Wales) (Chief Inspector)
Prisons (Scotland)
Roads (Scotland)
Royal Fine Art Commission for Scotland
Scottish Land Court
Security Commission ("matter" reports)
Social Security Advisory Committee (reports on statutory instruments)
Top Salaries Review Body
Works of Art Export Review Committee

Reports and Accounts

Criminal Injuries Compensation Board

Accounts

Development Agency (Northern Ireland)
Housing Executive (Northern Ireland)
United States Mutual Defence Programme Equipment Disposal

211

INDEX

AFTERGLOW

(AFTER #2)

E. DAVIES

London Borough of Hackney	
91300001088365	
Askews & Holts	
AF ROM	£11.99
	6348591

Publisher's Note: This is a work of fiction. Names, characters, places, and incidents are a product of the author's imagination. Locales and public names are sometimes used for atmospheric purposes. Any resemblance to actual people, living or dead, or to businesses, companies, events, institutions, or locales is completely coincidental.

Afterglow / E. Davies. – 1st ed.
ISBN: 978-1-912245-07-9